The publisher and the University of California Press Foundation
gratefully acknowledge the generous support of the Constance
and William Withey Endowment Fund
in History and Music.

We Have Always Been Minimalist

We Have Always
Been Minimalist

THE CONSTRUCTION AND TRIUMPH
OF A MUSICAL STYLE

Christophe Levaux

Translated by Rose Vekony

UNIVERSITY OF CALIFORNIA PRESS

University of California Press
Oakland, California

© 2020 by Christophe Levaux

Library of Congress Cataloging-in-Publication Data

Names: Levaux, Christophe, 1982– author. | Vekony, Rose, translator.
Title: We have always been minimalist : the construction and triumph
    of a musical style / Christophe Levaux ; translated by Rose Vekony.
Other titles: Nous avons toujours été minimalistes. English
Description: Oakland : University of California Press, [2020] | Includes
    bibliographical references and index.
Identifiers: LCCN 2020008789 | ISBN 9780520295261 (cloth) |
    ISBN 9780520295278 (paperback) | ISBN 9780520968080 (epub)
Subjects: LCSH: Minimal music—History and criticism. | Music—20th
    century—History and criticism.
Classification: LCC ML197 .L4413 2020 | DDC 781.68—dc23
LC record available at https://lccn.loc.gov/2020008789

Manufactured in the United States of America

29 28 27 26 25 24 23 22 21 20
10 9 8 7 6 5 4 3 2 1

Contents

Acknowledgments

My deepest thanks go to friends and colleagues who gave this book the benefit of their attentive reading: Émilie Corswarem, Mark Delaere, Michel Delville, Marc-Antoine Gavray, Bernard Gendron, Jérôme Gierkens, Olivier Julien, Philippe Vendrix, and especially Christophe Pirenne. I am indebted as well to those researchers who laid the groundwork for an approach to music based on science and technology studies, and actor-network theory in particular, and who kindly offered their perceptive insights, especially Antoine Hennion and Benjamin Piekut. Thanks also to several of the protagonists of this story for the invaluable information they provided, as well as for their willingness to be part of a study in which their work occasionally comes in for a bit of rough handling: Larry Austin, Jonathan Bernard, David Cope, Henry Flynt, Paul Griffiths, Richard Kostelanetz, John Perreault, Keith Potter, Eric Salzman, Greg Sandow, Elliott Schwartz, and David Smith. I extend my gratitude to Rose Vekony for her judicious advice and meticulous work in translating this book, as well as to Kim Robinson and Raina Polivka at the University of California Press for their patience and assistance during the final phase of its writing.

This study would not have been possible without the support of the Interuniversity Attraction Poles Programme of the Belgian Science Policy Office and its Literature and Media Innovation project, initiated by Jan Baetens in 2012. Nor could I have undertaken the research without the help of the Music Department at Columbia University—namely, Giuseppe Gerbino, Susan Boynton, Kevin Fellezs, Elizabeth Davis, and Nick J. Patterson—which hosted me three times, in 2014, 2015, and 2018. I also thank Brian McHale and the members of Project Narrative in the English Department at Ohio State University for welcoming me in 2014. Last, I extend my thanks to New York University, the New York Public Library, the Museum of Modern Art in New York (in particular Jennifer Tobias), and the Mela Foundation, as well as the Royal Academy of Music in London (notably Rosalind Cyphus) for granting me access to their magnificent collections. This work was supported by the Fonds de la Recherche Scientifique – FNRS under Grant No. 1.P008.18.

Introduction

OPENING THE BLACK BOXES

From spontaneous generation to global warming, from cold fusion to the memory of water or the age of the Earth, numerous controversies have punctuated the history of modern science. Similarly, major debates have regularly swept through the humanities, sometimes spilling over to the public sphere, such as those recently focused on migration history and the integrity of elective democracy. In musicology, experts have argued over the provenance of the Codex Medici (Staehelin 1980), the practice of vibrato (Neumann 1991), and the authorship of Giacinto Scelsi's oeuvre (Drott 2006). They have debated the place that one composer or another should be given in the history of music (recall the opposition between the defenders of John Cage and those of Karlheinz Stockhausen in the 1970s; see Nyman 2013), one music or another (as in the fight for academic recognition of "popular music studies"), and even one genre or another—if indeed they could agree on what differentiated those genres (Moore 2001).

How are such controversies settled? The standard response is to recognize the most objective and rigorous works, peer-reviewed and endorsed by prestigious editorial boards. But if we look behind the controversies to reconstruct the lineage of those theses and theories that established the present facts, we uncover an array of truths that, however solid they may seem, fail to converge in a single direction. During the second half of the twentieth century, relativist and postmodern thinkers in the humanities and social sciences rightly rejected the positivist rationality that science attempted to don, as would the so-called New Musicologists who followed them in the 1980s and after.

Thus, in 2002 Daniel Leech-Wilkinson demonstrated, drawing on Thomas Kuhn (1962), the inherent subjectivity of the facts produced by musicologists. In *The Modern Invention of Medieval Music,* he argued that the interpretation of medieval music evolved, from the concept of polyphony with instrumental accompaniment to that of an a cappella polyphony, less in response to tangible new "proof" than to the efforts of prominent academics and performers seeking to validate modes of thought that supported their own ideologies and musical tastes. A musicological theory was thus largely determined by the predilections of the researchers who elaborated it. Promoted via networks of influence, this theory gained credibility thanks to the institutional power behind the researchers, just as it gained cogency through their rhetorical manipulations (Leech-Wilkinson 2002, 215–46). This process opened the discipline to the dangers of ideological manipulation for personal or institutional ends. Leech-Wilkinson cites the incursion of Nazi ideology into medieval music research and its academic framework during the Third Reich (246–52). He reveals, as the extreme opposite of the positivist tradition, a musicology reduced to the social forces at play, to a belief or a set of beliefs. For Leech-Wilkinson, the notion of neutral objectivity is a delusion. Research is, and indeed must claim to be, a fundamentally subjective endeavor. From this perspective, one can only conclude, sadly, that "musicology is whatever musicologists do as musicologists" (216).

Nonetheless, various propositions have been made between the extremes of an objectivist science that recognizes little human interference in its normal operations and a relativism that sees in scientific facts only their aspect of social construction. One school of thought in particular puts forth another way to consider the question of scientific truth. This school has received different labels over the years and has undergone numerous, widely varied developments. Most often it is associated with "actor-network theory" and Bruno Latour. Among Latour's many works, *Science in Action* (1987) presents the most complete and detailed program of research in this protean field (see also Latour 2005). There Latour takes up Norbert Wiener's concept of "black boxes" to metaphorically designate scientific facts and techniques—from cosmological theory to the microprocessor or an economic model—that run "by themselves," without their users needing to question how they work. Latour tries to open these "black boxes" and describe them in action in the course of their construction.

In the world that Latour describes to his readers, new facts and theories do not appear from thin air as the result of a simple discovery, any more than they spontaneously gain recognition. Once elaborated by scholars, findings must then be backed by peers. To that end, these new facts usually need to be based on preexisting ones that have already won peer support. Recourse to theories already accepted as true and to facts already established is one of the techniques used to buttress a theory and ward off controversy. This reference to previously confirmed theories, however, provokes subtle changes in them; indeed, it is rare for a theory to be applied in exactly the same way as before. By relying on an established fact to develop a new one, the researcher steers the first fact in a slightly different direction. Latour calls these refashioned scientific arguments "modalities." He gives an example of these modalities in his book:

(1) New Soviet missiles aimed against Minutemen silos are accurate to 100 metres.

(2) Since [new Soviet missiles are accurate within 100 metres] this means that Minutemen are not safe any more, and this is the main reason why the MX weapon system is necessary.

(3) Advocates of the MX in the Pentagon cleverly leak information contending that [new Soviet missiles are accurate within 100 metres].

In statements (2) and (3) we find the same sentence (1) but inserted. We call these sentences **modalities** because they modify (or qualify) another one. The effects of the modalities in (2) and (3) are completely different. In (2) the sentence (1) is supposed to be solid enough to make the building of the MX necessary, whereas in (3) the very same statement is weakened since its validity is in question. (22; brackets and bold type in the original)

Thus the status of a statement depends on the subsequent statements that establish, transform, or abandon it. A theory can be categorized as "fact" or "fiction" based on how it fits with another theory. A fact, if ignored, will never become accepted as fact. For that reason a scholar needs to "recruit" other scholars to bolster it, at the risk of these latter transforming the fact in the process. This is the Latourian concept of "translation of interests": for a theory to be adopted by others and achieve posterity, it must arouse, and "translate," their interests. "We need others to help us transform a claim into a matter of fact. The first and easiest way to find people who will immediately believe the statement, invest in the project, or buy the prototype is to tailor the object in such a way that it caters to these people's explicit interests," Latour writes (108). Actor-network theory thus reveals the performative value of the arguments that constitute theories. For Latour, each scientific argument becomes a proposition whose fate depends on the authors who come later, who may adopt, transform, or reject it. Their works, in turn, are adopted, transformed, or rejected. In this perspective, scientific fact becomes a collective object that undergoes continual mutation at the hands of various authors, as well as a process of layering or stratification. Once any fact or theory is established in this way, contesting it can mean opposing such an entanglement of alliances, conciliations, and writings, each implicated in another, that the task proves almost impossible. The new theories have become things; the scholars seem to have discovered what had always been there. We witness this reification, itself based on a series of other reifications and soon, potentially, the basis for further ones. Layer upon layer, ideas have solidified into things. They have become *real*—at least as long as no one is there to contest them. Ultimately the great lesson to be learned from *Science in Action* is that if facts are made, then it is possible to escape the circular logic of "objectively demonstrated" and "socially constructed," whereby all is determined either by objects or by subjects. The facts are no less solid. Indeed, they are more solid, but it is up to us to decide their fate.

As mentioned above, the school of thought that Latour founded in the early 1980s—alongside Michel Callon, Madeleine Akrich, and John Law—underwent a number of developments, some of which addressed the question of music. Antoine Hennion—a member, like Latour, of the Centre de sociologie de l'innovation in Paris—was one of the first to confront the theory with music.

Actor-network theorists had learned an important lesson while examining science in action: the Weberian opposition between the scientific and the political was no longer tenable. Likewise the inhumanity of science and the humanity of societies and, finally, the human and nonhuman—this "Great Divide" between nature and culture, as Latour would call it in *We Have Never Been Modern* (1993). Hennion quickly assessed the benefit of such an approach for the sociology of music:

> Researchers in the sociology of music, fearful of the accusation that their statements would amount to no more than unsubstantiated aesthetic judgements, have chosen to ignore the aesthetic arena and to concentrate their efforts on an analysis of the ways in which musical objects are produced. What has emerged is a relativist sociology, focused on the interactions between the various actors who influence the production and reception process, and examining the interwoven human complex of "art worlds." My aim has been to show that there is a whole other aspect to a constructivist sociology—namely the influences exerted by the non-human elements in the production process. (1997, 432)

Hennion seeks to break away from the "false dilemma" between aestheticism, which isolates works of art from their social context, and sociologism, which reveals the social construction of the aesthetic object but provides little analysis of the results of artistic production. The reintegration of "nonhuman elements"—scores and texts, sound, instruments, repertoires, staging, concert venues, and media—would thus allow music to be envisioned "not directly in terms of aesthetic content or social authenticity, but in terms of the way in which, by rejecting certain mediators and promoting others, both are collectively constructed" (1997, 432). Other texts resonate with Hennion's thinking. In *Rationalizing Culture* (1995), on the institutionalization of the Parisian musical avant-garde, Georgina Born postulates that meaning is inherent in the social, theoretical, and technological aspects of music and its visual mediations just as in its sound. In *Music in Everyday Life* (2000), Tia DeNora likewise attempts to illuminate the way in which heterogeneous unions of people and objects are formed, interact, and structure each other. In *Experimentalism Otherwise* (2011), Benjamin Piekut approaches experimental music as a "network, arranged and fabricated through the hard work of composers, critics, scholars, performers, audiences, students, and a host of other elements including texts, scores, articles, curricula, patronage systems, and discourses of race, gender, class and nation" (19). With Nick Prior (2008),

Jonathan Sterne (2012), Eric Drott (2013), and numerous other scholars over the years, the ranks of those defending actor-network theory as an approach to music have grown. Most often their works seek to take into account those unjustly neglected "mediators"—a focus that reduces Latourian thought to this single aspect, at the risk of caricaturing it. Few attempt to apply the radical study program of *Science in Action* to the facts of music history. There have also been few efforts to open the black boxes of historical events in order to produce an "empirically justified description . . . that highlights the controversies, trials, and contingencies of the truth," as Piekut urges, "instead of reporting it as coherent, self-evident, and available for discovery" (2014, 3).

Indeed, it seemed that after *Foundations of Music History* by Carl Dahlhaus (1983) and *Music and the Historical Imagination* by Leo Treitler (1989), both of which anticipated many directions of the recent major developments in historical musicology, the question of the reality, multiplicity, or nonexistence of a "profound nature of the musical work" (see Dahlhaus 1983, 150–65, in particular) remained partly unresolved. Just as epistemology was often limited to the study of the lineage or circulation of facts once they were formed (see Latour 1989, 13–17), music history was often confined to the reception, impact, or context of a work, style, or genre. Seldom were these aspects viewed as entities or shifting substances, the fruits of an eminently collective work subject to continual mutation and renegotiation, acting and being acted upon within a diverse network of actors. Rarely would one attempt to tell the story of their making or to rehabilitate the experts and their imprint on such stories.

But in fact the experts—journalists, scholars, composers, and performers, or combinations thereof—are among the main actors in a story inspired by actor-network theory. Indeed, even though facts in the humanities are conventionally considered more malleable, with a wider range of critical possibilities than those in the hard sciences, the requirement of neutrality remains a condition of their scholarly integrity, and thus of their universality (Callerdo and Girard 2011, 243–45). Therefore, the humanities too—more paradoxically than other disciplines—have been subject to what Latour called the "Great Divide" of modernity: that separating facts from values, or the individual from science. This divide is precisely what partisans of actor-network theory have criticized.

From the perspective of actor-network theory, the requirement of neutrality, much like the utopian project of separating facts from values and the individual from science, is the source of the most intense controversies, ones that would impact musicology as well, as seen above. In particular, one controversy became especially heated over the last decades of the twentieth century. It had to do with a music called *minimalist* and with the work of its four well-known representatives: La Monte Young (1935–), Terry Riley (1935–), Steve Reich (1936–), and Philip Glass (1937–).

At the turn of the third millennium, the second edition of one of the most respected music encyclopedias, *The New Grove Dictionary of Music and Musicians,* devoted several pages to this music. According to that entry, minimalism constitutes a twentieth-century "style of composition characterized by an intentionally simplified rhythmic, melodic and harmonic vocabulary" (Potter 2001a, 716). Its accessibility, its tonal or modal nature, its rhythmic regularity and continuity, and its structural and textural simplicity define it. Minimal music, the entry further states, is characterized by two distinct but nonetheless related tendencies or approaches: the elaboration of "sustained sounds," on the one hand, and repetition, on the other. The first tendency owes mostly to Young; the second was developed by his successors Riley, Reich, and Glass. Although at its inception the movement was closely associated with minimal art (it goes back to 1958, we read), it was subsequently deemed "the major antidote to Modernism, as represented by both the total serialism of Boulez and Stockhausen and the indeterminacy of Cage" (716). Not only did it lead the way toward the destruction of cultural barriers, but it also met with great popular success, writes Potter, becoming one of the most remarkable developments in twentieth-century music. Indeed, this music had a substantial impact on a wide range of concert musics, including rock and the panoply of hybrid and postmodern forms that would become (again, according to *New Grove*) a major feature of music at the end of the century. Keith Potter's definition of minimal music leaves little doubt as to the recognition of this style: after all, his entry appeared in one of the major musicology encyclopedias of the world, sanctioned by a substantial bibliography of books issued by the most reputable publishing houses. Behind this definition, however, and behind the books on which it was based, lurk numerous polemics, debates, and all manner of contradictions.

In fact, as we study these texts more closely, the initial obviousness of "minimal music" diminishes. Having read in *New Grove* that minimalism was born in 1958, we discover elsewhere that it dates to 1953 (Sabbe 1982b). Some even trace the emergence of minimalism to Maurice Ravel's *Boléro* or Erik Satie's *Vexations* (Schaefer 1987, xii, 65). Whereas Potter considers minimal music a major antidote to the modernism of John Cage or Karlheinz Stockhausen, others see it as the future of experimental music (Nyman 1974) or the final stage of the European musical revolution launched by Arnold Schoenberg (Mertens 1983). Some authors evoke minimal music's borrowings from popular music or the impact of minimalism on the latter (Strickland 1993), while others completely ignore these connections, and still others refute them (Goodwin 1991).

Designating the main representatives of the "style" defined in *New Grove* is no less controversial. Michael Nyman first identified Henning Christiansen's music as minimal in 1968 (article reprinted in ap Siôn et al. 2013, 41–43), and a few years later that of Young, Riley, Reich, and Glass (Nyman 1974). Before classifying the work of these last four as minimal (1982), Tom Johnson saw minimal music as Californian, encompassing the aesthetic of Harold Budd or Michael Byron (1973). Over the years the foursome of Young, Riley, Reich, and Glass came to be universally recognized as minimalist, sometimes with the addition of Dick Higgins (Hitchcock 1974, 269), Morton Feldman (Salzman 1974, 187), or even Cage, acclaimed as a "minimalist enchanted with sound" in his *New York Times* obituary on August 13, 1992 (Kozinn 1992).

But even the term *minimal music* with reference to Young, Riley, Reich, and Glass was contested; hypnotic school, trance music, modular music, pulse, and space music were among the many variants associated with the music of all or some of these composers. Indeed, the four composers themselves never accepted the label being attached to their music, as Potter points out in *New Grove*. Moreover, the very terms of his definition can be questioned as well: how could the style have been *at once* modern and postmodern? How could the music have been *at once* minimal and of great richness? One might go so far as to doubt the existence of this minimal music: it is thanks to an "accident of musical history" that the term was ever used, according to John Schaefer (1987, xii).

We could, of course, attempt to follow the traditional approach of science in order to resolve the tangle of controversies that minimalism brought with it, and thus give credence to only the most factual, objective, and methodical works. But that task is complex, to say the least, since musicologists, historians, and critics base their studies on reasoning, facts, and objects. And if the reader cannot always assess their veracity, publishers, editorial committees, and universities, along with notes and bibliographies, will vouch for it. Indeed, many works have been recognized by new generations of authors, who validate them by citing them in their own studies, which are subject to the same academic vetting.

Perhaps, then, one might put the controversies to rest by considering only the most recent works on the topic, assuming they represent a higher level of information. But to do so would be to subscribe to the idea that facts are ephemeral; all truth would thus be provisional. By definition, however, what is "certain" cannot be temporary. Would it be better, then, to assemble the range of conceptions and discourses in an attempt to synthesize them, making minimal music a genre inspired as much by Webernian serialism as by the jazz of John Coltrane or Indian raga, belonging at once to modernity and postmodernity, and in turn influencing both serious and popular composers? In many ways, that is what the definition in *New Grove* did in 2001. That approach, however, disregards the fact that the oppositions, sometimes radical, are what shaped the various stances on both sides: for some, minimal music is serious precisely because it is in no way popular; for others, it has no Western roots because it owes everything to the East; and so on.

Thus, it is anything but easy to break free of these controversies. *New Grove* presents a calm musical landscape, where the concept of minimal music was established on the strength of the music alone. We initially imagine that we need only listen to one or another representative of the genre to confirm the validity of the concept. But once we dig a bit deeper, we find ourselves on a veritable postwar battlefield, with signs of struggle, weapons strewn on the ground, and the remnants of camps, destroyed or standing.

The present book has its precise origin in this chaos that, as a young researcher in 2012, I encountered while studying the links between minimalist music and popular music: thousands of works (articles in the press, scholarly articles, interviews, monographs, and edited volumes) intended to give an accurate and reliable description of minimalism failed to converge in a single direction. At that time the model developed by Latour for the natural sciences enabled me to slowly find my way through this set of antagonisms. Little by little, a twofold project of understanding the controversies around minimalism and testing the Latourian model on the history of music took shape. Its aim would be to bring to light the construction of a "musicological discovery"—that of minimal music.

I thus set out to trace, in the literature on minimalism, those modalities that transform established facts into new facts and ultimately into proven facts. I examined how those writing on music history, like Latour's scholars, sought to lead their readers down a single path; how they tried to patch up holes that their opponents might exploit; how they translated the interests of others in order to reinforce their arguments; and how the musical fact could be conceived as a layering or stratification, as a collective phenomenon, and ultimately as a reified object. Finally, I asked whether the profound epistemological upheaval provoked by actor-network theory might resonate in musicology. To find the answers, I had to reach into the black box and reopen the controversies of an established musical fact: the arrival of so-called minimalist music—that of Young, Riley, Reich, and Glass—on the twentieth-century musical landscape. I followed the network of ideas that developed around this event, exploring the texts generated at each node beginning with the first ones written about the four composers' work from the late 1950s to early 1960s, when "minimal music" did not yet exist.

To capture minimal music in the making, we must set the stage and revive the moments that immediately preceded the first published mentions of the music of its originators—Young, Riley, Reich, and Glass—to return to the cultural state as attested in the literature of the early 1960s, without questioning or analyzing it. Thus, in the first chapter of this book, we do not try to find out, for example, why serialism was recognized as the main trend in twentieth-century music or how Cage was at that time becoming one of the most prominent musical figures in the United States. Instead we take these statements for what they were at the time: facts. Indeed, the construction of future facts forms the heart of this study. Consequently, this book is structured by a succession of brief surveys on the history of these concepts, with occasional interruptions to consider what musicology on American minimal music tells us about specific points. These "freeze-frames"—chapters 4, 10, 18, and 21—are intended to systematically present the state of minimal music's development in the wake of

seminal publications that recount its history or that of its main protagonists: in 1967, shortly after the publication of "One Sound: La Monte
Young" by Cornelius Cardew (1966); in 1975, following *Experimental
Music* by Michael Nyman (1974); in 1984, a year after the English-language
translation of Wim Mertens's *American Minimal Music*; in 1994, following *Minimalism: Origins* by Edward Strickland (1993); and finally in
2001, with the definition in *New Grove* (Potter 2001a). We conclude with a
wide-ranging chapter that looks at the evolution of conceptions of minimal
music over the course of the twenty-first century.

As I have already indicated, this history of minimal music, from the
birth of the concept to the moment when it became "music itself," draws
on works in science and technology studies and in particular on actor-
network theory—a theory notably elaborated over the course of the 1980s
and 1990s at the École nationale supérieure des mines de Paris, an
engineering school founded in 1783. In a more general way, the present
work is an attempt to apply this approach to the historiography of music.
The technical concepts of modalization, translation of interests, stratification, and reification, though abundantly employed in this field of research,
will operate only on an indirect level, so as to preserve the fluidity of the
text, letting its methodological outlines appear progressively.

1. 1960

BEFORE MINIMALISM

What did *contemporary American music* mean at the dawn of the 1960s? What views on the subject were deemed accurate? The major encyclopedias and music dictionaries of the day held few answers to these questions. *Die Musik in Geschichte und Gegenwart,* a German encyclopedia of music begun in 1949, had not yet published its entry on the United States ("Vereinigte Staaten"); that would appear only in 1966 (Broder 1966). Nor did the fifth edition of *Grove's Dictionary of Music and Musicians* in 1954 contain an entry for "United States." What we do learn of the music panorama at mid-century is that most countries had adopted the twelve-tone technique; that the French were focused on musique concrète; and that the Germans, much like Edgard Varèse in New York, were trying their hand at electronic music (Searle 1954, 1961a, 1961b). The French *Encyclopédie de la musique* (Michel 1958–61) better documents the subject of American music. There we read that the United States had recently seen "the incorporation of the main European tendencies" and the progressive emergence of several different currents. One was the "mathematical" style of Milton Babbitt; another, a mode anchored in the complex music of Roger Sessions, Andrew Imbrie, and Leon Kirchner; and finally, the style of Harold Shapero, following the work of Paul Hindemith (Michel 1961, 3:946–48).

While the encyclopedias and dictionaries transmitted a blurry image of contemporary music in the United States, monographs on twentieth-century music allow us to sharpen the picture somewhat, at least by deduction. The British study *Musical Trends in the Twentieth Century* by Norman Demuth (1952) explained, for instance, that Impressionism and Romanticism now belonged to the past; that the symphonic tradition lived on in many countries; and that for some years the twelve-tone technique had remained a constant feature almost everywhere. The German works by Hans Stuckenschmidt (1958) and Rudolf Stephan (1958) likewise noted that the twentieth-century world had progressively been won over to the twelve-tone technique. Their compatriot Werner Oehlman (1961) explained that twelve-tone music was followed by the serial and electronic trends, with Nicos Skalkottas in Greece, Luigi Nono in Italy, and Pierre Boulez in France among their most famous representatives (289–303). In the French-speaking world, the *Atlas historique de la musique* (Collaer and Vander Linden 1960) affirmed that music after the Second World War was essentially characterized by the development of the twelve-tone technique that originated with Arnold Schoenberg and Anton Webern. It added that young composers had nonetheless set out to find new means of expression: electronic music in the case of Boulez or Karlheinz Stockhausen, concrete sound for Pierre Schaeffer, and tonal expansion for Varèse and John Cage (117, 120). Also in the Francophone world, André Hodeir painted an entirely different picture of the music of his day. According to *La Musique depuis Debussy* (*Since Debussy: A View of Contemporary Music*), published simultaneously in Paris and New York in 1961, the only noteworthy contemporary music was that of Olivier Messiaen, Boulez, and Jean Barraqué. The only good music from the United States was jazz, he wrote, even though several young composers such as Chou Wen-chung or Robert DiDomenica had displayed a certain audacity in distancing themselves from neoclassicism and twelve-tone music (222–23).

Contemporary music elicited the interest not only of British, German, and French authors but also Americans, who published numerous monographs on the subject between the late 1950s and early 1960s. In *The Complete Book of 20th Century Music,* David Ewen (1952) portrayed composers who initiated new approaches in instrumentation (Cage with prepared piano), harmony (Henry Cowell and his clusters), and rhythm (Messiaen in particular). He further maintained that some composers favored excessive complexity (such as Sessions or Charles Ives), while others turned to musical languages of the past (Norman Dello Joio, among the most recent) or opted for economy of expression (Francis Poulenc). Still others preferred a style that could be understood by "unsophisticated audiences" (xxiv). Such was the case of Aaron Copland. In *An Introduction to Twentieth-Century Music*, Peter S. Hansen (1961) argued that Webernism had triumphed after the war and that Boulez and his contemporaries had then sought to understand the serialization of durations, dynamics, and articulations, leading to the "total control" of music and ultimately to electronic music. Added to these were parallel currents such as French musique concrète, the aleatoric music of Cage and Stockhausen—who were also composers of electronic music—and computer music (345–58). In his *Introduction to Contemporary Music*, Joseph Machlis (1961) divided contemporary music into two camps: the twelve-tone composers, on the one hand, with the central figures of Luigi Dallapiccola in Europe and Mel Powell in the United States; and the experimentalists, on the other, with Stockhausen or Boulez in Europe and Varèse in the United States. Varèse's work was followed by Cowell and by Cage, an influential composer, but one whose experiments would probably be surpassed by advances in electronic music (632).

From one monograph to the next, the definition of American music is, if not contradictory, at least nebulous. Many works specifically dedicated to the music of America nonetheless aimed, in the late 1950s to early 1960s, to give a more precise idea of it. Among these, the third edition of John Tasker Howard's famous work *Our American Music* (1954; originally published in 1931) figures prominently. "Anyone who has had occasion to study the music of America's past has sought out John Tasker Howard's book," we read in *Notes* (Bellows 1957, 501). In the third edition of that book, a new chapter covers the period 1945–54.[1] There we learn that except for a movement inspired by Parisian electronic music (A68–A69), American postwar music preserved its allegiance to established cultures. The new composers thus took the path of Webern's chromaticism and Igor Stravinsky's neoclassicism, or alternatively the exoticism of foreign cultures and diatonic folk music that arose in opposition to one or the other. Alexei Haieff, Shapero, Elliott Carter, Kirchner, Irving Fine, Lukas Foss, Ben Weber, Babbitt, Henry Brant, Peter Mennin, Imbrie, Louis Calabro, and Leonard Bernstein were the leading lights of the new continent. In another work *A Short History of Music in America* (1957), Howard and coauthor George Kent Bellows sketched an even clearer portrait of the American music of his day. Music in the middle of the century was experimental with Ives and Cage, electronic with Otto Luening, twelve-tone with Wallingford Riegger and Weber, traditionalist from Vincent Persichetti to Shapero, eclectic from Howard Swanson to Alan Hovhaness, and operatic with William Schuman, Kurt Weill, and Bernstein. For Howard, even though American music was beginning to overtake European music, which had run out of steam (400), it remained in many respects anchored in the Old World tradition. Also in 1957, in the second edition of Howard's *Modern Music,* American modern music was either that of Cowell, Varèse, and John Becker, in an experimental vein; or that of Vladimir Ussachevsky, electronic. It still tended to find its precedents in Europe, and furthermore, it was essentially serious. Not all musicologists shared that opinion. Indeed, David Ewen, the author of *The Complete Book of 20th Century Music* (1952), published *Panorama of American Popular Music* in 1957. It was, he affirmed, the first time that a "complete" history, or at least one exclusively devoted to American popular music, was published. For Ewen, this music—Tin Pan Alley, jazz, folk music, and musical theater—was the best expression of the "native" culture of the United States.

In fact, Ewen's work was not the first to examine American popular music.[2] It was part of a recent trend, notably represented by *America's Music* by Gilbert Chase, who had recently called the "genteel tradition" his *bête noire* and the idea of "aesthetic progress" a fallacy (1955, xvii–xviii). On the heels of Charles Seeger, who founded the Society for Ethnomusicology the same year that Chase's book was published, Chase aspired to discover an authentic and traditional American music style. Thus he closed his panorama of American music—after the experimentalism of Harry Partch and Cage, the twelve tones of Babbitt and Weber, and Broadway and the operas of Bernstein and Schuman—with Charles Ives. The composer managed "to discern and to utilize the truly idiosyncratic and germinal elements of our folk and popular music," Chase asserted (659). Chase's message thus contrasts, in part, with that of Howard: the richness of American music, as opposed to European music, perhaps could be heard not so much inside concert halls as outside of them—namely, in the folk and popular tradition.[3] This idea was even more fervently supported by Henry Pleasants. The same year that Chase's book came out, Pleasants published *The Agony of Modern Music* (1955), announcing the advent of jazz and the decline of modern music. For Chase and Pleasants, a virtual boundary separated the two worlds. When the British musicologist Wilfrid Mellers celebrated the music of the "New World" at the end of his *Romanticism and the 20th Century, from 1800* (1957), he said the same: one could not expect there to be any connection between "artistic" and "commercial" music. In the end, this conception is one of the few to have enjoyed a consensus: various currents of modern music existed, but the only ones that did not interact were "popular" and "serious."

What do we find if we dig even deeper—if, after searching the encyclopedias, the more general monographs, and those specifically devoted to the music of the United States, we examine the periodical literature? What do the *Musical Quarterly, Notes, Journal of Music Theory, Perspectives of New Music, Music & Letters, Tempo,* and the *Musical Times* have to say about American music? Based on these journals, consensus appears to have been rare: whether from one journal to another or within the same journal, the portraits of contemporary American music are conflicting and even contradictory. Efforts to synthesize the general state of contemporary music are likewise rare. Contributors regularly shy away from any attempt at exhaustiveness, the province of encyclopedias and monographs. The evident interests of authors or groups of authors (often composers) are even regularly criticized: in 1963, Joseph Kerman denounced *Perspectives of New Music* for being concerned only with the "new music" of the journal's collaborators; he was replying to Charles Rosen's claim that one should listen only to the composer's perspective to understand a piece of music (Kerman 1963; Rosen 1962). Indeed, it is usual for each journal to favor one style, one school, one tendency, or sometimes even one music publisher's catalogue. For example, over the course of the 1950s, the Boosey & Hawkes journal *Tempo* tended to provide a forum for its own composers' views rather than those of others. In June 1955, when *The Score* published its twelfth issue, intended as an overview of American music, it presented a panorama that was mixed, to say the least: from Babbitt's "twelve tones" to Cage's experimental music, together with the music of "commerce" described by Wilfrid Mellers, the versions of the "American style" sometimes diverged widely.

The development of "commercial music" addressed by Mellers was also covered in music magazines and newspapers of the day: *Melody Maker* and *New Musical Express* in Britain, *Down Beat* in the United States.[4] These publications were even less inclined than their scholarly counterparts to synthesize the general state of the music of their time. At best, the reader can glean information on new trends and noteworthy figures within specific genres or territories. The same goes for the music sections in influential US news publications such as the *New York Times, New York Herald Tribune, New York Magazine, Newsweek,* and the *Atlantic.* As conventional wisdom would have it, the press is too local, too close to the present, too focused on its subject, too unstable. It is too "human," lacking the necessary distance to "tell the truth."

This excursion through the literature demonstrates how difficult it is to understand American contemporary music around 1960. For some, European influence is major; for others it is trivial. The popular is sometimes absent, sometimes celebrated. American music is described sometimes as essentially twelve-tone, sometimes as experimental or electronic. The definitions of the different genres, styles, schools, currents, or tendencies characteristic of North America overlap and intertwine, when they don't conflict. A certain current may be seen as having given rise to another (or not); it may be connected to another (or not); and a specific composer may sometimes be viewed as part of one current, sometimes another, and sometimes both. For example, we never quite know whether Cage was largely influenced by Schoenberg, whether he created his own American style, or whether he simply had no place to claim in the contemporary music panorama.

But since we must nonetheless try to assemble, almost statistically, a series of constants, we can surely highlight the disappearance or decline of Impressionism, realism, symphonism, and the "neo" movements (-baroque, -classical, -mystical, -primitive, -romantic). We can also note that the twelve-tone technique and its successive developments, whether in electronic or experimental music—the distinction remains difficult to establish—reigned supreme around the world, and partly in North America, and that its developments were fundamentally opposed to the popular currents largely represented by jazz. This imperfect synthesis formed the foundation on which the future history was to be built.

What is minimal music? We asked earlier what the response to this question might be at the turn of the third millennium. We read that for some this music, emblematic of the United States, existed since 1958; for others since 1953 or even since Erik Satie and his *Vexations* at the end of the nineteenth century. But when we ask what this "minimal music" meant in 1960, we are hard put to respond: we find absolutely nothing on the subject at the time. Nor do we know anything more about the major minimal composers; history had yet to unveil its ways to those who attempted to interpret it. Indeed, perhaps this delay explains the controversy in the early 1970s surrounding a work composed at the beginning of the previous decade by an American named La Monte Young.

2. Taking Root in Modernity

NEW MUSIC

[*X for Henry Flynt*'s] repeated sound is of the crudest and
most undifferentiated kind and nothing else happens.

(Smalley 1967a, 143)

There is also . . . a fascinating section "On the Role of the
Instructions in the Interpretation of Indeterminate Music."
This is principally concerned with La Monte Young's *X for
Henry Flynt* and should be required reading for those
critics who dismiss this music with an air of philistine
indifference.

(Smalley 1972, 593)

Five years separate these two quotations. Both are by the British musicologist and composer Roger Smalley in the *Musical Times*. The first is
from a letter sent to the journal in which Smalley virulently attacks an
article by his colleague Cornelius Cardew on the American composer La
Monte Young (Cardew 1966). Smalley calls Young "Lilliputian" and says
that his music "annoys" and "bores" him, in particular the piece *X for
Henry Flynt*, which, he asserts, is in no way even "musical" (Smalley
1967a). The second is from an enthusiastic review of a collection of essays,
again by Cardew (1971), titled *Treatise Handbook*, in which *X for Henry
Flynt* has now become a piece of "music."[1] Moreover, Smalley strongly rec-
ommends the work to those who denigrate Young's aesthetic. It is a radical
reversal, even more surprising because between 1967 and 1972 *X for*

Henry Flynt, a piece dating to 1960, remained unchanged by the composer: it still consisted of the repetition, at regular intervals and at high volume, of a cluster produced on piano using the forearms. In the *Musical Times,* through Smalley's assessments, it seems nonetheless fundamentally different. What happened over the course of the second half of the 1960s? How did Young's work, widely disparaged at first, turn into "music"? These are the questions we will address here.

"NOT LIKELY TO BECOME MORE THAN A PART OF THE *AVANT-GARDE* INFLUENCE"

To understand Smalley's about-face, we must go back to 1960. In June of that year, the name La Monte Young appeared for the first time in the *Musical Times.* At that time the journal constituted one of the pillars of the institution of British classical music. It had been published for more than a century, giving voice to established authors and composers and addressing the "general reader" as much as the scholar or practicing musician.[2] Young's name came up in a column titled "The Avant-Garde in New York: Spring 1960," authored by Peter Dickinson (1960), a British composer, pianist, and musicologist newly converted to the aesthetic of Cage, Cowell, and other "leading American composers" (Norrington 1965, 109). When Dickinson published his column in 1960, Cage was not yet, for many, a "leading American composer." He was only beginning to regain, in the eyes of the music establishment, the credibility he had lost by turning to the music of chance and indeterminacy.[3] A handful of American composers (in large part his own students at the New School for Social Research), publishers (such as Edition Peters), institutions (such as Wesleyan University), and theorists (such as Leonard B. Meyer, see esp. 1963) contributed to his recognition over the course of the 1960s.[4] Dickinson, on the other side of the Atlantic, also contributed, particularly in the *Musical Times.* Indeed, his review of a series of concerts given in New York in spring 1960 sought to remind the reader that "whatever aesthetic objections are raised against [Cage's] music, it is undeniably more human than electronic music, and each performance is unique" (Dickinson 1960, 377).

The "unique" character of each performance of his works was what, according to Dickinson, linked Cage's music to that of Cardew, Christian Wolff, Toshi Ichiyanagi, and Young, whose compositions were also presented in New York in spring 1960. Although the music of these last four was performed with "sensitivity and restraint," their music faced the same predicament as electronic music: it was "not likely to become more than a part of the *avant-garde* influence" (Dickinson 1960, 377). We learn nothing more at this point about the aesthetic of the "haphazard" that guided Young and his colleagues: the performer, we read, plays from a "design" that prescribes neither notes nor rhythm. Although the interest that Young and the other three composers elicited was marked by reservations in that issue of the *Musical Times*, these composers nonetheless carved a place for themselves in an influential journal, in which Dickinson presented them as heirs to one of the great figures of the future of American music. Thus Dickinson, from the pulpit of the *Musical Times*, accorded Cage the merit of posterity.

"LAMONT" YOUNG

The following year, Young's name appeared in another pillar of the British musical press: *Tempo*. Cardew mentioned him in an essay on his own compositional ideas titled "Notation: Interpretation, etc." (Cardew 1961a). At that time, the journal *Tempo* belonged to the music publisher Boosey & Hawkes, with contributions that notably established certain contemporary composers whose works it published and whose views the journal featured (see esp. Blaikley et al. 2001). These composers were Erwin Stein, Anthony Payne, Smalley, and Alexander Goehr. Cardew, the young British performer and composer newly returned from Cologne, where he had assisted Stockhausen, would now be part of that group. He had attracted the attention of *Tempo*, which "has always prided itself," as evidenced here, on "its scrutiny of contemporary music of every school" ("Notes: Tempo and the 'New' Music" 1961).

From 1961 on, when Cardew presented his "remarks" on music for *Tempo*, they effectively became "an important statement of practice and belief" ("Notes" 1961). The interests of the musician and the journal proved mutually beneficial: *Tempo* laid claim to a prominent composer's work and enriched its exploration of the avant-garde; Cardew enjoyed the journal's support and strengthened his position in the landscape of contemporary music. While Cardew relied on this powerful ally to defend his own conceptions, he also relied on an aesthetic that was gaining authority: that of John Cage. Indeed, it was partly in line with the American composer that his British counterpart tended to position his own work. And by mentioning the work of a certain "Lamont [sic] Young" in his twelfth numbered remark (Cardew 1961a, 25–26), he gave Young the leverage of association with *Tempo* and Cage, as well as his own support, gradually recognized by the music establishment.

In Cardew's twelfth remark, in contrast to what Dickinson had implied the year before (1960), Young emerged as the leader among those who placed "more emphasis on the human aspects of notations," preceding Cage, Wolff, Earle Brown, or Feldman (Cardew 1961a, 26). For Cardew, this quality of Cage's music was not even subject to discussion; it constituted a fact, as well as the unifying thread among the music of American composers such as Young. By associating his own aesthetic with Young's, Cardew underlined the same quality in the music he composed. This music, we also read, largely consisted of abandoning the predetermination of the traditional system of music notation. "The relation between musical score and performance cannot be determined," proclaimed Cardew (1961a, 22), who from then on would incessantly defend the idea of creative notation. The "graphic score" marks the culmination of Cardew's struggle for the performer's liberation from the constraints of notation: to that end, he composed *Treatise* from 1963 to 1967.

IN RE

Meanwhile, Cardew continued to promote Young's aesthetic. In 1962 he wrote an article on the composer in the magazine *New Departures*, for which he was the music editor. That article, titled "In re La Monte Young," presented Young's *Compositions 1960 #1, 3, 6, 7,* and *10* in the form of several lines of instructions to be given to the performer (see sidebar 1). He thus offered the first illustration of Young's works.

Sidebar 1

COMPOSITION 1960 #3

Announce to the audience when the piece will begin and end if there is a limit on duration. It may be of any duration.

Then announce that everyone may do whatever he wishes for the duration of the composition.

5-14-60

COMPOSITION 1960 #10

to Bob Morris
Draw a straight line and follow it.

October 1960

La Monte Young, *Composition 1960 #3 and #10.*

The article gave a glowing report on a series of works by Young: *Poem* (1960) was his most interesting piece, "a long and technical instruction manual";[5] while he saw *X for Henry Flynt* (1960) as an "ill-intentioned but salutory insult."[6] Young's work was in no way an exhibitionistic act, Cardew wrote; it demanded all the performer's resources (Cardew 1962, 75). In addition to the music's emphasis on the human aspects of notation and its Cageian roots, Cardew introduced a new term relevant to the assessment of Young's music: the performer's competence. From *Tempo* to *New Departures*, Cardew solidified Young's place in the musical landscape, while also laying the foundations for his own musical discourse.

He soon moved from theory to practice, expanding his campaign to promote Young's music by actively participating in the organization of concerts that celebrated the music of the American composer as well as his own. Two announcements appeared in the *Musical Times* in 1963 and 1964: Young's works were to be performed at the University of London and at the theater of the American embassy.[7] For both concerts Cardew was one of the performers, and he presented his own works as well. But at that time it appears that Cardew was not yet satisfied with the fruit of his efforts. In September 1964, he devoted an article to the works of Cage and Merce Cunningham. Here again he brought up Young, reproaching the "more powerful pundits of musical taste" for "unwaveringly" rejecting or ignoring the New Yorker's work. It was nonetheless enjoyed by audiences, he wrote (1964, 659), thus endowing a future ally with authority.

ONE SOUND

Two years after this remonstrance in 1964, Cardew was named a Fellow of the Royal Academy of Music. No longer was he an unknown in the eyes of the British music establishment. Besides his columns in the *Musical Times* and *Tempo,* his name—as an author, a translator of musicological works, and especially a composer—had appeared in *Music & Letters,* the *Musical Quarterly*, and *Notes.* In 1966 he published "One Sound: La Monte Young" in the *Musical Times,* including a biographical sketch of the composer and an analytical overview of his music. In this article Cardew sought to enshrine new facts: Young was indeed a great figure in music, of the same caliber as Stockhausen, as guaranteed by a recognized musicologist and composer addressing the music world through an eminent journal that aimed to cover the most recent developments in music. Since 1960, thanks especially to Cardew, his pronouncements, and his concerts, Young's music was indeed part of the contemporary musical landscape.

The status that Cardew accorded to Young in 1966 was further bolstered by new arguments. Even the inevitable influence of serial music was summoned: Young had studied with Leonard Stein (Cardew 1966, 959). In addition to being taught by the well-known former assistant to Schoenberg (Morgan 2001), he benefited from Stockhausen's teachings in Darmstadt in 1959. Moreover, although "it was difficult for the two composers—both 'giants' of new music as it has turned out—to find a level of communication," Cardew asserted, "there must have been some important interchange of a non-verbal kind" (959). Thus, Cardew wrote, "Stockhausen's *Piano Piece IX* [is] a weak, aesthetic version of the piece *For Henry Flynt*—and conversely the complex manipulations of random number tables that constitute the groundwork of La Monte's early pieces surely owe something to the 'statistical field' theory that Stockhausen was elaborating at the time"

(959). *Vision* by Young (1959), Cardew continued, was based on the use of a "random number book" (959), while *Poem* relied on an evolution of the same methods: the work now included any type of activity, whether it involved sound or not. Indeed, according to Cardew, that was what accounted for the connection between the "complex early compositions" and the "utter simplicity" of subsequent works by Young (959).[8]

Through Cardew's analysis, the works became the fruit of mutual exchanges: Stockhausen borrowed repetitions from Young, while Young borrowed the manipulations of number tables from Stockhausen. Although Cardew did not make it explicit, he seemed to justify Young's passage from the complex to the simple by the fact that Young, partly thanks to Stockhausen and his statistical fields, concentrated on a complex form of numerical randomness; this randomness led him to include any activity, so that "all being and happening" finally came down to "a single performance," and thus to simplicity (959). And if Young was impressed by Stockhausen, he impressed the German composer as well, Cardew asserted. That declaration, coming from someone who associated with both composers in Darmstadt, is hardly insignificant, which is perhaps why Cardew did not need to explain how this exchange between the "giants" took place. Against the new support from serialists (Stein and Stockhausen), Cardew ultimately pitted Cage, who, "in a humorous moment," denied Young's authorship of a series of works (959). The anecdote highlights the importance of Young, who was also followed by composers such as George Brecht and Toshi Ichiyanagi and then published a "great *Anthology*" (959; see also Young and Mac Low 1963). Young was on his way to becoming a leading figure in modern music.

Since then, however, Cardew continued, Young wrote almost nothing: "The *Henry Flynt* piece and a *Death Chant* on the death of a friend's child are the only compositions known to me. Instead of composing he took to improvising long concerts with various associates," namely his wife, Marian Zazeela; Tony Conrad; and "a Welsh musician who was responsible for introducing the tape [of a performance by Young] into this country," John Cale (960). With amplified instruments and voice, these musicians produced "variations of timbre and texture . . . by tuning and intensity of the various partials of a single fundamental tone" (960). And if for some these sounds were the most horrible that one could imagine, they moved us (or "should" move us, he added) more than "any merely artistic or intelligent attempt to shake the foundations of our complacent normality" (960).

LILLIPUTIAN

Roger Smalley's response to Cardew's convergent rereading of the aesthetics of Young and Stockhausen was not long in coming: his letter to the editor appeared in the *Musical Times* at the beginning of 1967 (1967a). Like Cardew, Smalley was a well-known figure in the British music establishment. He was one of the pianists most active in performing contemporary music, particularly that of Stockhausen, with whom he had studied composition two years earlier.[9] In his letter, Smalley addressed not so much the influence of *X for Henry Flynt* on *Piano Piece IX* as Cardew's reading of it. Unlike Young, Smalley asserted, Stockhausen made music; one need only listen to what followed the 227 repetitions of the same chord in the German composer's piece. But in Young's piece, "nothing else happens." Stockhausen, Smalley added, "is certainly a giant—probably the tallest; La Monte Young is, by comparison, a Lilliputian." The former's conceptions "are expressed in a musical language of sovereign assurance and power." For their part, Young's later compositions "have no interest whatsoever as far as musical construction, development or form are concerned," and in fact some of his works could not even "be expressed in musical notation"; indeed, Smalley added, "I don't even see how they can be performed." As for Cardew's verdict with regard to "our complacent normality" and his justification of the chaos in Young's work, Smalley retorted that "a composer may be obsessive but is never chaotic, and . . . his ideas may come from life but never just *consist* of life . . . they must be expressed in a musical syntax." In any event, he concluded, hearing Young's work "either slightly annoys or thoroughly bores me."

It appears that Young's recent works interested no other British critics besides his habitual champion. For Cardew in 1966, Young's body of work seemed to end in 1962, with *X for Henry Flynt* and *Death Chant* (1960). Mentions of Young in Cardew's subsequent articles again referred to his pre-1962 compositions rather than his work with his "various associates" (Cardew 1967; 1968).

IMPROVISATIONS

The connection between Cardew and Young did not, however, disappear; instead, it operated at a different level. Some of the characteristics that Cardew had formerly attributed to Young's music can, in fact, be noted in Cardew's descriptions of his own works in the late 1960s.

In 1966, Cardew joined a group whose music was described as "continuous improvisation which admits all sounds" (Parsons 1968, 430). The group was AMM, with Keith Rowe, Lou Gare, and Eddie Prévost.[10] Like Young's group, as described by Cardew (1966, 960), AMM used amplification to transform sounds and produce new ones (Parsons 1968, 430). In spring 1968 Cardew's own group—the Cornelius Cardew Ensemble— performed Young's music (*Death Chant*) along with that of another American composer, Terry Riley (*In C*, 1964).[11] A year later he founded his own improvisation group, the Scratch Orchestra, and published the ensemble's "Constitution" (Cardew 1969). There he again emphasized his interest in Young's music as well as Riley's. Both figure prominently in the list of works played by the ensemble (Cardew 1969, 619). Once again, the aesthetics of these composers, as Cardew conveyed them, seemed intimately linked to his own: for example, the Scratch Orchestra's music, like Young's, was concert music in which each of the members was encouraged to contribute accompaniments "performable continuously for indefinite periods" (617). The notation was free, and its place was secondary, while improvisation played a decisive role (619). One important element, however, seemed to distinguish the Scratch Orchestra from Young's group: the former indulged in the performance of "popular classics"— Beethoven, Mozart, and even John Cage—cut up or freely rearranged, particularly through improvisation (617–18).[12]

When he published his "Constitution" in 1969, Cardew had been teaching at the Royal Academy of Music, Morley College of Art, and Maidstone College of Art for several months. The composers Michael Parsons and Howard Skempton were students of his whom he invited to join the Scratch Orchestra. Many others joined as well: Gavin Bryars, Michael Chant, Brian Dennis, Brian Eno, Christopher Hobbs, Michael Nyman, Jill and Tom Phillips, Hugh Schrapnel, Dave Smith, John Tilbury, and John White figure among the students or collaborators of Cardew who swelled the orchestra's ranks.[13] Many of these would themselves become teachers: Bryars and Parsons at Portsmouth; Nyman at Trent Polytechnic, Maidstone, and Goldsmith's College; Tilbury at South West Essex Technical College, Kingston, Portsmouth, and Falmouth; White at Leicester Polytechnic. Most of them created their own groups in Cardew's footsteps: White, Hobbs, and Schrapnel were together again in Promenade Theatre Orchestra; Bryars, Eno, and Nyman in Portsmouth Sinfonia.[14]

It was the end of the 1960s and beginning of the '70s. Cardew's work of musical militancy was about to take a political turn, in the literal sense, when he turned his back on the avant-garde to focus on the creation of music to serve the Marxist cause.[15] At that time any aesthetic bonds he had managed to forge between his work and Stockhausen's broke. In 1974 Cardew gave a talk that was broadcast on BBC radio and published in its magazine, the *Listener*; he then republished it in a collection of his essays (1974). The lecture (as well as the book) was titled "Stockhausen Serves Imperialism" and denounced the composer's participation in imperialism through his cosmic composition *Refrain* (1959), which Cardew saw as disconnected from the painful contradictions of the real world. The aesthetic union of Cardew and Stockhausen became even more difficult when a former student of Cardew's who was active at the *Listener* published a book titled *Experimental Music* (Nyman 1974). In it Nyman solidified the contrast between the hypercontrol characterizing Stockhausen's music and the freedom that marked that of Cardew, Cage, and the "experimentalists." The book was a resounding success, and the notion of a link between the two composers faded into oblivion.[16]

AFTER CARDEW

In the wake of Cardew, many others stepped up to fortify the standing of Young or that of their former teacher in the landscape of contemporary music. Howard Skempton defended his teacher as well as Young against Smalley's criticisms in 1967;[17] in 1968 in the *Musical Times*, Jill Phillips described a gathering of "extraordinarily talented and devoted" musicians as well as the "good moments" in the performance of *Death Chant*, a "minimalist" work by the American composer (Phillips 1968a), while students from Morley College and Maidstone College of Art presented Young's *Trio for Strings* in May 1969 at the Round House (*Musical Times* 110, no. 1515 [May 1969]: 552).[18] One of the most fervent defenders of the aesthetic that Cardew promoted was one of his first students, Michael Parsons. Parsons focused his attention on a composer whom Cardew had closely associated with Young: Terry Riley. In May 1968, Parsons reviewed a concert of works by Young and Riley performed by the Cornelius Cardew Ensemble at the Institute of Contemporary Arts. In this review, he established a connection between Riley's *In C* (1964) and Cageian chance by appealing to the audience to link them (Parsons 1968). For *In C*, Riley had specified a series of musical cells transcribed in traditional notation; he also provided a long series of instructions as to the structure and performance of the piece.[19] Parsons reinterpreted the composer's musical text to highlight its indeterminate aspects.[20] Indeed, it is up to the listener, he wrote, to "find his own significance" in the direct experience he has of a work (429). The repetitions of *In C*, Parsons asserted, had nothing to do with a structuring into motifs or an attempt to organize sound. These continual repetitions became lost in a jumble of sound that had to be seen "as a world of immediate sensation." Thus, by mobilizing the audience and its direct experience of the sonic jumble, Parsons managed to reconcile the repetitions, cells, and structures with Cageian chance.[21]

Cardew's work in promoting Young's music (and that of some of his associates, such as Riley) in Britain over the course of the 1960s, continued by some of his disciples, clearly paid off. Over the years Smalley, who had stood up for Stockhausen to castigate Cardew and Young in 1967, gradually revised his judgment. Already in 1968 he seemed much less critical of Young. He asserted that Stockhausen's *Hymnen*, stemming from his search for a "World-music," was particularly influenced by the American composer (563). In 1969, on the model of AMM (Mark 2012, 99–100), Smalley founded Intermodulation, an improvisation group, with Tim Souster, a composer who had promoted the work of Cardew and Young on the BBC Third Programme as well as in the journal *Tempo* (Souster 1968–69, 6).[22] The group played Cardew, Riley, and Stockhausen.[23] In 1972 Smalley dubbed Cardew "the most important English composer since Dunstable," or at least "the first composer since that time who has radiated rather than absorbed influences" (1972c, 593). He then asserted that the section "On

the Role of the Instructions in the Interpretation of Indeterminate Music,"
published in *Treatise Handbook* (Cardew 1971, xiv–xvi) and "principally
concerned with La Monte Young's *X for Henry Flynt* . . . should be required
reading for those critics who dismiss this music with an air of philistine
indifference" (593).[24] Some months later, again following Cardew in his
Treatise Handbook (1971, xx), he posited that "perhaps it is the simplification rather than the elaboration of musical language which is now the most
fruitful way forward." Riley's music and especially Young's had convinced
him (Smalley 1972d). The former detractor laid down his arms.

LA MONTE YOUNG, COMPOSER OF ART MUSIC

In the Britain of the late 1960s and early '70s, as we have seen, a range of
forces combined to validate Young's standing as a member of the music
establishment. What happened in Britain from 1967 to 1972 that might
have helped change the perceived nature of an American body of work
from 1960? Interconnected actors in all fields (musicologists, critics, composers, and musicians), along with their artifacts (articles, courses, programs, and institutions), mounted a collective effort around the figure of
Young and his aesthetic, as presented by Cardew and his successors, that
grew until it became hard to ignore. After Smalley's conversion, the "state
of music" as it was known in the early 1960s subtly changed. A "new
music" appeared.

   The presence of Young and his work in the American contemporary
music landscape as seen from Britain now rested on a solid mound of facts
whose legitimacy was questioned less and less. If there were still those
who would dispute Young's place in the music establishment, they would
have to confront a long chain of alliances formed over the entire decade.
The importance that some wished to give to Young had been realized: in
the British music establishment of the early 1970s, Young had clearly
become a composer to be taken seriously. "Seriously," too, because even
though *jazz, improvisation, group, performer/composer,* and *audience* are
among the many terms that dot the pages written on Young and his associates, their work still tends to be placed on the serious side of the boundary separating popular and serious music.[25]

The La Monte Young who was promulgated in Britain through Cardew's campaign was essentially the pre-1962 composer (with his *Compositions of 1960, Poem, X for Henry Flynt,* and *Death Chant*). Although the emergence and success of improvisation groups seen as sharing some of the qualities of Young's later experimentations were recognized, this trend received less attention. An aesthetic relying on the collective playing of one or two sustained sounds—electrified, no less—remained difficult to defend, even through a Cageian "analysis grid." In the early 1970s, however ill-defined the outlines of his music may have been, it was the early Young who, in Great Britain, won his place in the world of art music.

3. Transcribing Music

NEW YORK AVANT-GARDISTS
AND MONOTONALITY

NEW YORK AVANT-GARDISTS

The American music establishment, like the British, did not fail to note Young's first steps into the avant-garde at the beginning of the 1960s. In 1962 the composer was mentioned in the *Musical Times*' American competitor, the *Musical Quarterly*. At that time the latter journal was directed, as it had been since 1915, by the music publisher Schirmer. Like the *Musical Times*, it sought to reach both professional musicians and music lovers. Hugh Wiley Hitchcock, a specialist in Marc-Antoine Charpentier teaching at Hunter College in New York (Morgan 2001b), was a regular contributor. He gave Young a far less favorable welcome in the journal than his British colleagues did. Reporting on the "ultra-modern" concert series ONCE—A Festival of Musical Premieres, he wrote that the pieces by Young and by Terry Jennings, musicians associated with the "Cage-Tudor-Maxfield New York Group," "communicated not a shred of novelty, iconoclasm, or even good old nonsensical Dada. Their self-conscious and slightly sheepish doings were tired, effete, lacking in conviction, humor, anger, involvement—or, indeed, any expression or evocation of human emotion. They seem to have confused inaction with oriental tranquillity, lack of responsibility with the detachment of Zen" (Hitchcock 1962, 245–46).

Paul Cooper, a composer who, like Hitchcock, had studied at the University of Michigan, also attended the concert of Young and Jennings. His review, published in the *Ann Arbor News*, was even harsher. "Total indignation," "thoroughly degenerate," "in brinkmanship of insanity" are the terms he used to describe the performance of these "two over-aged juvenile delinquents [who] slouched into town attempting to represent the avant-garde of New York" (quoted in Flynt 1996, 73). Their approach was not new, he wrote: "The Dadaists and surrealists of the 20's and 30's were infinitely more imaginative." In any case, Cooper continued, "I for one refuse to believe that a movement based on combined negative philosophies of East and West filtered through talentless, unprincipled personalities should achieve more than an agonized reappraisal from serious composers. . . . Some pianissimo pokings at the piano . . . some exploration of the squealing possibilities of a single reed saxophone; . . . reciting of 'words, words, words . . . ' for approximately 10 minutes"—for Cooper, this list spoke for itself. "At times we succumbed to oral ridicule, needless to say," he commented. "But . . . there can be no question of its having any value either for music, theater, or humor." For Cooper, as for Hitchcock, the clear lack of savoir faire and the inability of Young and his collaborators to transcend the aesthetic limits that others had crossed before them denied their music any credibility.

Three years later, in 1965, Hitchcock again wrote on a concert by Young for the *Musical Quarterly*. This time the concert was given at the Carnegie Recital Hall as part of a series organized by Lukas Foss, inviting the "best young American performer/composers" (Hitchcock 1965, 530). Even though Young had recently "turned to classical Indian acoustical and intervallic theory for inspiration" (538), Hitchcock introduced him via his association with Cage.[1] Young, he wrote, presented one of the "farthest-out" pieces in the series: *The Second Dream of the High-Tension Line Step-down Transformer*. Hitchcock offered a brief analysis of the piece, describing the intervallic construction of its drones as well as the resultant "static 'harmonic' music" (539). He then translated the work in the form of a staff with no bar line, presenting four whole notes whose ratios were 36/35/32/24—on this staff, more or less G/F#/F/C (fig. 1).

Figure 1. La Monte Young, *The Second Dream of the High-Tension Line Stepdown Transformer*, transcription by Hugh Wiley Hitchcock (Hitchcock 1965, 539).

Hitchcock's piece rendered a triple reduction: through his own words, through the transcription of the score, and when just isolating the "ten minutes'-worth" performed. Through it, Young's work appeared rather unconvincing, to say the least. These four notes—deprived of their harmonics, the arrival of which Hitchcock admitted not having the patience to wait for;[2] stripped of their volume, their indeterminate nature, and their significance in Indian symbolism; uprooted from their performance context to be analyzed in a journal of the music establishment—would long be ignored. By approaching Young's music solely in terms of harmonic analysis (without, however, considering the subject of harmonics itself), Hitchcock led the reader down a single path. In so doing, he helped exclude the composer from an "avant-garde" of his own design.

MONOTONALITY

Over the second half of the 1960s, a series of New York art critics sought to promote a pictorial and sculptural trend that they called *ABC Art, reject art,* or *minimal art.*[3] These critics were Jill Johnston, Barbara Rose, John Perreault, and Lucy Lippard. They wrote in *Art News,* the *Village Voice, Art International, Artforum, Arts Magazine,* and *Art in America.* Most of them did not conceive this trend within strict disciplinary boundaries. For some, minimalism was indeed not only artistic but also musical.

It all began in 1964 with an article by Jill Johnston, a critic for the journal *Art News* and the news weekly *Village Voice.* Johnston covered painting and sculpture for the former and dance for the latter.[4] On November 19, however, she ventured out of her usual fields and authored a music column in the *Village Voice*. Her piece, titled "La Monte Young," famously marks the composer's first appearance in that weekly paper (Johnston 1964). Johnston, who a year earlier had mentioned the visual art of one of Young's former music partners, Walter De Maria (1963), did not explicitly link the two modes of artistic expression: apart from his "Neo-Dada" pieces in 1960, Young's work—"that may well be, as [Young] says, a major new development in musical history"—evoked above all, in her view, the musical stasis of the East, or even of Morton Feldman's work (14). Nevertheless, the fact that a New York art critic was attentive to Young's music was hardly insignificant.

A year later another art critic, Barbara Rose—a regular contributor to *Art International, Artforum*, and (as Johnston would also become, some years later) *Art in America*—established a clear connection between Young's music and the visual arts.[5] Rose, at that time married to the painter Frank Stella, whom she helped to become one of the great representatives of pictorial minimalism, wrote "ABC Art," an essay devoted to a "new sensibility" (1965, 58), in which she traced its lineage.[6] For Rose this "new sensibility," whose "blank, neutral, mechanical impersonality contrasts so violently with the romantic, biographical abstract expressionist style which preceded," had taken root in the work of Kazimir Malevich and Marcel Duchamp, whose procedures "radically altered the course of art history." For some, we learn, this sensibility went by the name of *minimal art*. Rose borrowed the term from the philosopher Richard Wollheim, who had written about it a few months earlier (Wollheim 1965). Indeed, she shared a number of his views: if the public resisted this art, it was essentially because of "the spectator's sense that the artist has not worked hard enough or put enough effort in his art" (Rose 1965, 58). Although these works were perceived as inferior, their art content was "intentionally low." She quoted John Ashbery: "What matters is the artists' will to discover, rather than the manual skills" (58). If visual artists such as Darby Bannard, Larry Zox, Richard Artschwager, and Andy Warhol owed a debt to Kazimir Malevich or Marcel Duchamp, then dancers and composers— for they also participated in the movement—were all indebted to Cage. Rose considered Young one of these composers, or even the only one. His *Dream Music* concerts, which lasted several days, could be likened to Andy Warhol's film *Sleep* (1963), as well as to Satie's music, in particular his *Vexations* of 1893. This aesthetic of experimentation and inertia, Rose added, "seems applicable to a certain amount of avant-garde activity of the moment" (65).

To which part of the avant-garde? We do not find out. Nor would we find out when John Perreault, art critic for the *Village Voice* and *Arts Magazine,* followed in the footsteps of Johnston and Rose three years later. Perreault (1968), too, discusseed Young's work. He borrowed a number of analytical elements from the two critics:[7] the influence of Cage and Duchamp, as well as that of the East, in particular.[8] He also took up the link between music and the visual arts—the unchanging sound of Young's pieces, he wrote, invited the listener to an aesthetic experience resembling that of painting (29)—but he likewise did not extend his argument to encompass other artists. This music, which he called "monotonal," in reference to monochromes, was Young's alone.[9] That same year Lucy Lippard, another critic associated with *Art Forum, Art International,* and *Art in America,* and also the wife of another minimal artist, Robert Ryman, made her contribution in the *Hudson Review* (1968). There she associated Young with the visual art of Larry Poons. But for Lippard it was not a question of "minimalism" or "ABC Art," but rather "reject art."

The attempt to translate Young's aesthetic in terms of visual art and to integrate the composer with pictorial minimalism surely helped to form his cultural cachet in the 1960s New York art scene (just as it helped, by invoking the figure of a prominent composer, to reinforce the foundations of the pictorial movement). But this attempt did not extend beyond his own work, which was regularly portrayed as that of a former neo-Dadaist converted to the musical charms of the East (see esp. Perrault 1968).

4. 1967

What did *contemporary American music* mean at the twilight of the 1960s? What ideas were established on the subject at the time? Having considered this question for the beginning of the decade (chapter 1), let us now look at where matters stood some months after Cardew's article on the "giant" Young appeared in the November 1966 issue of the *Musical Times*.

The American contemporary musical landscape had changed since the beginning of the 1960s. Seven years had passed; new musicians, new composers and their works had been grafted onto the stock. But more than that, if we look closely, we see that the foundations of the former landscape, which had seemed so stable, had shifted. It seems, for example, that Cage's position and the place of popular music had perhaps been ill-defined in the former cultural panorama.

MUSIC IN A NEW FOUND LAND

In 1964, Cage's name—the Cage of chance and indeterminacy—was inscribed in gold letters in *Music in a New Found Land*, a book by Wilfrid Mellers, a composer, prolific author, and head of the music department at the University of York.[1] The recent importance of Cage's aesthetic in American music was not the only new fact that Mellers presented; his work also emphasized the notion that popular music constituted one of the country's most significant musical features. The second part of *Music in a New Found Land* is thus devoted to "the world of commerce" (237), encompassing the jazz of King Oliver, Louis Armstrong, Duke Ellington, and John Coltrane, as well as George Gershwin's musical comedies and Leonard Bernstein's musical dramas. According to Mellers's 1964 account, the image of the previous decade's music as portrayed by others had subtly changed. Indeed, he was not content merely to transmit the more or less established conceptions of authors such as Chase (1955); he slightly modified their nature. Previous authors had omitted Cage's aleatoric and indeterminate work; Mellers corrected their "error." He also established the dominant place of that "world of commerce" that many authors had left out.

In 1964, when Mellers published his book, the fine adjustments he had made to the portrait of the musical landscape were as yet valid only for him, along with his publishers, Barrie & Rockliff in London and Alfred A. Knopf in New York. The predominant place he accorded to Cageian chance and indeterminacy, as well as to popular music over the course of the 1950s, needed to be confirmed by others before it could firmly take root. And for other authors to take up Mellers's views, he needed to incite their interest. That is precisely what happened over the following years: in the *Musical Times,* for example, Peter Dickinson, the "pro-Cageian" theorist and composer, delighted in seeing his mentor appear in Mellers's book (1964, 660). While most other authors, Dickinson wrote, had quite simply left Cage's recent developments in the shadows, Mellers finally treated it "seriously." Dickinson's was but one declaration of support among others: little by little, thanks to their validation by other authors, the paradigms presented in *Music in a New Found Land* would become staples of contemporary musical thought.[2]

THE TWENTIETH CENTURY WITH YOUNG

In 1967, Young's position in American music was similar to that of Cage a bit earlier: his "greatness" was self-evident only in the eyes of certain people, namely Cardew and a few New York art critics. They were, at least, almost the only ones to have publicly affirmed that view. For that claim to gain wider recognition, Cardew had to incite the interest of other protagonists, who would then adopt and transmit his conceptions. As we have already seen, Cardew did so through his students and collaborators over the last third of the 1960s. But what was the situation beyond his circle of initiates?

Prior to 1967, Young appears to have attracted little interest among other authors. The ninth edition of *The International Cyclopedia of Music and Musicians* by the musicologist Oscar Thompson (1964),[3] one of the most complete and popular music encyclopedias,[4] makes no mention of Young in 1964. The same is true of the fourth edition of *Our American Music* by John Tasker Howard the following year (1965), even though its aim was to give an almost exhaustive history and to include recent music developments in the United States, particularly in popular music.[5] In 1966, when William Austin presented an overview of music since Debussy, published by Norton, he likewise made no place for Young.[6] The most interesting developments in American music were, according to Austin, to be found in the compositions of Walter Piston, Henry Cowell, Roger Sessions, and Elliott Carter (442). Austin's work marked a milestone; in Hitchcock's words, "For the first time, twentieth-century music has been treated with the same scholarly standards, the same bibliographical controls, the same careful historical method as earlier periods of Western music history" (1966, 254).[7] That same year the thirteenth volume of *Die Musik in Geschichte und Gegenwart* came out, containing an entry on the United States ("Vereinigte Staaten," cols. 1467–86). There we find no very different content from what one was wont to read at the beginning of the decade: experimental, electronic, and twelve-tone musicians as well as a bit on the musical comedy—these were all one needed to know about American music (Broder 1966, cols. 1478–79).

In 1967, some months after the publication of Cardew's article on Young in the *Musical Times,* Mellers took up the twentieth century where he had left off in 1964. He published a work on "renewal in twentieth-century music" titled *Caliban Reborn.* It aims to give a "fresh vision of reality" (ix). Here the boundary separating art from commerce in his earlier writings further diminishes: Harry Partch and Cage stand alongside jazz and Eastern music, Stockhausen and Feldman, the Beatles and Bob Dylan. The young generation of American composers includes, among others, Harold Shapero and Alexei Haieff, who follow the tradition of Stravinsky and Copland; Milton Babbitt and Mel Powell, who fall under Schoenbergian postserialism; Lukas Foss, an eclectic; and even Seymour Shifrin, who draws on jazz. Young still does not participate in the great march of the twentieth century, regardless of what Cardew and his peers have said of him.[8]

Also in 1967, Peter S. Hansen published the second edition of his *Introduction to Twentieth-Century Music,* its scope limited to "those composers who have been most influential in the period" (vi), up to 1964. The names that appear here are Varèse, Boulez, Stockhausen, and Cage. Apart from Stockhausen, Henri Pousseur, and Feldman (374–76), no one is mentioned after Cage. That same year Barney Childs, who had highlighted the link between Cage and Young the year before in *Texas Studies in Literature and Language* (1966, 437), published *Contemporary Composers on Contemporary Music* with Elliott Schwartz (Schwartz and Childs 1967). The collection of essays gives pride of place to experimentalism and that music "in which the performer's role is enlarged" or that makes use of chance techniques (xv). Nonetheless, it presents no writings or interviews of Young. The composer's name appears only in the credits, for having first published two essays by Richard Maxfield that are reprinted in the book (349–61, originally in Young and Mac Low 1963), and in an interview with Cage, who confirms his interest—even as he emphasizes the difference between their respective works—for Young's music (335–48, reprinted from Reynolds 1962, 45–52). Although this homage is not insignificant, the students, concertgoers, and musicians for whom the book is intended (vii–viii) learn nothing more about Young.

Two years later, a pedagogical work by Robert D. Wilder titled *Twentieth-Century Music* (1969) bespoke the impact that the directions taken by these various authors had on music instruction: in 1969, music ended with Cage, or at the latest with Foss.[9] It seems that only Cardew and some of his close associates definitively recognized Young's qualities. Wilder perhaps sided with Hitchcock, who some years earlier had shown very little interest in the composer's creations, which to him were devoid of any "shred of novelty" (1962, 245–46).

Indeed, the Dadaist connection that Hitchcock made is precisely what certain critics retained through the second half of the 1960s. Some authors chose this approach to write Young's name into the history of music. In 1966 Gilbert Chase, who had contributed to *The International Cyclopedia of Music and Musicians* two years before, published the second edition of *America's Music: From the Pilgrims to the Present*. There he continued to postulate that the major styles in American music had taken root outside the concert hall—all the more so for folk and popular traditions. This new edition now included Young, who is mentioned as a member of the "neo-Dadaist" wing of avant-garde music, along with George Brecht and Terry (incorrectly referred to as Peter) Jennings (663).[10]

In 1967 Eric Salzman published an introduction to twentieth-century music in the Prentice-Hall History of Music Series at the request of the series editor, Hitchcock. The series, Hitchcock noted in the foreword, aimed to give a "panoramic view of the history of Western music" (Salzman 1967, v). He mentioned Young in the context of a movement described as antirational and aleatoric, epitomized by Cage. The essence of these compositions consists in their "lack of identity," Salzman wrote (168), returning to the views he had expressed in *The New American Arts* two years earlier (1965). The works "proceed in short, inevitable steps from long sets of meaningless directions for meaningless and useless 'existentialist' actions to a kind of 'neo-realist' Theatre of Aimless Activity, and then to 'Happenings' and perhaps on to meaningless, useless real life" (168). Young's appearance in Salzman's volume is tentative and hardly laudatory, but nonetheless it marks the second time in two years that the composer figured in a monograph devoted to contemporary music.

Also in 1967, Peter Yates published a work on the evolution of twentieth-century music "from the end of the harmonic era into the present era of sound"—that is, up to performance art and the experimental tradition that brought up the rear toward the end of the decade. Yates was a critic at the magazine *Arts and Architecture*. His book, he asserted, did not have a musicological orientation; recounting the evolution of twentieth-century music did not call for the traditional notated examples (xi, xiv). He posed the end of the harmonic era as his premise, citing Young's just-intonation work as proof. "One of his 'Dream Tortoises'" thus became a ritual experience that was "deliberately unmetrical or out of phase" (247, 248). The piece evoked the Hindu *Om,* Yates found, and it required the listener, in order to understand it, to let go of all preconceived judgments.

It was Young's third appearance in an account of twentieth-century American music. In the first, he was quite neo-Dadaist; in the second, quite post-Cageian; in the third, he was a harmonist and a ritualist with a "unique" aesthetic. To the extent that we can rely on these authors, we find that in 1967 Young enjoyed a place in the contemporary music landscape, despite the fact that the nature of his music was still poorly understood. Richard Kostelanetz's writings, however, would soon shed light on its essence, as we will see in chapter 5.

5. Creating Genres

THE THEATRE OF MIXED MEANS
AND DREAM MUSIC

THE THEATRE OF MIXED MEANS

In 1968 Richard Kostelanetz, a critic and essayist who wrote for the *New York Times*, the *New York Herald Tribune*, and the *Village Voice*, among other periodicals, published the first book in the United States to have an entire chapter devoted to Young: *The Theatre of Mixed Means* (1968). Kostelanetz linked the New York composer to the latest developments in modern music, as Cardew had done; to harmonic theory, as Hitchcock had done; and to the visual arts, following Barbara Rose and some of her colleagues. But here the connections were superficial. For Kostelanetz, as for Smalley in the beginning, Young's work was not musical. Kostelanetz's explanation differed from Smalley's, however: Young's work was instead part of "the most interesting recent development in American theatre" (xi). The approach taken by Kostelanetz largely contrasted with what was already known about Young. It did not, however, appear out of the blue, having been elaborated on the margins of the music establishment for almost three years. Since 1965 a handful of theorists had enlisted Young and his music in their campaign to recognize new forms of artistic activity transcending the division of art—from film to music, dance to poetry—in fixed categories. Some dubbed these forms *happenings, events,* or even *new theater.* Let us take a closer look at them.

New Theatre

To understand the emergence of Kostelanetz's concepts, we must briefly turn to the *Tulane Drama Review,* a mouthpiece for the discipline of performance studies that emerged in American universities in the early 1960s.[1] In that journal, Young's work, snubbed by the American music establishment, found its first theatrical and academic celebration in the United States. It won acclaim from Richard Schechner, who would found and direct the Performance Group some years later, and Michael Kirby, who subsequently joined him.[2] The two editors devoted the winter 1965 issue of the *Tulane Drama Review* to a "new theatre," naming Young one of its main representatives, following Cage, in particular. For after Cage had enabled silence to become music in *4'33,* "any activity or event may be presented as part of a music concert," we learn. Thus, "Young may use a butterfly as his sound source" (Kirby 1965, 25).

Young himself was among the issue's contributors. There he presented "Lecture 1960" (Young 1965), the transcription of a talk he gave at a summer workshop held by the choreographer Ann (now Anna) Halprin. It consisted of a series of commentaries on his early works, in particular—for example, *Composition 1960 #5,* with the butterfly (see sidebar 2). Published in the form of an article in a university journal, Young's lecture enabled the academy, to whom the talk was now addressed, to assess, through the artist's own words, the theatrical nature of his so-called word pieces.[3]

Neither the lecture nor Kirby's introduction to the issue explicitly made an aesthetic connection between Cage, the word pieces, and Young's interest in continuous sounds (which had drawn Hitchcock's attention; see chapter 4). The connection was at most implicit: it was in 1960, during Young's theatrical or Cageian period—Cage having, in effect, authorized "any activity or event" to be part of a concert (Kirby 1965, 25)—that Young had confirmed his turn to "extended sounds."

Nor was the link between "any activity or event" and Young's "extended sounds" what interested Kirby and his collaborators. In their writings,

Sidebar 2

Turn a butterfly (or any number of butterflies) loose in the performance area.

When the composition is over, be sure to allow the butterfly to fly away outside.

The composition may be any length but if an unlimited amount of time is available, the doors and windows may be opened before the butterfly is turned loose and the composition may be considered finished when the butterfly flies away.

La Monte Young, *Composition 1960 #5*, in Young and Mac Low (1963).

Young above all fit within the framework of the "new theatre," which, we read, shook up the relation between performer and audience and integrated the work in its environment.[4] For Kirby, Young's 1960 *Compositions*, conceived in the form of instructions, primarily highlighted the interpretative act and the performer's relation to space and audience. When Susan Sontag mentioned Young in the same journal two years later,[5] she translated his aesthetic in the same way: in terms of the recent idea, in theater as in cinema, of art as an act of violence, reversing the audience's former passive relation to the work (1967, 37).[6] Kostelanetz confronted the New York composer's work in a similar vein.

"Cisum"

Earlier on, however, Kostelanetz understood Young's work differently. Indeed, in 1965, as the editor of *The New American Arts,* he advocated a more strictly musical approach to Young's work: that of Salzman, the composer and critic assigned to the chapter on music. Salzman had already mentioned Young's music in hardly complimentary terms in the *New York Times* (1961). In his chapter for the 1965 anthology, although he included Young among the representatives of a "new American art," Salzman did not revise his opinion: Young's work was a pathetic successor to that of Cage, who himself only told "90 tiny funny stories" on his recording

Indeterminacy (Folkways 1959). Such works, Salzman asserted, were "non-music music [that] takes everything that music does and does it backwards" (1965, 261).

Although highly critical of Young, Salzman offered an argument linking the composer's work with Cage's aesthetic of sound: "Where music may be defined as an organization of sound, a piece of 'cisum' may consist of non-sound or silence;[7] where a piece of music would be a finite event in time, there are compositions which imply an indeterminate or possibly infinite length; there is even a piece which consists of two notes with the direction: 'Hold this for a long time.'" Thus the link between the Cageian silence of *4'33"* and Young's *Composition 1960 #7* was formed.

Toward Another Theater

Although Kostelanetz sided with Salzman's musical ideas in 1965, soon after he chose a different path, one mapped out in particular by those who defended a theatrical conception of Young's work. Just one year later, Kostelanetz published an article in the theater section of the monthly magazine *Art Voices* in which he rehabilitated Young's aesthetic. He presented Young as one of the principal representatives of a current that he himself was gradually constructing: the Theatre of Mixed Means (Kostelanetz 1966). Kostelanetz campaigned for the use of that name instead of *happening*. The latter term, Kostelanetz argued, created after the works of Allan Kaprow, referred to unplanned results that characterized only certain branches of the movement. By contrast, the concept of Theatre of Mixed Means isolated the movement's central feature: the use of elements as varied as music, dance, sculpture, and film (23).

To make the connection between Young's work and theater, Kostelanetz focused not on the word pieces mentioned by Kirby but rather on *The Tortoise, His Dreams and Journeys,* from Young's Theatre of Eternal Music. This piece, Kostelanetz asserted, lay at the center of this new aesthetic: it was multisensorial and contained visual and olfactory dimensions. Like Kirby—and unlike Salzman—Kostelanetz proposed an approach to Young's work that moved away from a strict musical reading. He himself was unconvinced that the musical meaning of Young's sound would be relevant to the audience. He preferred a theatrical conception of Young's work. Thus, according to the critic, Young's precursor was no longer so much Cage as Antonin Artaud. Like the latter, Young exploited electronic sensorial overload to move his audience. Lacking a greater openness to the sensorial qualities of art, he continued, the audience or the critic, indifferent or scandalized, could not properly grasp Young's work.

In 1967 Kostelanetz confirmed his admiration for Young in *Perspectives of New Music*, where he wrote an entire article castigating his colleagues in music literature for their incompetence, ignorance, and nepotism (125–26). In between two sections of criticism, he reiterated his interest in Young's piece *The Tortoise, His Dreams and Journeys*, which he professed to "enjoy and admire as mixed-means theatrical events in which the composer's 'notes' are a partial contribution to the total experience" (123–24).

Young's Mixed Means

In 1968, these "mixed-means theatrical events" were precisely the subject of Kostelanetz's book *The Theatre of Mixed Means*. The "genre" forged by the critic (xii) brought together artists as well-known as Cage, Halprin, Robert Rauschenberg, Kaprow, Claes Oldenburg, Ken Dewey, Young, Robert Whitman, and the USCO collective; it also constituted "the most interesting recent development in American theatre" (xi). In this work, Kostelanetz finally distanced himself from critiques he made in *The New American Arts*: "My opinion . . . was based upon inadequate research, some unfortunate experience, and a bias toward the theatre of literature I had learned about in college. Since then, I have seen many more examples of mixed-means performances, most of which pleased and excited me considerably" (xii). Kostelanetz explained his past error as a result of having "split the critical work into categories—cinema, fiction, dance, poetry, painting, theatre, and music," whereas "so much that is currently artistically advanced today straddles, if not transcends, these traditional divisions" (xii–xiii). Since the publication of *The New American Arts* in 1965, the work of performance studies advocates had clearly made an impact.

In his portrayal of Young, Kostelanetz relied on the writings of Cardew (1964, 1966), Yates (1967), Johnston (1964), and Jean Vanden Heuvel (1966). But the conclusions he drew about Young were very different from theirs. Cardew had placed Young's work within chance music and linked the composer to serialism, while for Johnston and Vanden Heuvel his music was a hallucinatory experience inspired by the East, and for Yates it was a ritual-harmonic experience that was "deliberately unmetrical or out of phase" (Yates 1967, 248). Kostelanetz, however, translated Young's aesthetic in other terms, framed by other conceptions. For him Young was, without a doubt, one of the representatives of a new Theatre of Mixed Means; his piece *The Tortoise, His Dreams and Journeys* figured "among the most exciting theatrical presentations" (Kostelanetz 1968, xii). Kostelanetz's high praise for Young elevated his own concept, even as he subtly drew on the works that preceded him.

He returned to earlier observations regarding Young's serial training with Stein and Stockhausen, Young's electronics experience with Stockhausen as well as with Richard Maxfield, and his interest in classical Indian and Japanese music (184).[8] In his interview with Young, he also brought in the composer's first music experiences and his involvement with jazz in the 1950s.[9] Indeed, we learn, as a saxophonist Young had made the rounds of clubs for a time with such figures as Billy Higgins and Don Cherry. Subsequently, however, he was no longer interested in the genre except "from a listening and speaking point of view" (187). Although his high school ambition was to break through in jazz, he gave it up in favor of "more serious composition" (187). Jazz was merely a biographical detour. Young was a skilled artist, an educated composer who could discuss and theorize on his work—work in which, regardless of what the critics said, all sensual reference was banished. Extreme volumes were simply a means of putting sound under a microscope, not a condition for hallucinatory bodily experiences or even a provocation.

Ultimately, the other aesthetics that Young subsequently touched on amounted to biographical detours as well. Webern drew Young away from jazz at the end of the 1950s. The discovery of classical Indian and Japanese music enabled him to turn his back on the twelve-tone technique. Cage's aesthetic offered him another exit: Young's pieces from 1959 and 1960 were in large part the product of the "immediate impact" of his exposure to Cage's music (194). This discovery led to *The Tortoise*, a "performance" in which Young and his associates chanted a chord "of intrinsically infinite duration, amplified to the threshold of aural pain" (212). The demonstration has reached its destination.

On reading Young's interview, however, we find that the nature of his connection to theater remains nebulous. What interested Young above all were the sound and the manifestation of its harmonic components (197), much more than the centrality of the performer, the audience, and their environment evoked by Kirby or the "multi-sensory involvement" and theatrical mixed means mentioned by Kostelanetz (184, 183). Moreover, Young did not fit within any preexisting movement: "The Theatre of Eternal Music is establishing a tradition of its own," he asserted (216).

The thirty-five pages of analysis and interview with Young, unprecedented at the time, formed part of a work attempting to build this new Theatre of Mixed Means. The cultural establishment, however, greeted them with an indifference similar to Kostelanetz's own vis-à-vis that group in *Perspectives of New Music* the year before. His book received almost no reviews in periodicals that were still rigidly divided among theater, music, and poetry. The existence of a genre that would shatter these "traditional forms of classification" (xiii) was not discussed further or adopted, at least in the short term. *The Theatre of Mixed Means* remains merely a book written in 1968 by Kostelanetz.[10]

DREAM MUSIC

In the period when, almost simultaneously, Cardew, Hitchcock, the New York art critics, and Kostelanetz seized on Young's work—portraying it in contrasting, if not contradictory, ways—the composer too strove to define his own music. He did so in a series of texts collected in *Selected Writings*, published by Heiner Friedrich in Munich (Young and Zazeela 1969).[11] *The Tortoise, His Dreams and Journeys* appears regularly at the center of his writings, but in a completely different framework from that designed by Kostelanetz to support his theatrical conception of Young's work. In fact, the composer refers more often to *Dream Music* and *Dream House*. And although *Dream House* incorporates luminous creations by Young's wife, the light artist Marian Zazeela, in Young's writings it is above all a place that holds sound. His music, Young asserted, constituted "a radical departure from European and even much Eastern music" (15). The cards were reshuffled once more.

Young maintained that the foundation of this music was harmony: "not European harmony,"[12] but that which emerged via harmonics "when any simple fundamental is produced" (5). This harmony was heard even before humans made music. The drone was thus the first sound, and dream houses were those places where the drone could be ceaselessly (re)incarnated for tens of thousands of years. This music could thus be played eternally, "just as the Tortoise has continued for millions of years past" (16). The music was produced by sine wave oscillators that generated a continuous live electronic sound environment and a series of chants that added other frequencies (11).

As opposed to Kostelanetz, who, to develop his mixed-means genre, emphasized the hybrid nature of the composer's work, Young underlined its sonic nature. Even so, since 1965 Zazeela's work in the piece had acquired its own importance (13). The visual dimension was indeed present, notably in *The Tortoise*, which Young sometimes defined as "a total environmental set of frequency structures in the media of sound and light" (11): the work combined the dissemination of sinusoidal signals and chants with the installation of "floating sculptures" and "dichroic sources" favoring color frequencies that corresponded to the music (11). The listener also participated in the play of frequencies, the composer maintained, by producing slight air currents, for example, that subtly shifted the mobiles and the luminous frequencies (14). This description meshed well with the theatrical genre of Kostelanetz, who was unsure that the musical meaning of Young's sound would be relevant to the audience (Kostelanetz 1966, 23).

At the end of the 1960s *The Tortoise* was the subject of at least three different readings (not including the various approaches to Young's complete works): a strictly musical and harmonic reading, by Hitchcock in the *Musical Quarterly;* a theatrical one, by Kostelanetz in his writings; and finally Young's own, focusing first on the sonic aspects and then on the visual ones. In all three cases, conceptions clashed: music versus theater, European harmony versus natural harmonics, and so on. The more the New York composer's work was studied, the less any consensus on the content and meaning of his music seemed possible.

6. Taking Sides over a New Medium

ELECTRONIC MUSIC

At the end of the 1960s, serial music and the developments in so-called aleatoric or indeterminate music that arose in the wake of Cage's works continued to divide the contemporary landscape outlined by the music establishment. Indeed, Young's music was often read and understood according to one orientation or the other. Meanwhile, however, a medium that many authors ignored had recently begun to take shape as a genre in its own right: electronic music. Apart from the writings of Schaeffer ([1952] 2012), Stockhausen (in his journal *Die Reihe*, since 1955), and Cage himself (1961), little had been published on the subject. Even then, as Robert Emmet Dolan attests in *Music in Modern Media* (1967), most of those works focused on technical considerations. In 1968, however, Hugh Davies published the *Répertoire international des musiques électroacoustiques*, a work that sought to inventory the production of electronic music at the time. Surprisingly, it associated Young with the movement, whereas critics up to that point had conceived the evolution of his music in quite different spheres. Davies's inventory describes certain of his *Compositions* from 1960 as "electronic creations" and characterizes *The Tortoise* as an "amplified" work. Young was in fact an electronic musician, according to Davies, and he was, moreover, far from being the only musician to be recruited by the defenders of the medium. New names appeared in articles and works devoted to the subject. Among many others, we note especially Terry Riley and a composer named Steve Reich. What is the history of this "alternative" reading of Young's work? How could a conception so far from what had been said about the composer up to that point have emerged at the end of the 1960s and, moreover, firmly take hold over the following years? By exploring the network formed around the writings of those who championed the electronic medium, we begin to see how.

ELECTRONIC CREATIONS

When Davies published the *Répertoire international des musiques électroacoustiques* (1968b), he had already spent at least four years campaigning for recognition of the genre. In 1964 he published "A Discography of Electronic Music and Musique Concrète." Between 1964 and 1966, he succeeded Cardew as Stockhausen's assistant, and in 1967, when Cardew was named professor at the Royal Academy of Music, he became the director of the electronic music studio at Goldsmiths' College (University of London). At that point it had been one year since Cardew mentioned Young's work in "One Sound" (1966) and even longer since he had been organizing concerts of the American composer's work in London. In 1968, pieces by Young, Cardew, and Davies were featured in a concert series in the capital (see *Musical Times* 109, no. 1499 [January 1968]: 94). That same year, Davies founded his own group, as Cardew had done with AMM. But unlike AMM, Davies's group, Gentle Fire, was "electronic" (Davies 2011, 53).[1] Davies was indeed an electronic musician; he said so loud and clear in the *Musical Times*, where he also announced his intention to promulgate these new sounds, which he himself represented, in England (Davies 1968a).

Davies's mission in publishing the *Répertoire* was to encompass "all the electronic music ever composed in the almost twenty years since composers first began to work in this medium" (1968b, iv).[2] Included among these pieces are *2 Sounds* from 1960, described as a "realization by Terry Riley and La Monte Young" (169, 239), along with Young's *Poem for Chairs, Tables, Benches, etc.* and *Composition 1960 #9* (also from 1960) and "electronic realizations" by Young (212, 218, 239). The electronic realizations, we read, were performed by a group called the Theatre of Eternal Music. That ensemble, we also learn, performed a series of "amplified" works by the composer, such as *The Second Dream of High-Tension Line Stepdown Transformer* (1962), *Studies in the Bowed Disc* (1963), and *The Tortoise, His Dreams and Journeys* (1964). While his colleague Cardew was presenting Young's work in connection with Stockhausen's theory of statistical fields, Davies focused instead on Young's medium of communication. In so doing he subtly modified the nature of Young's work, turning Young into one of the representatives of this new movement that he sought to promote.

Riley's individual works, regularly seen in conjunction with Young's in London concert announcements, also appear in Davies's book. Davies includes his *Concert for Two Pianists and Five Tape Recorders,* from 1960 (177), and the piece *I Can't Stop,* from 1966, which Davies labels "pop" (220). He also lists a "jazz" piece by Riley, *Shemooshe* (from 1966), as well as *Dorian Reeds* (from 1965), which he calls a "tape feedback loop" (220). In the *Répertoire,* Young and Riley stand alongside a good number of New Yorkers, notably Tony Conrad, Dick Higgins, Toshi Ichiyanagi, and Cage. Among them we also find the name Steve Reich. Four of Reich's works from 1966–67 are cited but not described: *Come Out, Melodica, Saxophone Phase, Four Pianos.* and *Buy Art Buy Art* (220).

In the months following its publication, Davies's work—copublished by the Groupe de Recherches Musicales of l'ORTF (the French public radio and television agency) in Paris, the Independent Electronic Music Center in New York, and MIT Press in Cambridge, Massachusetts, and London—won recognition as an authority, eliciting the interest of many champions of electronic music (Emmerson and Smalley 2001). It was reprinted, with no added commentary, in one of the pioneering journals in the field, *Electronic Music Review.* Meanwhile, Davies took part in another publication that was to become equally indispensable: *A Bibliography of Electronic Music,* by Lowell M. Cross (1968). It included *The Anthology of Chance Operations* by Young and Jackson Mac Low (1963), which contained both Young's and Riley's works (121). Two years later Davies furthered his campaign, this time working outside the confines of the musicological establishment. He contributed to the electronic music discography in the summer 1970 issue of *BMI: The Many Worlds of Music* (Frank 1970). In particular, Davies added works by Cage, Ichiyanagi, Maxfield, and Pauline Oliveros, as well as by Riley (*Reed Streams* [1965], *A Rainbow in a Curved Air* and *Poppy No Good and the Phantom Band* [1969]) and Reich (*Come Out, It's Gonna Rain* [1965] and *Violin Phase* [1967]).

ELECTRONIC MUSIC REVIEW AND THE COMPOSER

Among the earliest defenders of the genre that Davies helped to forge in the late 1960s was Robert Moog, who had recently invented the eponymous synthesizer, and Reynold Weidenaar, an electronic music composer (Kostelanetz 2001, 659). Together the two published the *Electronic Music Review*, which reprinted Davies's *Répertoire* in 1968, marking the first appearance of Young, Riley, and Reich in the journal.[3]

In July 1968, in the journal's seventh issue, the composer Roger Reynolds continued the work of positioning Young in the electronic genre. At that time Reynolds was known for having founded the group ONCE with Robert Ashley and Gordon Mumma (Sollberger 2001) and for conducting the interview in which Cage expressed his admiration for Young. Reynolds, like Davies, was also known as an electronic musician (see, in particular, Clarke 1965). In an article for the *Electronic Music Review*, "It(')s Time" (1968), he contributed to the association of *The Tortoise* with electronic music. Young's connection to the genre solidified—and so did Reich's. In the same issue of the journal, Tod Dockstader wrote about a compilation titled *New Sounds in Electronic Music* (1967), in which Reich's piece *Come Out* appeared alongside compositions by Maxfield and Oliveros (Dockstader 1968, 33).

In June 1969, a year after *Electronic Music Review* published its final issue on the East Coast, *The Composer* made its debut on the West Coast. The journal was published at the instigation of David Cope, who was one of the editors along with Allen Strange, among others. The journal's aim was to "establish the elements of dialogue between the factions (radical and moderate) of those individuals concerned with the craft and art of creating with sound" (see *The Composer* 1, no. 1 [1969]: 3). As the articles and reports that made up the journal's first issue suggest, this "creat[ion]" with sound" essentially meant machine-assisted creations. The journal was published for six years, until 1975. In the course of *The Composer's* fifteen issues, Young, Riley, and Reich were among the many who appeared in its pages. There Reich was sometimes associated with "live electronics" or cited among the composers for "solo ensemble" whose pieces "use a combination of live and pre-recorded music" (Turetzky 1970, 67).

MAGNETIC TAPE

Although the connection between electronic music and composers such as Young, Riley, and Reich did not amount to much in 1970—an inventory, a bibliography, and mentions in two journals—a 1972 book by Allen Strange provided a bit more support. At the time Strange had just been named professor and director of the electronic music studios at San Jose State University (Ruppenthal and Patterson 2001). His book *Electronic Music* was published by William C. Brown Company (1972), the publisher of *New Directions in Music* by David Cope, a work that associated Riley with "live electronics" groups (1971, 48). Here, instead of offering an aesthetic discussion of electronic music, Strange opted to present different techniques used by a series of composers representing the genre. Unlike his colleague Cope, Strange mentioned neither Riley's manipulation of electronics in live performances nor Young's "electronic creations" that Davies had inventoried four years before. He did, however, discuss Reich, whom he described as the composer making the most imaginative use of tape loops (1972, 120).[4]

The year that Strange's monograph came out, Herbert Russcol published his own introduction to electronic music, *The Liberation of Sound* (1972). Russcol relied especially on the works of Lowell Cross (1967) and Davies (1968). Unlike them, however, he saw Young not as an electronic musician but rather as a representative of mixed-media composition, as Salzman (1967) and Kostelanetz (1968) had also seen him. Young, we read, was one of the figures who had recently opened the borders of music (Russcol 1972, 114). The old divisions, particularly between "classical" and "popular" music, were coming down, thanks to the general availability of electronic materials that were now used in both (115). The composer whom Russcol associated most with electronic music was Reich, with *Violin Phase* and *It's Gonna Rain,* in particular (220–21)—works that recalled Riley's *In C,* he wrote, and that "allow us to hear things that ordinarily escape us—rather as a microscope enlarges tiny fragments and reveals hidden beauties that we could not otherwise behold" (221).

ELECTRONIC MUSIC

In 1973 Elliott Schwartz helped to further interest in the electronic movement with his book *Electronic Music: A Listener's Guide* (1973). Schwartz was a graduate of Columbia University and had studied and worked with Otto Luening, Henry Brant, and Edgard Varèse. In the mid-1960s he began composing works that made use of tapes as well as aleatoric instruments, games, and processes (see Godfrey 2002 and www.schwartzmusic .com). According to *Electronic Music,* in their lengthy works Reich and Riley invited the audience to participate, or at least to leave behind their passive position of listeners ensconced in their armchairs (165). The same was true with Erik Satie in *Vexations,* Cage in *HPSCHD,* and Young and David Rosenboom, the author asserted. The integration of the audience into the work was what these composers had in common, wrote Schwartz, who tended to do likewise in his own compositions (Godfrey 2002).[5] The audience's freedom was also a condition for the success of a long composition such as *In C*: if the audience was constrained by "artificial concerthall restrictions," its only reaction was to flee (Schwartz 1973, 166). Furthermore, audience participation was partly what brought Riley and Cardew closer to popular music (174). Indeed, Schwartz wondered whether Riley was classical or pop. The question was all the more pertinent for works such as *A Rainbow in Curved Air, Poppy No Good and the Phantom Band,* and *Church of Anthrax* (with John Cale in 1971); these electronic works, even more experimental or avant-garde than *In C,* were categorized as "pop-rock" by certain critics. *Classical* and *popular* had lost their traditional meaning, Schwartz argued, especially because serious and popular music coincided in the electronic medium. Although Reich did not figure among the standard-bearers for the style, he was included with the avant-gardists who married electronic music with live music—in particular those with an "utterly perfect" grasp of the idea of the echo in *Echoi* (1960–63) by Lukas Foss.

In the early 1970s, many composers were enlisted in the effort to win recognition for electronic music. Young, whose work had been used to support the foundations of performance art as well as the validity of a new movement in the visual arts, was among these composers. So were Riley and Reich, who had received little mention before then. At the time, however, the general public knew of no connection between the composers. At most a connoisseur might be aware that Young and Riley had collaborated in the Theatre of Eternal Music or that Riley and Reich had worked together in the context of the premiere of *In C* in 1964. All three may have been electronic musicians, but dozens of other composers made use of the same medium. Soon, however, another author would postulate that the music establishment had overlooked a major detail: all three were part of the same New York Hypnotic School, which had very little to do with electronic music. This author was Tom Johnson.

7. The New York Hypnotic School

FOUNDING A MOVEMENT

By the beginning of the 1970s, Young, Riley, and Reich had been active on the American musical scene for almost ten years.[1] Critics and musicologists followed their work closely. Although many of them had celebrated the works of each of these composers, few had established a clear connection between these works. At most, the composers were discussed together in analyses of electronic music (as well as in a few articles in the New York press, such as Henahan [1969a; 1969b; 1969c] and Davis [1970]). Not everyone, however, recognized their inclusion in the electronic movement. As we have seen with Young, very different, sometimes contradictory, readings of a composer's work coexisted. One New York author had nonetheless recently declared that a single aesthetic united these composers. That author was Tom Johnson, who worked for the popular newsweekly the *Village Voice*. For him, they formed together the New York Hypnotic School. In 1972, he even asserted that "the term define[s] one of the more important areas of new music. [It] should refer primarily to La Monte Young, Steve Reich, Terry Riley, and Philip Glass. . . . They all have the same basic concern, which can be described as flat, static, minimal, and hypnotic" (1972, repr. in Johnson 1991, 29).[2] Far from being discouraged by the profusion of divergent readings of the composers' works or by the complete absence of a proven relation among them, the critic outlined his own stylistic genealogy: "There is a direct line of influence from Young, to Riley, to Steve Reich and Phil Glass," he claimed (1973, repr. in Johnson 1991, 56). This genealogy, unlike those that had often been proposed, began with neither Cage nor Stockhausen; the latter had in fact made no impression on Young, Johnson told his readers (1974, repr. in Johnson 1991, 81). The Hypnotic School, as he defined it, quite simply broke with the past (1991, 29). What, then, is the history of Johnson's extravagant proposal?

THE *VILLAGE VOICE*

After the contributions of Jill Johnston and John Perreault on Young in the mid-1960s (see chapter 3), the *Village Voice* regularly mentioned the composer. Riley and Reich were not left out, either. Before Johnson, however, few writers in the *Village Voice* had attempted to unite them in a single "school." Although Carman Moore evoked Reich's "reiterative" work several times (1966; 1967; 1969), he never related it to the stasis of Young's music or that of Young's disciple Terry Jennings, on whose work he also commented (1968). Also, unlike Johnston and Perreault, Moore did not develop the analogy with the visual arts; he focused solely on the composers and their music. Like Perreault, however, Moore alluded to their aesthetic connections with jazz, raga, and even rock. The critic—a composer who would become known for incorporating elements of jazz and blues in his own music (Wyatt 2001)—noted as well that the composers shared certain traits with popular music, such as the use of repetition and high volumes.

Thus, in Moore's writing we find no mention of Cage, the aleatory, or indeterminacy among the future "hypnotics." Ron Rosenbaum, another critic for the *Village Voice*, confirmed in 1970 that for years already, Young's music was no longer seen in the context of Cage, Fluxus, or Dada (6). The composer, we read, no longer needed to incorporate any sound or any gesture in his music to expand its frontiers. The battle had been won long ago. Young's "Dream Music" now unfolded beyond it, focusing essentially on a single, eternal sound.

At the dawn of the 1970s, Johnson had not yet made the connection between those whom he would soon call the "hypnotics." When he reviewed

Reich's *Drumming* on December 9, 1971, one of the rare "long complex piece[s] of new music [to receive] a standing ovation," he described the performers' "amazing precision," the "unity" of the piece, and its "unpretentious climax," but he did not broach any of the traits that would soon define the "school" to which the composer belonged (1971, repr. in Johnson 1991, 20).[3] At the time, the characteristics of Reich's music were, in Johnson's writing, shared by numerous other musicians: Alvin and Mary Lucier, whose pieces "all work on a static dynamic plane" (1972, repr. in Johnson 1991, 23); Frederic Rzewski and his repetitive music, simple and regular (1991, 25); Phill Niblock and his "sustained sounds" (1991, 26); Rhys Chatham and his drones (1991, 28); and so on. Indeed, an aesthetic appears to have emerged in Johnson's chronicles of music in the *Village Voice*: repetition, stasis, and minimalism were among the criteria uniting these "new musics" for which he had become the ambassador. Nonetheless, in the summer of 1972 the critic still saw only one "hypnotic" musician, strictly speaking, in New York: Philip Glass, a composer whose name the music establishment had barely heard before (1991, 24).

"LA MONTE YOUNG, STEVE REICH, TERRY RILEY, PHILIP GLASS"

In the September 7, 1972, issue of the *Village Voice*, Johnson published "La Monte Young, Steve Reich, Terry Riley, Philip Glass," the article that marked the birth of the New York Hypnotic School (repr. in Johnson 1991, 29). The designation had received scant attention in music literature up to that time. Its use had been occasional at best, and hardly complimentary (see especially Henahan 1969c). But for Johnson, the school constituted "one of the more important areas of new music" (Johnson 1991, 29). A typically New York school, it excluded Rzewski, Philip Corner, and David Behrman (because their work did not clearly fit the criteria set by Johnson), as well as Gavin Bryars (since he was British). It was defined by four terms: flatness, stasis, minimalism, and hypnotism. Beyond that, it mattered little whether the music featured traditional scales or not, a regular beat or the absence of rhythmic articulation, acoustic or electronic resources. The music was flat, Johnson explained, because there was no attempt to build to a climax or produce tension and relaxation. It was static because it was nondirectional, even though changes arose throughout its development. It was minimal in that it never evolved very far beyond its starting point. Finally and especially, it was hypnotic, Johnson asserted, because it lulled the listener into a trancelike state. According to Johnson, the music of the New York Hypnotic School was, moreover, easier to listen to than any other contemporary music. It focused not on intellectual devices but on sound itself, making it as accessible to the layperson as to the scholar.

In the two years that followed the September 1972 article, Johnson repeatedly evoked these various traits as they developed toward success—distinctive traits that were never boring, Johnson regularly affirmed—in the work of numerous composers of this new music. This music, however, was still only that of Young and his three colleagues.[4] These composers, moreover, completely broke from tradition; their music had nothing to do with either contemporary music or jazz (Johnson 1991, 29).[5] If their static, nondeveloping forms had roots anywhere, they were to be found in non-Western music (1973, repr. in Johnson 1991, 35–36).

At the end of 1974, a controversy arose within Johnson's own writings: until then, "minimalism" had been one aspect among others that characterized the four New York composers, while for him the "minimalists," strictly speaking, were California composers, such as Harold Budd or Michael Byron (1973, repr. in Johnson 1991, 58–59). These latter, heirs to Harry Partch, Lou Harrison, Silvestre Revueltas, and Dane Rudhyar, went "far beyond" the New Yorkers in their processes of sound reduction. Nonetheless, on December 30, 1974, Johnson labeled the music of the New York Hypnotics—with David Behrman now in their ranks—as minimal, further declaring that this minimalism was one of the major currents of new music (1974, repr. in Johnson 1991, 94). Shortly thereafter, this view would be reinforced by the British author Michael Nyman, whose book *Experimental Music* had just come out in the United States (1974). In that monograph, Nyman too grouped Young, Riley, Reich, and Glass under the "minimalist" label.

The story of Johnson and the Hypnotic School is in some ways a variant of that of Cardew and his ties to Young: after having promoted a typically

New York movement deserving of a place in the Western art music tradition, the critic put on his composer hat, largely influenced by the movement he had defended. In 1972 Johnson premiered his *Four-Note Opera* in New York, a piece whose static and minimal nature the *New York Times* did not fail to note (Ericson 1972). At the same time, he exhorted music teachers to turn toward the creative possibilities of avant-garde music, publishing two of his pieces in that vein, by way of example, in the *Music Educators Journal* (Johnson 1972). In 1974 the *New York Times* described his 1971 composition *An Hour for Piano* as "meditative."[6] It belongs, we read, within a general movement of "austerity," employing "modular repetition" and "deliberately limited materials," in the wake of Reich and Glass (Rockwell 1974a). In 1976, *Spaces* and *Septapede* (1969) were described as "free from the concept of climax as a structural necessity" (Burge 1976). These compositions by Johnson, a former student of Morton Feldman, seem to have taken a hypnotic or minimal turn. The opportunity was not slight, as he himself had noted: this music would probably "reach a wider audience than most contemporary music has" (Johnson 1991, 29).

8. Untying the Bonds

PROCESS MUSIC

Books by composers, including this one, are probably
of most interest to those already interested in the
composer's music.

(Reich 1974, vii)

By 1974, Reich's name had been appearing in publications on American contemporary music for several years. Authors such as Hugh Davies, Allen Strange, and Elliott Schwartz (chapter 6) categorized him among electronic music composers, while Tom Johnson suggested that he be seen as part of the New York Hypnotic School (chapter 7). The former approach appealed to many defenders of the medium but failed to generate much interest outside their circle. Likewise, the latter view did not yet seem to have convinced many beyond the pages of the *Village Voice*. The composer himself did not confirm his affiliation with either category. When he published his *Writings about Music* in 1974, Reich set the record straight regarding the observations and analyses that had been made about his music: it was not defined by any medium at all, nor did it stem from any Western tradition or school. His aesthetic, moreover, was shared by no one else. Reich declared right from the introduction to his collection of texts that it was above all his "intuition" that had guided his steps through the music scene of his day (vii).

What, then, did Reich's music consist of, according to Reich himself? He went on to explain this, particularly in his 1968 essay "Music as a Gradual Process" (9–11). This music consisted of a process that determined not only each detail from one sound to the next but also the overall structure of the piece. This process must be understandable by all, with no "hidden structural devices." To be perceptible, it must unfold gradually. The composer thus professed to turn his back on all forms of musical elitism, thereby denying any roots in the Western classical tradition: his musical processes, completely controlled, had nothing in common with Cage's, which he said were inaudible when the piece was performed (10).[1] Nor did they have any link with serialism, which likewise masked the connection between "the compositional processes and the sounding music." His music furthermore had no ties to Indian music or rock 'n' roll, the composer asserted. While these genres focused on sound details as they unfolded in the present—they were built on a single key, featured hypnotic drones, and were repetitive—they remained, above all, bases for improvisation (11). Reich, however, maintained that "one can't improvise in a musical process—the concepts are mutually exclusive."[2]

Reich, like Young in 1968 (chapter 5), thus claimed to establish his own tradition, regardless of what authors such as Johnson had written. In his later texts gathered in *Writings about Music,* he drove the point home. After dismissing improvisation, Cage, and serialists in his "Postscript to a Brief Study of Balinese and African Music" (1973, 38–40), Reich reiterated his uniqueness with respect to rock groups and their "chinoiseries" that did nothing more than import non-Western instruments into their music (40).[3] He responded no differently to the exoticism of those who "[sing] 'Indian style' melodies over electronic drones." Unlike Young (he may as well have written), Reich sought to draw on the East from a structural perspective.

By 1973, however, Reich's musical conceptions had evolved somewhat. He had definitively rejected the music of his hemisphere: "Non-Western music is presently the single most important source of new ideas for Western composers and musicians," he now asserted (38), and his visit to Africa had confirmed his intuition that acoustic instruments could be used to produce a more authentic music than that produced by electronic instruments (58).[4] The composer's turn toward the East was inimical to his first medium of expression: electronics. For even though in 1968 it mattered little to Reich whether the "process" was electronic or human (9–11), in his "Optimistic Predictions about the Future of Music" (1970, 28), for example, the first medium clearly waned with the rise of the second: "Electronic music as such will gradually die and be absorbed into the ongoing music of people singing and playing instruments." Subsequently too, Reich never ceased to declare his lack of interest in electronic music, which he even claimed to have abandoned in 1969 (55), at the very time that the champions of the medium were making him their ally (chapter 6).

In the course of Reich's writings, his passage from electronic to ethnic music is not the only observable change; there is also a shift toward attention to pulse, rhythm, and regularity. We witness the change that he announces retrospectively in the introduction to his collection of texts: music is of no interest if it is simply based on a system (vii). The concept of process thus tends to disappear from his language. His music is built instead around a steady pulse created by human beings (25). And it is precisely "the pulse and the concept of the clear tonal center" that are the future of music, according to the composer, something he announced in his "Optimistic Predictions" (1970, 28).

Essentially, the 1970 "Predictions" announced changes that Reich himself was undertaking in his own music. Indeed, he imagined a brilliant future for the pulse just as he was reviving it, the end of electronics when he was turning his back on it, and the advent of non-Western music when he began to take a keen interest in it. The predictions, moreover, confirm a final movement taking place in Reich's music: his growing interest in composer/performer groups (28)—an interest that, he would write a posteriori, went back to the beginning of the 1960s (45).[5]

Thus in 1974, in his *Writings about Music,* Reich broke with the Western tradition, moving from electronics to the East, from process to pulse. He closed the door on the possibility that his music could be rooted in the Western classical tradition, with the exception of his strong interest in early music and, in a different vein, Riley's *In C,* which had heightened his interest in repetition (50). In many respects Reich's writings had already received the approval of a certain cultural establishment: they had been published in concert notes, sometimes at prestigious halls, as well as in respected newspapers and eminent journals on both US coasts and in France, Great Britain, and Germany.[6] By collecting his conceptions on his music in 1974, Reich gave them a bit more weight; he was aided in that endeavor by reviewers such as William Austin, Paul Griffiths, and Peter

Dickinson.[7] The narratives of the electronic music advocates may have been true at one time or another for certain people, while Johnson's had perhaps been only a fiction. Reich was truly a maverick who owed his aesthetics to no one, at least in the West.

The debate would have ended there if the British critic Michael Nyman had not published his book *Experimental Music* the same year that *Writings* came out. In it, he in turn took on the composer's music.

9. Transfiguring Experimental Music

We know about Johnson's theory, in the middle of 1974, of a hypnotic school developing in New York, with Young as its initiator and Reich as one of its main protagonists. We have also read about Johnson's comments on a California movement that was strictly minimalist, going far beyond the New York composers' attempts in terms of reductive procedures. Its representatives were Harold Budd and Michael Byron, its mentors Harry Partch and Lou Harrison. Whereas the definition of the hypnotic school came into conflict with a series of explanations of Young's and Reich's music, that of California minimalism had not, for its part, been subject to debate—at least up to this point. At the end of the year, however, Nyman's *Experimental Music* was published in Britain, its last chapter devoted to minimal music (Nyman 1974, 139–71). For Nyman, unlike Johnson, the term did not designate the work of Budd or Byron but that of Young and Reich, as well as Riley and Glass. Nyman also pointed to the work of a group of British composers that in some respects was supplanting that of the Americans. Their music came neither from the East nor from the composer's intuition alone, as Young and Reich, respectively, had affirmed of their own music. Instead, it was rooted in Cageian indeterminacy and extended its principles. Thus, a new, competing approach had come on the scene, one whose history we will trace here.

IN THE WAKE OF CARDEW

When Nyman published his first monograph, in 1974, he was far from unknown to the British music establishment. Since the end of the 1960s, his many publications had appeared in the *Spectator*, the *Listener*, the *New Statesman*, *London Magazine*, *Music and Musicians*, *Tempo*, and the *Musical Times*. These publications often attested to his admiration for the "liberating" nature of Cage's music, which he regularly opposed to the "authoritarianism" of Stockhausen: "One would be grateful to Cage simply for seeing his present function as a composer not as a dictator's," he wrote in 1969 (repr. in Nyman 2013, 65). At that time Nyman, a former student at the Royal Academy of Music and onetime disciple of the Manchester School of Alexander Goehr, Harrison Birtwistle, and Peter Maxwell Davies, had effectively turned his back on serialism.[1] He discovered Cardew's work and *The Great Learning* (1968–71), "one of those rare works of such power and freshness that they seem to reinvent music from its very sources by somersaulting musical history" (Nyman 2013, 67). Thereafter he ceaselessly celebrated the music of Cardew and his Scratch Orchestra, as well as their ability to reconnect the listener to the physicality of sound.[2]

Since the end of the 1960s, Nyman had also become a more or less regular reporter on "popular" music: in an article for the *Spectator* on October 11, 1968, he delighted in mentioning the music of The Fugs or Spooky Tooth (repr. in Nyman 2013, 42). That article also contained his first mention of the existence of minimal music, a label he used for a happening by Charlotte Moorman and Nam June Paik at the Institute of Contemporary Arts and in particular for the work *Springen* (1968) by the Danish composer Henning Christiansen. "Simple idea, straightforward structure, intellectual control, theatrical presence and intensity in presentation" characterized the piece, which, Nyman continued, "consisted of nothing but a series of parabolas traced by the fingers, arm and eyes" from one C to another (43).

Introduced in 1968, the expression *minimal music* would be revised only a year later: in November 1969 in the *Listener*, Nyman wrote of a so-called minimal music that was American this time, represented by figures such as Riley and Reich. Nonetheless, this music still consisted of illustrating a "single idea," thereby "revealing a vibrating inner life" (repr. in Nyman 2013, 80).

In 1970, in *Tempo*, Nyman again mentioned Riley's work, this time in his review of a concert given at the BBC Proms on August 30, 1970, that brought together the music of Riley, Tim Souster, and the group Soft Machine.[3] The association of serious and popular musics did not fulfill its promise, Nyman maintained.[4] It nonetheless revealed the aesthetic quality of Riley's music. His work, the critic wrote, belonged to the "nouvelle vague" inaugurated by Young around 1962, "when he gave up his Fluxus events." The *Keyboard Studies* (1968) by Riley are "tonal, or rather modal," he continued. On paper, they "resemble [a succession of the type] tonic–dominant–tonic" (1970, repr. in Nyman 2013, 204); to the ear, however, the modulations are drowned out by the persistence of the tonic and the absence of any directional feeling. The *Studies* unfold over the course of permutations, repetitions, and sustained sounds. And although such an analysis could seem "infantile," Nyman wrote, what creates the unity and the revolutionary character of the piece is precisely the limitation of the chosen pitches, the inexorability of the structural method, and the adherence, without digression, to the process underlying the work. As a result, we hear "totally new relationships" and a "marvellous microcosmic changing of colour" within a static continuum. The sustained notes, he asserted, "glow magically," and their progressive ascent is "of quite extraordinary power and simplicity" (205).

Nyman was thus full of praise for Riley, whom he considered the heir to Young. The latter, in Nyman's texts, was the initiator of a nouvelle vague whose aesthetic principles needed no explanation. Cardew's writing since the early 1960s helped position Young in this role, even though the Young that interested Cardew was very different from the one that interested Nyman. Cardew had focused on Young's Fluxus period, whereas Nyman touted the post-Fluxus Young. Soon, however, Nyman's attention would be drawn in a different direction. John Tilbury, his colleague in the Scratch Orchestra, introduced him to Reich's music, which Nyman mentioned in his article in the *Listener* in 1969. Beginning in March 1971, when he organized a concert of Reich's works at the Institute of Contemporary Arts in London and published an article on Reich in *Time Out* as well as an interview in the *Musical Times*, Nyman would ceaselessly promote the composer's music.

REICH

In his March 1971 article on Reich in *Time Out*, Nyman no longer called the composer minimalist, as he had in 1969. He now preferred to classify his music as live electronics. The critic nonetheless continued to forge a link between Reich's aesthetic and those of Riley (whose work he had just promoted) and Young (who had already won recognition, thanks to Cardew).[5] Like them, Nyman wrote, repeating almost word for word his assertions on Cardew and *The Great Learning* (1969; 1971 article, repr. in Nyman 2013, 67), Reich went back "to the ritual sources of music, to the pulse and the drone, to the use of constants which Western Music lost with Culture" (Nyman 2013, 85). His music was partly inspired by Africa, but unlike "the sitar in rock trip," there was no trace of exoticism. Like Riley's music, Reich's too made use of loops, but not in a merely repetitive manner. As with his composition *Come Out* (1966), in the end Reich's music was, above all, simply "fantastic."

In Nyman's interview with Reich that appeared in the *Musical Times* in March 1971 as well, the critic was no less laudatory: like Peter Maxwell Davies, Harrison Birtwistle, Goehr, and Cardew, he declared, Reich had, "quite remarkably, concentrated intensely small areas of musical activity which [he] subject[s] to a microscopic scrutiny" (repr. in Nyman 2013, 229). To these great names of the British contemporary music establishment, Nyman added other authoritative figures: Darius Milhaud and Luciano Berio, who were Reich's teachers; the San Francisco Tape Music Center, which he had frequented for a time; Young and Riley, once more; as well as Glass, for the first time. Following on Cage, with whom Nyman also associated them, Reich and the last three composers had "replaced silence by a completely unbroken continuum, improvisation and indeterminacy by freedoms within severely circumscribed limits" (229). He thus solidified the association of these composers without yet calling them *minimalist*. The closest Nyman came to that label was in mentioning Reich's use of "an absolute minimum of musical material" (230).

Reich, too, made no mention of the label in the interview. When Nyman asked him to name his music, he chose the expressions "Live/Electric music," "pulse music" (229), and even "developmental music" (230). Reich said nothing about the origins of his art or whatever aesthetic points he had in common with the other composers, preferring to concentrate on technical descriptions of his "gradual processes" and the progressive shift of his own interest from machines to instruments. Serious attention to non-Western music represented the future of composers, Reich asserted. And while he was interested in the freedom that playing in a group produced, he was not interested in improvisation—nor in jazz, which, he said, was merely an adolescent preoccupation.

A month later, however, Nyman returned to the connection between serious and popular musics—between pulsed music and pop—in the April 1971 issue of the *New Statesman*, where he commented on the association between John Cale and Riley in *Church of Anthrax* (1971). "Pulse, repetition, modality" were features common to pop, Nyman contended; yet Riley's association with Cale proved to be a "near-disaster" (repr. in Nyman 2013, 114). For Nyman, the true meeting point for pop and serious music lay in *A Rainbow in Curved Air* (1967–68), not in the "cosy cliché" of *Church of Anthrax*, where Riley's music was "spun directly into the pop orbit." Nyman further opined that the two realms should remain closed off from each other, or mostly so: Cale was effective only when he imported Riley's aesthetic to Nico's music, or Young's to that of the Velvet Underground, whereas the opposite was apparently inconceivable.

In his subsequent writing, Nyman would continue to lavish praise on those whom he was soon to call minimalists, definitively this time. In May 1971, in the *Musical Times*, he celebrated the freshness and beauty as well as the richness and complexity of the drones and repetitions of Reich and Glass (repr. in Nyman 2013, 120). In August, in the *New Statesman*, he castigated the record industry for ignoring the "new 'classical' music of unprecedented vitality and strength of purpose" by Reich, who now "extends beyond the frontiers of the Cage-Stockhausen era" (126). In October, for the first time in *Music and Musicians*, he announced that "melody rides again," evoking the "post-Cardew" scene and within it the "new total determinacy" of John White or of Brian Dennis, whose music shares certain traits with that of Reich and Riley (126, 128). The term *minimal* reappeared here, this time in reference to the visual arts and the music of Gavin Bryars (131).

The year 1971 was an important one for Nyman: he mentioned the work of Riley, Reich, and Glass in numerous articles, associating them with Cage—whom they always surpassed—and with others such as Cardew. In 1972, the critic went a step further. Nyman had taken part in Cardew's Scratch Orchestra; now he would even perform with Reich's ensemble in a concert of works by the composer that he organized in February at the Hayward Gallery (repr. in Nyman 2013, 19n).[6] Immediately thereafter, he published "SR—Mysteries of the Phase" in *Music and Musicians*, in which he offered a technical description of Reich's *Drumming* (1970–71) and his phasing processes. Nyman no longer needed to establish the legitimacy of the composer's music, which he called "fascinating" and "magical" (Nyman 2013, 224). A year later Nyman himself turned to composition. He presented *Bell Set No. 1* (1974) in London, a piece that his friend Dominic Gill (Nyman 2013, xi–xii) called "a neatly knit permutation of rhythmic structures for four bells" (Gill 1973, 57), recalling the "unexpected chain of cross-rhythms" in *Drumming* that Nyman described in 1972 (Nyman 2013, 225). In 1973 Nyman explicitly recognized his "own involvement" in the "new tonality," as well as in the aesthetic of "ritual repetitions" after Reich or Riley (Nyman 2013, 155).

EXPERIMENTAL MUSIC

In 1974 Nyman signed and sealed what had, by his own writing, become a "fact": minimal music was indeed the last link of the experimental chain. Moreover, the future, and perhaps the demise, of the concept of experimental music was in the hands of the minimalists—now especially in those of a new generation of British composers who had expanded on the Americans' work.

Experimental Music: Cage and Beyond was above all an attempt to define the experimental aesthetic and its developments since the work of

Cage. At the time, the label *experimental* had taken on several meanings: a range of composers and authors appropriated it in ways that varied, and sometimes conflicted, from one to the next.[7] Nyman, for his part, proposed a definition of experimentalism revolving around the figure of Cage and partly based on Cage's appropriation of the concept, as expressed in *Silence* (1961) and *A Year from Monday* (1968). In these two collections of texts—especially *Silence*—Cage celebrated the liberation of sound, enjoining others to let sound take its own course (Cage 1961, 10). According to Cage, electronics had revealed that "musical action or existence can occur at any point or along any line or curve or what have you in total soundspace" (9). This notion called for radically abandoning the former "musical habits" based on "scales, modes, theories of counterpoint and harmony," instead seeking out means to let sounds be themselves rather than vehicles for man-made theories or expressions of human sentiments (9–10). The experimental action thus became "simply an action the outcome of which is not foreseen." It was composed "in such a way that what one does is indeterminate of its performance" (69).

Although Nyman relied in large part on the concepts developed by Cage, he went beyond them, reshaping the experimentalism forged by the New York composer. The aspect of Nyman's reconstruction that would have lasting impact was his insistence on the contradictions between the experimental aesthetic and that represented by Boulez and Stockhausen (Piekut 2011, 4), as well as the extensive integration of British composers into the definition of the genre, particularly into the account of the latest developments of indeterminacy. Nonetheless, Nyman's goal in this book was also, or even especially, to fashion an experimentalism with minimalist touches (which would ultimately give rise to minimalism).

Having presented experimental composition as the process of "outlining a situation in which sounds may occur,"[8] Nyman identified five types of "process[es] of generating action": chance determination processes, people processes ("which allow the performers to move through given or suggested material"), contextual processes ("concerned with actions dependent on unpredictable conditions and on variables which arise from within the musical continuity"), repetition processes, and electronic processes (1974, 4, 6). From the start, then, Nyman brought repetition into the experimentalism that he had just defined as having no predetermined components or structure. Nyman neglected to specify here that Reich's gradual processes—which he included among the repetition processes (8)—"determine all the note-to-note (sound-to-sound) details and the overall form simultaneously" and must be perceptible, in contrast with the Cageian processes that "could not be heard when the piece was performed" (Reich [1971] 2011). Moreover, the processes that Nyman defined after Cage were presented as outlines of situations for the indeterminate emergence of sound, whereas those defined by Reich referred to musical pieces that were themselves strictly determined and perceptible processes.

By quickly passing over this crucial difference between Cage's processes and those of Reich, Nyman began to reshape experimentalism in order to subsequently align it with minimalist language. According to the British critic, experimental action could be determinate, no matter what Cage said; conversely, repetitive processes could admit indeterminacy, with all due respect to Reich. "In repetition processes the 'unforeseen' may arise," Nyman added (1974, 8). By slightly shifting the basis for this process on both sides, he achieved a preliminary unification of the two aesthetics.

The rest of the book presented further revisions, culminating in the seventh chapter, where Nyman definitively drove the point home and explicitly placed minimalism at the pinnacle of the music of his day. Consider, for example, the Cageian conception of time as expressed by Nyman: "A time frame may be chosen at random and then filled with sounds," the critic wrote (Nyman 1974, 12). Thus works of "indeterminate" duration, such as Young's *Poem* (1960), Reich's *Pendulum Music* (1968), or Riley's *In C* (1964), could fit within the constraints of experimental music. Note also the definition of the experimental "task": whereas Cage had opened the door to nonintentionality and turned his focus to the sounds produced by the environment, according to Nyman this task required conscious involvement on the part of the performer. Indeed, we find no unbridled "carelessness" (15) in Nyman's experimentalism; minimalism looms in the distance.

Nyman also linked Cage to Reich in considering the liberation of the instrument: Cage's prepared piano was but one step from Reich's drumming fingers in *Phase Pattern* (1970) (Nyman 1974, 20). For the critic, both composers conceived of the piano as a percussion instrument; little did it matter that for Cage the preparation of the instrument was meant above all to introduce "the unknown" (Cage 1961, 16). In terms of the organization of sound, since experimental processes did not have "the effect of organizing sounds and integrating them, of creating relationships of harmony," as Nyman wrote in his reading of Cage, what resulted was an "effect of flattening out, de-focusing the musical perspective" (Nyman 1974, 29–30). This approach, he continued, ranged from "maximum change and multiplicity," in the aesthetic of Cage or the Scratch Orchestra, to "uniformity and minimum change," in that of Reich or John White (30).

If Nyman regularly translated experimentalism in minimalist terms, he also seized on other aesthetics, isolating and sometimes remodeling their components to associate them with the musical movement that was the subject of the final pages of *Experimental Music*. Thus, "Satie's use of extended repetition . . . takes on fresh significance in the light of the new experimental music which uses multi-repetition, tape loops and the idea of endlessness" (Nyman 1974, 36). Thus, too, from Webern's serial procedure "there emerged indeterminate, extra-serial configurations, irrational non-lineal static spatial groups. This was due to Webern's technique of repeating notes of the same pitch, always in the same octave position, in different permutations and transpositions of the row" (38). Nyman even brought in Schoenberg, whose "Farben," from his *Five Pieces for Orchestra*, "involved stasis rather than climax" and intrigued Young (43).

Likewise, Nyman highlighted minimal features in the music of the experimentalists themselves: Morton Feldman, Earle Brown, Christian Wolff—those whom Cage identified as such. Among these traits were Feldman's "impressively simple method" (53), Brown's "total sound continuum" (52), and Wolff's "minimal serialism" (59). These areas, Nyman wrote, had begun to be explored systematically by Young and Reich (59).

Nyman similarly presented the Fluxus movement (chapter 4), electronic music (chapter 5), and indeterminacy (chapter 6) as further areas in which to connect experimentalism and minimalism. Thus he connected Young to Fluxus—a movement from which Young had ultimately proclaimed his independence—given that it involved, at least for George Brecht, a series of "minimal event activities" (76). Reich had already concluded the evolution of electronic music, with his loops and tape-delay systems (108–9). Indeterminacy, for its part, was seen in Cardew and Wolff's having "forsaken the cryptic for the direct" (110). Composer-performers (115), sustained sounds

(114), stasis (123), and loops (124) punctuate the chapter; minimalism is ready to make its appearance.

MINIMAL MUSIC

> One single word might sum up what appears, on the surface at least, to be the most significant quality of experimental music: limitlessness.
>
> George Brecht, La Monte Young and other Fluxus composers reviewed multiplicity, found its deficiencies, and chose to reduce their focus of attention to singularity. . . . Perhaps a reaction against indeterminacy was inevitable: the music of La Monte Young and Terry Riley, Steve Reich and Philip Glass—the three other American composers most closely associated with Young's minimal "alternative"—shows a many-sided retrenchment from the music that has grown from indeterminacy, and draws on sources hitherto neglected by experimental music. This music not only cuts down the area of sound-activity to an absolute (and absolutist) minimum, but submits the scrupulously selective, mainly tonal, material to mostly repetitive, highly disciplined procedures which are focused with an extremely fine definition (though the listener's focusing is not done for him).
>
> The origins of this minimal process music lie in serialism. La Monte Young was attracted by aspects of Webern's music similar to those that had interested Christian Wolff. . . . The stasis [Young] saw in Webern he also found in music from outside the Western tradition. (Nyman 1974, 139)

The first paragraphs of the chapter devoted to minimal music offer probably one of the best examples of the way in which Nyman reshaped the concepts and theories that preceded him—even as he drew on them—in order to make them converge toward his own musicological construction. In particular, Nyman needed to forge a link between the "limitlessness" of experimental music and the "highly disciplined procedures" of minimalism. How did he carry out his demonstration? How did he elevate minimalism to become the paragon of modernity?

The first element to which Nyman turned to support his argument was experimental music. This genre, already widely recognized by the music establishment, notably gave rise to Fluxus; Fluxus, after exploring multiplicity and "inevitabl[y]" scaling it down toward singularity, engendered the music of Young; and Young's "minimal 'alternative'" led to that of Reich, Riley, and Glass, here "closely associated."[9] Thus indeterminacy and hyperdeterminacy were now two links in the same chain. Finally, two new allies strengthened the bases of Nyman's construction: Webern's serialism, on the one hand, and the Eastern music tradition, on the other. Beyond their mention here, we read almost nothing about them. Webern's emergence is problematic, to say the least: once Nyman had demonstrated that Young's aesthetic was anchored in the experimental tradition, attempting to establish that it also went back to serialism—which, for Nyman, was at the opposite pole of contemporary music—was surely difficult.

The second argument that Nyman put forward to hitch minimalism to experimentalism relied on an oscillation between experimental freedom and minimalist determination: the frequencies to be used in a performance by the Theatre of Eternal Music were predetermined, but the moment at which each performer placed his frequency was free (141); Young's system was meticulously controlled, but it allowed sound to develop by itself (143). The same went for Riley, Glass, and Reich, each one attached to Young by virtue of repetition, which was present, Nyman wrote, "on a 'passive' level in *The Tortoise*" (144). The music of all three was determinate, but it possessed a certain measure of indeterminacy: Reich, for example, determined a process, but he did not interfere with its development (152). *Pendulum Music*, with its "uncontrolled, unprogrammed results,"[10] is thus a piece that ideally demonstrates the salience of indeterminacy for repetitive musicians.[11]

A final "adjustment" of the aesthetics in question closes the chapter on minimal music. It consists not only in linking the British minimalists to their American counterparts, as well as to experimental musicians, but also in presenting the British as the successors to the Americans. The Scratch Orchestra, the Portsmouth Sinfonia, the Promenade Orchestra, Hugh Schrapnel, John Tilbury, Christopher Hobbs, Howard Skempton, Gavin Bryars, and John White are names scattered throughout Nyman's work that now appear together to outline the future of experimentalism. Once again, Nyman used repetition as the link. From Cage to Young, from Young to the minimalists, Nyman's long chain of reasoning leads finally to Britain.

In the end only two points distinguish the British minimalists from the American ones, but these connect them all the more to Cage and experimentalism. First, the British do not demand technical prowess of the members of their orchestra (161–62); second, they tend to reuse Western classical works within their own creations. Nyman argued that Cage himself was the first "to consider the classics as just so much sound material to be used in its own right, not for its symbolic or associational value" (160). For Nyman this tendency was the distinctive trait shared by most of the British composers, and ultimately by Nyman himself, who several years later would write the piece "In Re *Don Giovanni*," his rereading of Mozart's work. As Nyman concluded, "The future, and perhaps disappearance, of the concept of 'experimental music' lies, I feel, in the hands of the younger British composers whose work I have briefly outlined" (171).

10. 1975

What is "contemporary" American music? What has been concretely proven on the subject? Over the course of this journey in pursuit of "minimalism in the making," we posed that question for 1960 (chapter 1) as well as for 1967 (chapter 4). Between those two dates, as we have seen, the description of the postwar musical landscape underwent sometimes large revisions: the Cage of the 1950s, as characterized by indeterminacy, is for example almost entirely absent from the music literature of the early 1960s, but he becomes inescapable seven years later. The same cannot be said for Young: unknown in 1960, he remained so in 1967 in many respects (see chapter 4). From then until 1975, where the present chapter ends, the situation nonetheless evolved: if in 1967 Young was a "giant" only for Cardew and his circle, by 1975 he had become for many one of the heroes of the 1960s avant-garde. Once again, history was transformed: the established, concrete facts slightly shifted, and Cardew's "fictions" were now part of that history.

The revelation of Young's importance did not arise from the "discovery" of hidden evidence, of a truth that had been concealed from the world. Nor was it an "invention" of Cardew alone; it was the fruit of a collective effort in which various protagonists joined in little by little to swell the ranks of the "allies" united in the same battle. Throughout these fashionings and refashionings, by dint of converging interests—whether aesthetic, ideological, or professional—Cardew's idea that Young was a major figure in the contemporary musical landscape eventually proved true. By 1975, any attempt to contest Young's greatness—or his place in the postwar American musical landscape—would require retracing a long series of books and articles, of arguments and battles already won. One would have to raise so many objections that the task would prove almost impossible. From 1967 to 1975, a network of defenders grew around Young—a musician often known only for his activity from the early 1960s—to the point where it became difficult to oppose his significance without deploying an arsenal of musicological arguments.

In 1975, Nyman's minimalism was thus in the same position as Cardew's "giant" Young had been eight years before. It was too soon for anyone to presume its success. Nyman could believe that the absence of Cageian limits led "inevitably" to the multiplicity in Fluxus, then to Young's "retrenchment," and finally to the "highly disciplined procedures" of Riley, Reich, and Glass; he could proclaim that "the concept 'experimental music' lies . . . in the hands of [specific] younger British composers" (1974, 171)—but unless he could convince his readership of specialists and laypersons to pass the word on, those views would never become truths. In 1975, the destiny of Nyman's proposal was not in his hands. The same held for Johnson's "Hypnotic School," Kostelanetz's "Theatre of Mixed Means," and the electronic music enthusiasts' view that Riley and Reich were above all representatives of their movement.

It thus remains worthwhile to ask: Which of the statements about the music of American composers—in particular those whom Nyman dubbed *minimalists*—were held to be true in 1975? Which conceptions had garnered the support of the music establishment? Did these composers deserve a place within it, and if so, what kind? As we have just confirmed, the music establishment had ratified Young's "greatness," but that was not all. Here we will first look more closely at the idea that Young, Riley, Reich, and Glass, over the course of successive campaigns in their favor, had a place to claim in the contemporary music scene. Next we will turn to the disparate nature of the descriptions of their work, the resistance these composers faced, and finally, the broad consensus on their work.

JOINING FORCES

After Salzman included Young in his 1967 book *Twentieth-Century Music: An Introduction*, Hitchcock did likewise in 1969 in *Music in the United States: A Historical Introduction* (published in the same series, for which he was the editor), abandoning, in turn, his objections to the composer. Following his colleague, Hitchcock presented Young among those composers who—like Joseph Byrd, Toshi Ichiyanagi, and Richard Maxfield—developed Cage's idea that "relevant action is theatrical" (Hitchcock 1969, 248).[1] Salzman's support for Young's aesthetic in 1967 no doubt had an impact on the place that Hitchcock accorded the composer's work two years later. But Salzman was not the only factor: in writing *Music in the United States,* Hitchcock was also partly influenced by Leonard Meyer's recent thinking in *Music, the Arts, and Ideas* (1967; see also Hitchcock 1969, 250). There Meyer announced the advent of a manifold cosmopolitan culture in which tonality, serialism, jazz, and popular music coexisted in the same work of art (208–9). He also predicted the emergence of a period of stasis, in which sociocultural development would no longer be the necessary condition for human existence; progress in the arts was moving toward its inexorable end, the philosopher asserted. Meyer also brushed aside serialism's tendency to claim a place at the forefront of culture: "Because its level of redundancy is extremely low, total serial music presents the listener with so much novel, densely packed material that even those parts of the musical message which might have been intelligible are often masked and confused by the welter of incoming information" (291). Criticism of serial complexity was met by the celebration of Young's simplicity noted by others;[2] the two positions tended to reinforce each other. Meyer's work gradually became indispensable,[3] as would Hitchcock's *Music in the United States.*

In 1971, for example, Virgil Thomson cited Hitchcock's book when he included Young among the most remarkable American composers of the twentieth century. Thomson was a "patriotic" critic for the *Herald Tribune*: for him American music was essentially defined by the nationality of its main actors, the composers, and not by a sound or a style.[4] In his work *Twentieth-Century Composers,* Young is nonetheless a leader of the indeterminate school (Thomson 1971, 106). That same year, the fourth edition of Nicolas Slonimsky's *Music since 1900* was published in New York. It, too, included Young's music among the "elements . . . that subtly but surely influence the entire future of music" (Slonimsky 1971, vii). His "descriptive chronology" mentions Young's compositions from 1960 as well as *Piano Piece #1, Poem* from 1960, and *Two Sounds* from 1961 (see 1078, 1165, 1205, 1211, 1320). Layer upon layer, the composer's place in the musical panorama was taking shape.

Also in 1971, David Cope published *New Directions in Music*, presenting new orientations in the music of the previous twenty years, particularly that of the avant-garde and "postavant-garde" (xii). There we find, among others, Young with his *Composition 1960 #7*, Cage with *4'33"* (1952), and Eric Andersen with *Opus 48* (1966). The three composers produced a "minimal art," based on a preference for "the smallest thought or act" (Cope 1971, 103).[5] Riley was included as part of an electronic music movement, since he played in one of the recent groups devoted to live performance, with David Rosenboom, Jon Hassel, and Gerald Shapiro (48).[6]

Among the various attempts to appropriate and institutionalize the music of these composers, that of John Vinton is noteworthy. In 1974, he edited *Dictionary of Contemporary Music*, covering the music from the preceding decades up to the time the book was in press, in particular concert music of the Western tradition. Young, Riley, and Reich appear several times in the dictionary. The various entries in which they are mentioned give no hint, however, of possible connections between their respective aesthetics. For instance, Young's music, "rigorously based upon just tuning, is perhaps the purest example of [microtonal] music in Western art," following Partch or Lou Harrison, according to Ben Johnston (483–84). Elsewhere Young's music, in particular his "word pieces" from 1960, is cited as one of the paradigmatic examples of "Prose Music," according to Frederic Rzewski (594). Along with the music of Riley and other West Coast composers, such as Joseph Byrd or Terry Jennings, Young's music was rather part of the movement of "indeterminacy" that subsequently led to "minimal art," simple, static, and repetitive, as Childs defined it (337–38).[7] For Salzman, Young, with his single notes and sustained intervals as well as his visual motifs, was instead the extreme representative of "mixed media," of "theater works or events that involve some merging of arts, forms, and electronic media" (489), whereas Riley, Reich, and Glass, for their part, had developed "live performance[s]" on "specially designed electronic apparatus" (491). The four composers, Rzewski wrote in another of his entries, produced "pulse music" that shared characteristics of non-Western music and sometimes contained repetitive figures (624).[8] Whether or not they associated the four, few authors would argue the credibility of these composers whom Nyman had recently dubbed *minimalists*.

The weightiest and most significant endorsement of the idea that Young, as well as Riley, Reich, and Glass, fully deserved to figure among the great names of the music of their time came in 1974, in the second editions of Salzman's *Twentieth-Century Music* and Hitchcock's *Music in the United States*. Both show how increasingly difficult it had become to neglect the work of these composers. In the first edition of both works, in 1967 and 1969, Young received only a brief mention, and Riley, Reich, and Glass simply did not exist. In the revised editions, however, all acquired considerable status. In the case of Young, to give but one example, what new works had he published that might explain this change in status? None at all: from one edition to the next, it was always the same *Compositions* from 1960 that the authors addressed. The featured works by Riley (*In C* from 1964) and Reich (*It's Gonna Rain* and *Come Out*, from 1965 and 1966, respectively) likewise predated the first editions of the two authors' books. In 1974, these works no longer had the same resonance as in 1967 and 1969. Or rather, they had now acquired resonance. It was not so much the "musical material" as the way that Salzman and Hitchcock viewed it that had changed.

This change may owe to Leonard Meyer's ideas, which, in the time between the old and new editions, continued to spread. This influence can be seen in Salzman's account, at least, in which aleatoric and serial music, which in 1967 had represented the absolute culmination of twentieth-century music, had now been surpassed. These works centered on a closed community of specialists, at a time when technology was making musical experience accessible to all. A third current, rejecting academic isolation as well as mass commercialization, was born. The early 1960s now represented a transitional period, destructive of the past, in the course of which the arts had been mixed, collectivized, and torn from their historical roots (Meyer 1967, 183–85). Thus, according to Salzman, minimalism was born as a response, through simplicity, to the modern excess of information (1974a, 186). This need for simplicity was also sensed, the author added, among the serialists, such as Webern (186); composers such as Varèse, Cowell, and Partch; and in Cage's Eastern music.[9]

Although he used the same label, Salzman's minimalism was not quite the same as Nyman's. For Salzman (1974a), the idea first arose in the music of Morton Feldman (187). Feldman, we read, not only used simple sounds that were sustained and isolated but also rejected all preestablished "processes," insisting on the "essential 'it-ness'" of the sound (187–88). Salzman obviously had not read Reich's writings on process music. Young did the same, he continued, by focusing all his energy on a minimum of sensory data. Works by Reich, Riley, Rzewski, and Glass were likewise products of slow transformations, phases, or cycles stemming from this return to simplicity. Thus, in 1974 Salzman in turn brought minimalism to the forefront of the contemporary music scene, taking care to distinguish it from "new pop culture" as well as from music theater—in spite of the fact that his colleague Kostelanetz, on whom he claimed to rely, had portrayed Young as one of the major representatives of the latter.

In the second edition of his *Music in the United States* (1974), Hitchcock—like his mentor Chase (x)—still sought to dispel the notion of American music's inferiority to that of Europe, while also emphasizing its distinctive popular vein as well as a range of new musical tendencies. Among the latter, Hitchcock identified "new virtuosity"; minimalism; collage, mixed-media, and music theater; and "new expressionism" (265–70, 273–76). In Hitchcock's first edition, as in Salzman's, Young held a minor place in the panorama of American music that the author portrayed in 1969. But again, as in Salzman, although not a single note had changed (Hitchcock considered a work from 1962), the composer's music took on a completely different dimension in 1974. Young was an experimentalist and antirationalist in 1969; in 1974, he was a minimalist (268–69). Salzman, whose new edition had just come out, surely had something to do with it (see Hitchcock 1974, 276–77). In his chapter on minimalism, although Hitchcock repeated almost verbatim the terms of his 1965 article, he left out the notion of boredom. Like Salzman again, he added the influence of Cage to that of Eastern music. The reasoning was the same: Cage permitted everything in music; therefore, he allowed Young's drones.

For Hitchcock, the drone musicians were Riley, Dick Higgins, and Glass, as well as Reich, who nonetheless focused more on pulse than on drones. For Reich, Hitchcock again looked at a work that preceded the first edition of his book, *Come Out* from 1966, connecting Reich to Young through its "hypnotic" character. From 1969 to 1974 Hitchcock, again like Salzman, primarily reconstructed the early 1960s.

DISPARITIES

If we follow the various lines of thought that developed around the music of Young, Riley, Reich, and Glass from the early 1960s to the mid-1970s, we find that several disparate readings of their works coexist. This disparity emerges even within the same work, such as Vinton's dictionary, or *Source,* one of the most respected journals on new music at the time.[10] The four composers are sometimes connected, sometimes not; sometimes isolated and sometimes associated with bigger groups. Only Cardew approaches Young as an isolated figure; Kostelanetz associates him with Ann Halprin, Robert Rauschenberg, and Allan Kaprow. Allen Strange brings Riley and Reich together, whereas Elliott Schwartz relates the latter to Lukas Foss. Salzman mentions Young first in conjunction with Cage and then with Riley, Reich, and Glass, together with Feldman and Rzewski; Hitchcock favors Higgins in place of the last two. For Nyman, these Americans are mixed with a good number of British composers. Finally, Young discusses only his own work, and Reich does the same. In 1975 the association of the four composers was far from factual, as Nyman presented it; there seemed to be as many different associations of composers as there were authors to advance them. Moreover, even when the association of Young, Riley, Reich, and Glass was explicitly affirmed, the label assigned to them was often not the same. From the time of its earliest mentions in the pages of music literature, their music received a variety of names: new music, neo-Dada, indeterminacy, multimedia, Theatre of Mixed Means, dream music, electronic music, live electronics, monotonality, or pulse, minimal, hypnotic, and process music, among others.

The wide array of names reflects sometimes deep-seated conflicts, concerning as much the methods and approaches of the writers as the content they describe. Parsons, for example, relies on listener experience to validate Riley's aesthetic, while Kirby, Kostelanetz, and Sontag later choose audience participation in the performance to explain Young's innovations. Kostelanetz also offers a reading of Young's works that reaches beyond the compartmentalized disciplines in art, while Barbara Rose and John Perreault apply the "minimal" analogy only to visual arts. Salzman and Hitchcock ultimately consider only the "musical" aspects of the four composers, as does Johnson, even though he confines his analyses to New York City in defining the "Hypnotic School." Some, like Strange or Schwartz, highlight the medium (electronics) as the aesthetic common denominator; others approach the musical material through Cageian precepts of the liberation of form; still others emphasize the limits and controls that the composers impose on this form or the type of ensemble that the works require.[11] Once again, the approaches and methods are manifold.

In the articles and books that deal more specifically with the origins of the four composers' music, the controversies are no less heated. Indeed, how is one to reconcile the image of Young inspired by the sound of the wind with that of Young, who owes everything to Cageian silence, and that of Young, who owes everything to himself, or even to Indian music, in explaining the birth of his aesthetics of stasis? How can one be inspired by Cageian freedom while at the same time producing a music with multiple restrictions? The reader in 1975 surely found it hard to sort through these differences. In considering only the link between Young and Cage—the most popular of the dozens of arguments advanced over the previous fifteen years—we find that even this premise remains tenuous: Cage permitted any sound or event to be music; therefore, sustained sounds constitute legitimate music. Likewise, Cage permitted silence to be music; conversely, continuous sound is music as well. Such reasoning presupposes a malleable interpretation, to say the least, of the Cageian heritage.

RESISTANCE

The confusion only grows the more we step back from it. By focusing our attention on the networks that developed around the music of Young, Riley, Reich, and Glass, these arguments have led us to believe that they held a predominant place in contemporary music. But when we delve into the reference books, encyclopedias, and contemporaneous accounts, we discover yet another controversy: for many authors, those four composers never dominated the musical panorama of the 1960s and 1970s. Young and Riley were of course active since the beginning of the 1960s and became known almost simultaneously; for many authors, however, Young, Riley, and Reich had no claim to a place in the cultural landscape. Not only had history bypassed their music in 1967, but it continued in many respects to resist it in 1975, after several iterations of works devoted to contemporary music.

From 1969 to 1970, two of the world's most prestigious universities— Oxford and Harvard—published, respectively, a "dictionary of" and a "companion to" music (Apel 1969; Scholes 1970). Neither mentioned the concepts of minimalism, hypnotism, process music, or music theater. That omission was not due to any failure to consider the United States (Apel 1969, 882–89) or the period in which these movements emerged (880; Scholes 1970, 477–79). Indeed, recent aleatoric and electronic music, for example, appears alongside neoclassicism and serialism, which were already known (Apel 1969, 26–27, 285–86). We note the same omission in France, where Edmond Rostand published his *Dictionnaire de la musique contemporaine* in 1970. Here the word *contemporary* did encompass electronic and aleatoric music, but it included no other current, nor the names of the four "minimalists." *Composers of Tomorrow's Music* by David Ewen presented a "non-technical introduction to the musical avant-garde movement." This avant-garde, however, still ended with Cage, followed only by Partch.[12] In *Music in Europe and the United States* by Edith Borroff (1971), which aimed in particular to present the representative forms of new music, as well as its most representative composers (vi), we learn only of serial, aleatoric, and popular music.

In 1975, the new edition of Wilfrid Mellers's *Music in a New Found Land* likewise illustrates the resistance faced by the music of Young, Riley, Reich, and Glass. Mellers's preface addresses a series of omissions that he made ten years before (xi–xii), but these concern only Varèse and his successors, George Crumb, and American folk music. Once again, Young and his associates are absent. Also in 1975, in the final reprint of the fifth edition of *Grove's Dictionary of Music and Musicians*, we read nothing of the four composers. Nor does the dictionary mention mixed media, indeterminacy, the Hypnotic School, or minimalism. That same year, a reader consulting the German work *Komposition im 20. Jahrhundert. Details—Zusammenhänge* (Gieseler 1975) would learn about improvisation, intuitive music, collage, live electronic music, process music, and multimedia. Apart from that, however, minimalism and minimalists are hardly to be found; the last great names of the twentieth century are Cage and especially Pierre Boulez, Mauricio Kagel, György Ligeti, Karlheinz Stockhausen, Krzysztof Penderecki, and Iannis Xenakis. In 1975, the 1960s did not yet include Young, Riley, Reich, and Glass.

CONSENSUS

Nonetheless, if we pass over the numerous, sometimes steadfastly opposed, readings of the music of Young, Riley, Reich, and Glass to assemble, almost statistically, a series of constants, what might we highlight? Besides the static or repetitive aspect of their music, two elements in particular come to the fore: its serious nature, on the one hand, and its Anglo-Saxon roots on the other. Indeed, it was not the "popularity" of their music that justified its incorporation by the music establishment, but rather its ability to offer a new development of "established musical concepts" (Strange 1969, 39)— after or, rather, "beyond" Cage, as the subtitle of Nyman's *Experimental Music* indicates; beyond Stockhausen for Cardew or Artaud for Kostelanetz; beyond the music establishment's officially recognized figures.

Through the 1960s and up to the mid-1970s, connections between the music of the four composers and the idiom of pop or rock would occasionally be mentioned. Authors such as Souster (1968–69), as well as Alan Beckett (1969) and Nyman, attempted to forge links between these musical spheres within the literature of the music establishment. Often, however, they ended up undoing those links. Their aim was more to differentiate aesthetics than to unite them around the stasis or repetition that was noted in both spheres. Souster, for example, construed Young's work not as a bridge between pop and art music but as a shield to defend the avant-garde from the popular menace. Over the course of these fifteen years, accounts of the repetitive or static music in both pop and serious genres were constructed in ways that excluded one sphere from the other. Young, Riley, Reich, and Glass were "serious" precisely because they were not "popular." Young and Kostelanetz agreed on this point: there was good and bad repetition: on the one hand, an objective strategy to produce a subjective effect; on the other, an admission of incompetence (Kostelanetz 1968, 187–88). For Young as for Reich, popular music was already ancient history.

Their own music was so serious that on the other side of the divide, in magazines such as *Jazz Monthly* (Knox 1967), *Friends* (Knox and Knox 1970), and *Crawdaddy* (McGuire 1968), Young and his colleagues were associated with the classical world. When Lenny Kaye mentioned Young in reference to the Velvet Underground in the *New Times* of April 1970,[13] it was only to remind the reader that the group's music, ultimately, was "all rock 'n' roll" (157). A bit later Lester Bangs, Dave Marsh, and Greg Shaw, like Kaye before them, also seized on the Velvet Underground to popularize the label *punk* by emphasizing its "unpretentious, unadorned, and pugnacious pop roots" (Gendron 2002, 228). They evoked multiple repetitions and deafening volumes, but once again, they excluded Young and his music.[14] Even Lou Reed, who had accompanied the release of the Velvet Underground track "Loop" with a text in praise of electronics and repetition in 1966, would renounce any interest in this conceptual music three years later.[15] "That was something John [Cale] did, and I'm not interested in that kind of thing, per se, very much," Reed explained (quoted in Martin 1969, 117). His bandmate Cale clearly represented nothing more to the music establishment than "a Welsh musician who was responsible for introducing the tape [of a performance by Young] into this country" (Cardew 1966, 960).

In monographs devoted to American music—particularly those by Chase and Hitchcock—that viewed popular music as a national distinction and claimed to approach it in the same way they did serious music, connections between the four composers and the rock or punk scenes were never established. The book *Serious Music and All That Jazz!* (Pleasants 1969) is a good example. The author attempts to show that the composers of serious music—unlike those of rhythm and blues, country, pop, or rock—are lost in the meanderings of noncommunication. Young—who had set fire to a violin filled with concert programs on stage—figures as the representative of the "obscenities" related by critics who, "behaving like ostriches," never protest

(229).[16] Another example is Charles Hamm's exhortation to revitalize the field of musicology by opening it to popular genres, lest the best students turn their backs on it. One must stop ignoring the fact that music ranges from Cage to Jimi Hendrix or from Riley to Simon and Garfunkel, he wrote (1971, 95), thereby associating the minimalists with the classical world.

Connections with continental Europe were similarly ignored. Over the years from 1960 to 1975, anglophone authors rarely looked to France, Germany, Italy, or Belgium, except to contrast the serious composers of the Old World, represented essentially by Stockhausen and Boulez, with Young, Riley, Reich, and Glass, whom they placed at the pinnacle of the music of their day (see especially Whittall 1970 and Rockwell 1972). For Americans, minimalism was an American affair; for the British, it was Anglo-American. Moreover, critics on the Continent said almost nothing about comparable aesthetics arising in France, Italy, or Belgium during the same period. Surely some should have drawn comparisons with such eloquently titled works as *Symphonie Monoton Silence* (1949) by Yves Klein; *Quattro Pezzi su una nota sola* by Giacinto Scelsi, who reportedly knew Young (Szendy 2002, 34); or the feedback pieces by Eliane Radigue, a former student of Pierre Schaeffer and Pierre Henry, including *Stress Osaka* (1969). But no analytical study of the links between these works and the music of the minimalists was produced.

At the time, experimental circles in France focused their attention on Schaeffer's work, in which repetition was merely a detour enabling him "to isolate the in-itself-ness of the sound phenomenon" (Schaeffer [1952] 2012, 13), thus leading to musique concrète.[17] After his experiments with the closed groove, Schaeffer and his collaborators moved away from bare repetition, which he had "discovered" at the end of the 1940s. Indeed, until the mid-1970s, no efforts to categorize the music of Young, Riley, Reich, Glass, and the British composers can be found in Western Europe. Research works, reports, and interviews are few and far between. The fourth issue of the Parisian magazine *VH 101* in 1970, for example, includes writings by Glass, Young, and Reich, among many other representatives of contemporary music, but makes no explicit link between the three composers, apart from the recurring mention of repetition (in Glass and Reich) and the influence of non-Western music (in Reich and especially Young).[18] Daniel Caux, the music editor for *Chroniques de l'art vivant,* took the greatest interest in Young, devoting an issue of the magazine to him in 1972. Once again, Young is described as a post-Cageian or neo-Dadaist now looking to the East, although he mostly drew his inspiration from within himself (Caux 1972, 24). In the musicologist's interview with him, Young cites only Scelsi among the composers who share his aesthetic interests (32).

The year 1975 offers no hint of what would finally become of the music of Young, Reich, Riley, and Glass. Indeed, in the middle of the decade, when the critic Johnson abandoned the designation *hypnotic* and called the four *minimalists,* the composer Robert Ashley firmly opposed that term, uniting some of the same composers within a new style that he called *ethereal.*

11. Fighting or Laying Down Arms

MUSIC WITH ROOTS IN THE AETHER
AND SIMPLICITY

Over the course of the 1960s and 1970s, the composer Robert Ashley's name, as well as that of his group *ONCE* and his collective Sonic Arts Union (with David Behrman, Alvin Lucier, and Gordon Mumma), appeared regularly alongside those of Young, Riley, Reich, and Glass. In 1962 Hitchcock asserted that Young and Ashley shared similar experiences and the same ideology (245–46), and in 1965 Kirby deployed the two composers in service of his concept of "New Theatre" (chapter 5, above). During the following decade, Johnson never failed to point out in the *Village Voice* the aesthetic similarities between spoken word pieces such as Reich's *Come Out* (1966) and Ashley's *She Was a Visitor* (1967) (1975 article, repr. in Johnson 1991, 56); to observe the "minimal slow-motion approach" of Alvin and Mary Lucier, evolving on a "static dynamic plane" (1972, repr. in Johnson 1991, 23); or to associate David Behrman with the "hypnotics" Young, Riley, Reich, and Glass (Johnson 1991, 29). Across the Atlantic, Nyman noted in *Experimental Music* (1974) the looped recitations and even gradual processes in Alvin Lucier (*I Am Sitting in a Room* [1969]: 108) and Ashley (*Fancy Free* [1971]: 109), as well as Behrman and Ashley's work with feedback (100–101).

Nyman's account in *Experimental Music* of the music of the members of the collective Sonic Arts Union mostly attests, however, to a rift between the respective aesthetics of which Ashley and Young were the leading figures. Indeed, in Nyman's book, works such as *The Wolfman* (1964) and *She Was a Visitor* (1967) by Ashley, *Runthrough* (1970) by Behrman, and *Vespers* (1968) by Lucier belong to a different category from that assigned to the four minimalists. No matter that the works contain loops and feedback effects, repetitions and gradual processes; they still do not make it into the seventh and final chapter of the book, "Minimal Music." Nyman's focus in the group around Ashley is instead the medium, electronics, including the use of magnetic tape and amplification, which the critic tends to pass over in discussing the music of Young, Riley, Reich, and Glass.[1] This split is likewise evident in the writing of the *New York Times* critic John Rockwell, who also reviewed the work of Ashley and his associates. Rockwell did not even point out the potentially repetitive nature of their music. Ashley's connection with the minimalists seems to have escaped Rockwell; what he described to his readers was simply electronic music (1973b; 1973e; 1973g).

This aesthetic divide also attests to the solidification of the networks built around Young, Riley, Reich, and Glass, on the one hand, and Ashley, Behrman, Lucier, and Mumma on the other.[2] Over the course of various reshapings and appropriations from one text to another, the music of the former group had become "minimal," while that of the latter was "electronic." Each was elaborated to the exclusion of the other, to the point where potentially similar traits no longer appeared. In 1976, however, Ashley contested this state of affairs, first in a letter to Nyman and then in *Music with Roots in the Aether*, a documentary film (an "opera-for-television" as Ashley called it) presented the same year at the Whitney Museum. Nyman, as a European, saw and singled out in American music only what would allow him to connect New York to his own continent, Ashley argued (see Nyman 1976d, 266). For his part, Ashley wished to "demonstrate the elements of a style of musical composition that originated in the US and that has come to have international significance" beyond the geographical limits set by the British critic in *Experimental Music* (Ashley quoted by Nyman in ap Siôn 2013, 266).

Music with Roots in the Aether was not an attempt to attach the group around Ashley to the minimalism that was soon to become established.

Nor did the film intend to emphasize the static or repetitive nature of its protagonists' music. It presented seven interview portraits, seven "landscapes," as Ashley called them: those of Behrman, Glass, Lucier, Mumma, Pauline Oliveros, Riley, and Ashley, all of whose music took root "in the aether." Broadcast in 1976 in festivals and museums and sold as a videocassette, the film explicitly assembled a group of composers around common roots. It nonetheless left it to the viewer to formulate the connections between these seven figures that Ashley had gathered. At the time, no supporting works came out to reinforce or define the elements of the music style that Ashley was constructing.

From one interview to the next, numerous links united the composers, all of whom actively participated in the elaboration of Ashley's "ethereal" style: rejection of the academy and of serial music, embrace of a physical approach to music, the practice of group composition and performance, and a marked interest in harmonics, improvisation, the electronic medium, long compositions, and simplicity. This style, however, did not catch on as hoped: even before the video was distributed, Nyman, defending the aesthetic of repetition that connected New York to London, swept aside Ashley's strictly American stylistic construction. In summer 1976, in *Studio International*, Nyman reasserted the validity of the European link and the lack of impact that West Coast experimentalism had had on the contemporary musical landscape. At most he agreed to add the drones of California composer Harold Budd—who was not part of Ashley's "aether"—to his minimalism (269–70). Once again, stasis and repetition were what interested Nyman, not the multiple stylistic elements presented in *Music with Roots in the Aether*, even though such elements had also been mentioned by Glass and Riley, who themselves were included in the style that Ashley defined.

Ashley's conceptions failed to echo the interests of Nyman or Rockwell. For the latter, Ashley's desire to "define a grouping of American composers that has neither been perceived as such nor been taken very seriously by the new-music establishment in this country" was certainly "lively and informative," although he questioned Ashley's approach of simply "mak[ing] a portrait of [his] friends"—excluding Reich, David Tudor, and Salvatore Martirano (Rockwell 1977d, 13). Whereas in this article Rockwell outlined and justified the links between the members of Ashley's group (they were, he wrote, united around an intuitive music without notation, simple techniques, a rejection of postserial excesses, and inspiration drawn from Eastern meditation or from theater), he made no mention of the group in his book *All American Music* a few years later (1983). There Ashley appears above all as a composer who has shown "that it is not only possible but fruitful to carry on the American experimental tradition of Cowell and Cage" (96), while Behrman remains a post-Cageian who "has become a leader of this school of newly humanized electronic music" (133). Rockwell failed to mention any connection between the minimalists and the "post-Cageians" of the Sonic Arts Union.

Like Rockwell, Johnson reviewed the presentation of Ashley's documentary at the Whitney Museum (on April 20, 1977). For Rockwell, while Ashley certainly shed light on the music of his artists, their association remained nebulous. In his opinion, if anything connected the composers' music, it was essentially its lack of historical roots and their refusal to employ notation. For Johnson as for Rockwell, the group that Ashley constructed was missing certain figures, American or British (1977, repr. in Johnson 1991, 161–62). Ashley's work did not pass the tests imposed on it. Furthermore, in 1977, when David Osterreich discussed *Music with Roots in the Aether* in his book *Perspectives of New Music*, he considered it not so much a style as a videographic "work" by Ashley; thus he analyzed its aesthetics rather than its musicological content (Osterreich 1977).

At the end of the 1970s, despite the criticism of his work, Ashley assembled several authors to help substantiate the style that he sought to create. He prepared an anthology of texts by Paul DeMarinis, Peter Gordon, Jill Kroesen, Maggi Payne, Margaret Ahrens, Paul Robinson, Craig Hazen, and Robert Sheff. The authors' mission was to bring the concepts elaborated by Ashley to life. Difficulties with the publisher, however, prevented the completion of his project.[3] *Music with Roots in the Aether*, the book as well as the style, remained unrealized. In the late 1970s, Ashley's project was finally no more than a set of videos presented from one venue to the next. In no way was it a musicological document describing a musical style; "Music with Roots in the Aether" would never gain recognition as a typically American style.

SIMPLICITY

In 1966 the composer Barney Childs was one of the first to contest the disparagement of indeterminate aesthetics, defending Young in particular, in

Texas Studies in Literature and Language. Although he did not select the composer for inclusion in *Contemporary Composers* (Schwartz and Childs 1967), he nonetheless celebrated his "indeterminate" work in 1969 in *The Composer*. In 1974, in Vinton's *Dictionary of Contemporary Music*, Childs included Young among the West Coast composers of indeterminacy who had moved to the East Coast, where this indeterminacy developed through Fluxus or ONCE. In New York, he wrote, the work of the second generation of West Coast composers led to a *"minimal art,* in which attention is directed to the simplest musical, verbal, or pictorial elements often extensively prolonged or repeated" (Childs 1974, 338).

Since 1971, Childs had been working at the University of Redlands, some sixty miles east of Los Angeles, where he composed his own indeterminate music while also teaching a series of composition courses (Swift and Attinello 2001). There he continued his work in defense of the American music of his day.[4] In his 1975 article "Directions in American Composition since the Second World War," he noted, "the last few decades of 'serious' music have brought an important change in the composer's view of the nature and function of musical process" (Childs 1975a, 35). This change might be summed up, he wrote—once again revealing his engagement with Cageian theories—in an interest in "the realization of a musical . . . concept in sound." For the period from 1965 to 1975, Childs identified three compositional orientations (43). The first, called "live electronics and intermedia" (43–44), concerned electronic composers such as Pauline Oliveros, Alvin Lucier, and Robert Ashley.[5] The second, which integrated "diverse sound sources" (44), pertained to polystylistic compositions, as in Salvatore Martirano or Philip Winsor. The third, "simplicity and minimalism" (44–45), unveiled what he had only briefly mentioned in Vinton's 1974 dictionary.

Although it went by the same name, Childs's minimalism radically departed from that described by Nyman the year before (1974). In many ways it resembled the California minimalism that Johnson mentioned in his 1973 writings for the *Village Voice* (Johnson 1991, 58–59, and see chapter 7); indeed, for Childs minimalism essentially concerned the West Coast. Its well-known representatives and its aesthetic content also differed from what one read in Nyman: a primary trend in minimalism, Childs asserted, was a focus on "elements of simple lyricism." That focus was found in Reich, as well as in West Coast composers such as John

Adams and Peter Garland. A second trend in the movement instead proposed the "reaffirmation of past tonal and structural vocabularies." Ben Johnston, Harold Budd, and Daniel Lentz were its representatives. Childs's article marks the first explicit evocation of the idea of "a revisitation of a past aesthetic ideal" (44) with regard to minimalism. Nyman had mentioned the quotation of classics, in the spirit of Cardew, as part of British minimalism; Childs, however, described another level of reference, one not limited to the "literal" quotation of a given work from the past but instead drawing more generally on its aesthetic possibilities. Moreover, for Childs, Britain was beside the point: "The European tradition that had shadowed most American music for decades has continued to fade." Indeed, that tradition had had no influence on the development of American new music (45). Thus it is not surprising to read, in the review of Nyman's *Experimental Music* that Childs published three months after his "Directions in American Composition" (Childs 1975a), a critique of Nyman's Eurocentrism (Childs 1975b). Childs also pointed to Nyman's error of failing to address the West Coast; in fact we find nothing in Nyman concerning Childs's minimalists (80).

But the battle between the two authors would never take place. That same year, Reginald Smith Brindle, a composer and professor at the University of Surrey who is remembered especially for his interest in serialism and electronics (Larner and Wright 2013), published *The New Music* (1975). The author fashioned a panorama of new music that ran from Webern to Boulez, Stockhausen, and Cage. The main topics he covered were pointillism, post-Webernism, integral serialism, the twelve-tone technique, indeterminacy, graphic notation, musique concrète, and electronic or theater music. Childs criticized him not only for characterizing Young's work as "pranks" (Brindle 1975, 184) and ignoring "the whole Steve Reich–Terry Riley–Phil Glass direction" (Childs 1977) but also for failing to mention the group of British experimentalists that Nyman "superbly" portrayed in *Experimental Music*. Nyman may not have conveyed Childs's interests, but nonetheless, Childs provided him his support.

12. Persevering

At the end of 1974, when Nyman presented Young, Riley, Reich, and Glass as minimalists whose aesthetic had been expanded in Britain via various attempts at rereading "Western classics," Brian Dennis proposed that the four were instead "repetitive" composers who had given rise to a "systemic" aesthetic, within which "the structure and note to note procedure are dictated by a numerically expressible construct" (Dennis 1974, 1037). Two years later, in October 1976, the composer Michael Parsons took it a step further in the *Musical Times*: many composers, American and especially British, were associated with the emergence of a music based on "systems." Nyman's minimalists were among them. Dennis and Parsons were not the only British composers to share this concurrent conception of the musical heritage of Young and his colleagues, which had begun to take shape in the mid-1960s. To understand its development in musicological literature, we need to look at another musical figure: the composer John White. In the same way that Nyman's writings were part of a large network whose roots went back to Cardew, the writings of Dennis and Parsons arose from a similar interconnection in which the name of White, a contemporary of Cardew's, regularly appeared.

JOHN WHITE

Like Cardew, White was born in 1936. Cardew studied at the Royal Academy of Music in London beginning in 1953; White enrolled in the Royal College of Music in 1955. Six years later, when Dennis too enrolled in the Royal College, White began to teach composition there. At the time, White was a prominent performer and composer. Among his students were Roger Smalley and William York. In 1964, the teacher founded the Composers' Ensemble with his students Dennis, Smalley, and York. Up to that time, White had primarily been known for his knowledge of Messiaen's music (Dennis 1971a, 435). In the Composers' Ensemble, he turned instead to Ives, Stockhausen, and Satie, but also to Cardew, whose name increasingly spread through contemporary music circles.

The connections between White and Cardew—and their respective aesthetics—progressively strengthened. "Only the occasional ad hoc performance of a Cardew work," Dennis (1971a) wrote, "provided any kind of catalyst for further objective analysis" during White's years of compositional isolation, when he drew ideas only from Robert Schumann and Anton Bruckner (436). Cardew fascinated White, Dennis added. The opposite was equally true: in 1968, Cardew commissioned a piece from White; the result was *Cello and Tuba Machine*. According to Dennis, the work attested to an unparalleled economy of means, evoking Satie's *Vexations* (436). Since the early 1960s, White had been pursuing the path of "anti-development," "deadpan harmonies," and "obsessive ostinatos" (435). He and White performed his *Cello and Tuba Machine* together in May 1971 at Queen Elizabeth Hall. In the meantime, the Composers' Ensemble had disbanded. Smalley and Dennis had left it to study, like Cardew, with Stockhausen. York joined Nadia Boulanger in Paris. White then founded the Promenade Theatre Orchestra with Christopher Hobbs, Alec Hill, Hugh Shrapnel, and David Smith—all members of the Scratch Orchestra; Smith was also a member of the 5 Piano Group with Nyman. They played their own compositions as well as those of Cardew, with whom they were in regular contact through the Scratch Orchestra. Unlike that group, which focused on improvisation, the Promenade Theatre Orchestra produced what Dennis described as an aleatoric but nonetheless "static" music of "impassive regularity" (437).

Through the years 1960–70, some of White's students followed their teacher's work. They showed enthusiasm for both his work and Cardew's, as well as that of Young, one of the latter's heroes.[1] Two of his students, Smalley and Dennis, also engaged in a broad effort to promote both their respective works and an aesthetic, many traits of which they seemed to share. In 1969, Dennis praised the prophetic nature of Smalley's work as well as its use of "regular pulse systems" and "extreme repetition" (30). In 1972, Smalley in turn presented a laudatory portrait of Dennis. Just as Dennis had celebrated Smalley's repetitions, Smalley extolled Dennis's ostinatos. In his 1972 article in the *Musical Times*, Smalley also recalled White's notable influence on Dennis (Smalley 1972b, 31). White had led him to turn his back on serialism and to set out, in the mid-1960s, in search of a harmonic language interspersed with multiple repetitions. Dennis's work, we read, relied on simple and regular materials and forms, while containing "structures of considerable complexity . . . often formed from the superimposition of these basic elements" (32). In 1974, Dennis synthesized their aesthetic conceptions in his article "Repetitive and Systemic Music," postulating the existence of a systemic current extending the principles of the repetitive music of Young, Reich, Riley, and Glass.

REPETITIVE AND SYSTEMIC MUSIC

When he published "Repetitive and Systemic Music," Dennis not only drew on the work he had undertaken with his colleagues to highlight the value of their drones, repetitions, and regular and symmetrical pulsations; he also relied on the aesthetics that were being established by his American counterparts.

According to Dennis, repetitive and systemic music was unique in that it induced perceptions and effects that varied from person to person, although composers insisted that this was not their goal (1974, 1036). That phenomenon was precisely what linked this type of composition to experimentalism and to Cage, whom he quoted as saying: "These are your sounds; you can do with them as you like."[2] This music produced four "experiences": the relaxation of the mind; the sudden awareness of a change that has taken place gradually; the exploration, at a personal level, of the interaction among musical modules; and a perception of pitch that varied from one listener to the next, provoking "the active aural exploration of harmonies, harmonics and their interaction." What especially defined repetitive and systemic music, Dennis observed, was the compositional technique that made these effects possible—that of Reich above all, in his *Piano Phase* from 1967 (1036–37). Also included were Riley's music, with an emphasis on instrumental color, as in *In C* from 1964; that of the British composer John Lewis, who rationalized the intuitive repetitions of *In C* by specifying the number of occurrences for each module; that of Glass, characterized as "linear"; and that of Rzewski in *Les Moutons de Panurge*, with its gradual development of a melody.

In addition to Reich, Riley, Lewis, Glass, and Rzewski, Dennis named Hill, whose procedures lengthened the measures in his compositions; White, who created "change-ringing permutations"; and Hobbs (a former student of Cardew's and founder of the *Experimental Music Catalogue*), who most clearly marked the transition from repetitive to systemic music (1037). This systemic music was directly linked to the repetitive trend but differed in that "the structure and note to note procedure are dictated by a numerically expressible construct" (Hobbs quoted in Dennis 1974, 1037). According to Dennis, chance was replaced by precise numbers, and the different sections were numerically derived. Thus defined, systemic music was above all his own music, in addition to that of his colleague Hobbs and even that of White. For Dennis, "the extreme economy" and audible processes of Reich and Riley could now give rise to the exploration of zones "where systems are partly heard and partly hidden."

Basing his argument on the "repetitive" composers most prominent in the music establishment of that year, Dennis in his 1974 article sought above all to promote his own systemic music. The leverage game carried on: Cage had been used as a support to elevate Young to the pinnacle of contemporaneity; Young had been used in the same way for Riley; and then Riley for Reich and Glass. Now the last two were propelling the British systematics to the forefront of the musical stage. Along the way, Cage and his aesthetic had almost completely disappeared. Hobbs, White, and Dennis himself had now become, according to Dennis, the representatives of this music exploring new zones where "chance and individual choice" were no longer at home (1974, 1037).

SYSTEMS

Almost two years later, Parsons, one of Cardew's former students and a cofounder of the Scratch Orchestra who regularly collaborated with Skempton and White, took up and then refashioned Dennis's theory (1976). Dennis had used the New York "repetitive" composers as leverage to establish his own music, as well as that of Hobbs and White. Parsons in turn would use Dennis's work on the systemic composers to establish his own music as well as that of Howard Skempton, John Lewis, and Dave Smith—a music that would break free of the American composers.

Parsons's demonstration also sought to broaden the connection with the visual arts that Dennis had hastily outlined the year before: the "musical system" described by Parsons, who eschewed the label *repetitive*, was in fact linked to British "pictorial systems," such as those of Jeffrey Steele and David Saunders. Their works, too, made use of limited means and numerical bases (1976, 816). Not only had Hobbs and White presented their works in systemic circles but also, in Parsons's view, they had numerous contacts with artists (just as Young, Riley, Reich, and Glass did with the representatives of op art), in terms of both theory and attitudes.[3]

The British systemic musicians, however, differed from the Americans Reich and Glass. For the British composers, Parsons contends, repetition was not used for its psycho-acoustic effects but rather to create a structured sense of time, with clear divisions based on numbers. In these pieces, wrote Parsons—who, like Nyman, drew on Cage—the "planned" coincided with the "unexpected" (1976, 816). And if some composers, such as White and Hobbs, we read, had turned away from systems in favor of an empirical mode of composition that drew on references to the music of the past, others, such as Lewis, Smith, Skempton, and Parsons himself, had, each in his own way, pursued that numerical vein (see table 1).

In what way, ultimately, did the writings of Dennis and Parsons make use of Young, Reich, Riley, and Glass? These composers furnished the bases for the development of a new aesthetic. By harnessing the reputation of the four composers, the two authors made the recognition of their aesthetic possible. In so doing, they also reinforced the connection of systemic music to New York repetitive music, thereby supporting Nyman's work as well. In the writings of Dennis and Parsons, however, the nature of this connection—essentially intended to promote systemic music—

Table 1   Rhythmic Phasing in Parsons's *Six Pieces in Counterrhythm for Two Drummers*, no. 1

	Section 1	Section 2	Section 3	Section 4
Player 1	36 × 4	48 × 4	60 × 4	72 × 4
Player 2	48 × 3	64 × 3	80 × 3	96 × 3
	144	192	240	288

Quaver [♪] = 240. Ratio of section lengths: 3 : 4 : 5 : 6
SOURCE: Parsons 1976, 817.

Sidebar 3

Minimal music. See System (ii).

Entry for "Minimal music" in *The New Grove Dictionary of Music and Musicians* (Griffiths 1980).

---

differed from, or even competed with, that established by Nyman. Some months later, Nyman addressed Parsons's work (Nyman 1976e). He strenuously opposed the idea of a connection with the visual arts but supported Parsons's musical conceptions. Parsons appears to have translated the interests of Nyman, who was expanding his landscape of American and British contemporary music to embrace the systemic music described by his colleague. For his part, Parsons did not wish to deconstruct Nyman's pronouncement.

Their differences were temporarily resolved. Four years later, when the entry "Minimal music" appeared in the *New Grove Dictionary of Music and Musicians* (1980, 12:3354), it merely referred the reader to the entry "System" by Paul Griffiths (1980): "A variety of new compositional practices, the common feature being an emphasis on repetition." In Griffiths's definition, the two labels have merged—or rather, one has absorbed the other (see sidebar 3). "The element of repetition may be governed by a system," he wrote, thus including the music of Reich and Glass with that of Hobbs and White, as Dennis did originally. The *New Grove*, following Nyman, agreed with Dennis and Parsons.

13. Giving Up Ground; Retaking It

MINIMAL MUSIC

In the mid-1970s, Nyman's chapter on minimalism in *Experimental Music* (1974, 139–71) constituted the last link in a long chain of alliances going back to the early 1960s. This conception of minimalism marked the culmination of extensive work in which numerous actors had taken part. At the time, however, the critical acceptance of this "minimalism," even of its existence, was no more guaranteed than that of concurrent theories referring, in whole or in part, to the same music, as well as to trends that were more or less related. The history of minimalism was in fact written after the publication of *Experimental Music*, as it was tested, reclaimed, and reworked by Nyman and other authors. After the publication of *Experimental Music*, minimalism quickly became the subject of sometimes virulent debates, accepted by some (explicitly or not) and variously appropriated by others. Meanwhile, its author continued to clarify and refine the concept.

CHALLENGES

In 1975 Smalley, the former detractor of Cardew who revised his assessment of Young in the late 1960s (see chapter 2), reviewed Nyman's book in the *Musical Times* (1975a, 23). Smalley's critique addressed not only the issue of minimalism but also Nyman's reading of Cage's aesthetic and even that aesthetic itself. At the time, Smalley had radically reoriented his compositional style (Smalley 1975b, 1054). He turned his back on the resolute experimentalism of his improvisation group, Intermodulation, and revisited serialism in an attempt to reverse the linear or contrapuntal logic so as to focus on its harmonic possibilities. In his music, he affirmed, it was now the chord, and no longer the melody, that dictated his twelve-tone technique. In his review of *Experimental Music*, Smalley did not dispute the "fact" that Cage and Cardew were the "leaders" of this music (1975a, 23). Nor did he contest the "fact" that the center of gravity for this music had, as Nyman asserted, moved from the United States to Britain (23). That, for Smalley, went unquestioned: experimentalism was a valid concept, which furthermore was rooted in the tradition of Western classical music. His disagreement lay at another level: that of values. Cage's work, Smalley wrote, misunderstood the nature of music by privileging ideas to the detriment of style (23). By letting sound relations develop naturally, Cage forsook integration, harmony, and balance. He had made himself the ambassador of a world of chaos (24). Experimental music, Smalley continued, destroyed style and promoted reactionary ideas. By allowing inexperienced musicians to perform, Cardew and others denigrated values such as skill.

The defects that Smalley pinned on minimalism were no less numerous than those he attributed to experimentalism. They were nonetheless quite different: the connection that Nyman constructed between Cage and the duo Reich and Glass was not "meaningful," Smalley claimed. The music of the latter two was precisely notated and demanded a high level of expertise and control. These two minimalists, to whom he added Feldman, dealt not with ideas, as their supposed predecessor had, but rather with style.[1] These composers make music. Meanwhile, pieces characterized by great simplicity—chiefly those of British composers (who were above all the ones mentioned by Nyman, Hobbs, and Bryars in the *Experimental Music Catalogue*)—tended, in Smalley's view, to produce an aesthetic not of innovation but rather of "inconsequential triviality" (25–26).

Some months later, when Smalley took part (with Peter Dickinson and Tim Souster, among others) in the discussion forum that closed the first

American Music Conference at Keele University in England, he reaffirmed his views: Cage's discourse had lost its initial intensity (Dickinson 1975, 188), and the "essentially American" aesthetic influence of Reich, Riley, and Young in Britain could lead only to a superficial cultural transplantation (196).

Nyman's interests thus failed to coincide with those of Smalley. The same was true with Richard Middleton. In *Music & Letters*, Middleton declared that Nyman's experimentalism aimed to banish the human from sound (but would not be able to succeed); that this experimentalism was full of means without an end; and that it was, moreover, difficult to distinguish from the avant-garde (1975, 86). For Bill Hopkins in *Tempo* (1975, 40) and Childs in the *Music Educators Journal* (1975), that distinction was likewise doubtful. Childs also complained that Nyman's book did not reflect the idea that he himself championed in Vinton's dictionary (Childs 1974): that the West Coast composers took part in the development of indeterminacy and subsequently of minimal art. Not one line about Pauline Oliveros or Larry Austin, zero on Douglas Leedy or the journal *Source*: indeed, he lamented, one found nothing at all in Nyman on the California colleagues mentioned by Childs (Childs 1975b, 80). In the United States, where the book was distributed in the middle of 1975, Larry Lockwood made the same criticisms of Nyman that Smalley had formulated a bit earlier: the opposition between Cage and Stockhausen was fragile; the connection between the Cageian lack of limits and the minimalists' predeterminations did not hold up. And if Satie tried his hand at repetition, it was out of sheer irony and nothing more. Nyman, Lockwood wrote, was merely promoting the music he liked (57).

In 1975, to judge only by reviews in the journals of the music establishment, one might conclude that Nyman did not succeed in convincing his peers. That, however, did not prevent him from campaigning for his experimentalism and his minimalism, through his teaching at Trent Polytechnic and the lectures he gave here and there. In April 1975, at the first American Music Conference in Keele and subsequently in the publication of its proceedings (Dickinson 1975), Nyman continued to insist on the division, though contested by numerous critics, between avant-garde and experimentalism, as well as between continental Europe and the United States. To the great dismay of his detractors, he reaffirmed the notion that minimalism flourished along a line that associated Cage and Feldman on one side and Young and Reich on the other (repr. in Nyman 2013, 243). In his lectures, he even rallied new support for his experimentalism through the figure of Anthony Philip Heinrich, one of the first great American composers. Heinrich's music, with "no progress, no climax, no discernible logic," became, for Nyman, a forerunner to experimentalism (249).

Logically, Nyman also solidified his proposal through his critical work. In winter 1976, in *Studio International,* he once again supported the inclusion of Glass in the experimental movement, citing "evidence of one's own ears" as proof that Glass's connection to Cage was valid. For further justification one need only read the writings of Glass or Wolff, he affirmed, to see that they shared the will to banish all "dramatic structure" from their music (Nyman 2013, 255–56). In the same issue of the magazine Nyman promoted the label Obscure Records, whose founder, Brian Eno, had over the past year been publishing the works of his colleagues in the *Experimental Music Catalogue,* particularly Hobbs and Bryars. That same year Nyman released his first album, *Decay Music,* with the pieces "1–100" and "Bell Set No. 1," as well as percussive works by Cage, which now represented for Nyman the American composer's "most interesting music" (2013, 260).

VICTORIES

In 1976 Nyman was confronted with a challenge he could not ignore. One year before, Ashley had sent him a letter to voice his discontent with the essentially geographical limits that Nyman had set in his description of American music. For Ashley, as for Childs before him, Nyman's book, which focused solely on New York and Britain, was written by a European for Europeans (see Nyman 2013, 266). At the time, Ashley was promoting the idea of an "American style" extending far beyond New York to the West Coast, a style he called "music with roots in the aether" (see chapter 11).[2] In 1976 he was producing his documentary video on that style, which encompassed Lucier, Mumma, and Behrman—Ashley's own colleagues, Nyman pointed out, returning his charge of nepotism—as well as Riley, Glass, and Oliveros.

If Nyman at first seemed tempted to ignore Ashley's letter, he had to respond once the composer's "counter-proposition" was released in the theaters. In doing so, Nyman gave up as much ground as he sought to regain. He admitted that it was indeed the connection between New York and London that had guided him in formulating his statement; the West Coast avant-garde had not managed to reach Europe, or even New York, whereas Cage, Fluxus, Reich, and Young had had an undeniable impact. Only the static work of Harold Budd—soon to be released on Obscure Records (270)—deserved fuller attention. Nonetheless, Budd still exemplified a major difference between West and East Coast composers: the former were intuitive, the latter intellectual. The debate thereby concluded—not only for Nyman, of course, but also for Ashley, who, after the release of *Music with Roots in the Aether*, gave up the fight.

CONCESSIONS

Meanwhile, Nyman and his theories continued to be challenged. As we saw in chapter 12, the year that Nyman published *Experimental Music*, Dennis proposed a different landscape of British new music: one that was not only minimalist but also, and above all, repetitive and systemic. Less than two years later, Parsons, one of the founders of the Scratch Orchestra, furthered and expanded his colleague's proposal in the *Musical Times*. He too highlighted the systemic nature of the music of a series of British composers, as well as the connections between their systems and the aesthetic of a series of British painters (Parsons 1976). After the publication of Parsons's article, Nyman again had to defend his theories. In his 1976 essay "Hearing/Seeing" in *Studio International*, he proceeded in two stages: first he rejected the connection with the visual arts, and then he allied Dennis's systemic theory with Parsons's.

> I have deliberately emphasised the *differences* between the visual and sounding arts because it seems to me that there is no point in making generalisations about interconnections and influences, since these tend only to oversimplify the essential nature of music and musical life, of sounds and structure, of scores and performances. Music's processes and materials, and its social, cultural and historical contexts, are entirely its own, if only because

the transmission and reception of sound is subject to its own (natural) laws and (cultural) organisation. Ultimately music—for better or worse, and no matter how beneficially it seems to be affected by the conceptual, aesthetic, philosophical, and procedural attitudes of the climate that the visual arts have created—essentially stands alone, feeding off itself. (repr. in Nyman 2013, 302)

To demonstrate the invalidity of the connection to the visual arts, Nyman extrapolated a subtle concession made by Parsons himself. Parsons had maintained that shared theoretical principles united the systemic work of artists such as Steele and Saunders with that of composers such as Hobbs, White, and himself, but that at a perceptual level no strict equivalence could be established (Parsons 1976, 816). For Nyman, even though the "lines" traced in Young's *Composition 1960 #7, #9,* and *#10* could evoke hard-edge painting (Nyman 2013, 279), they were not perceived the way that painting was.[3] In music, stasis led to harmonic variety, creating "psycho-acoustic effects" that gave rise to the "unpredictable," Nyman wrote, basing his argument on Reich's remarks as well as his own definition of experimentalism (280). For the author, the "game" of linking music to the arts was not only impossible but also dangerous (282). The desire to treat sound as an autonomous and impersonal entity defined only the first generation of experimentalists (283).

Although Nyman dismissed the visual connection, he nonetheless left a bit of leeway for Parsons, whose systemic theory seemed to have succeeded in translating some of Nyman's own interests. In *Experimental Music,* Nyman defended the idea, with regard to minimalism, of a "many-sided retrenchment from the music that has grown from indeterminacy" (1974, 211); like Parsons, he saw a shift in the concerns of British composers, from hyper-freedom toward hyper-restriction and, now in 1976, toward "systemic music" (repr. in Nyman 2013, 284). But Nyman was not so much going back on his earlier writings as extending their scope to encompass other works. Having thus sided with Parsons, Nyman now viewed a specific "attitude towards time and form/content" (288) as what differentiated the British from their American counterparts, rather than the borrowings from classics that he mentioned in 1974. And in fact, according to Nyman, this systemic conception of music—an "objective" conception, where music was not a mouthpiece for subjectivities but expressed itself freely—was what rendered the analogy with the visual arts obsolete: unlike their supposed visual equivalent, modular musics did not necessarily exclude lyricism (289–91).[4]

Thanks in particular to Nyman's work in *Studio International,* he largely overcame the regular challenges to his theories in the late 1970s. Ashley did not take his debate with Nyman, or even his defense of his own ethereal style, any further. The defenders of systemic music saw their theory reappropriated by Nyman, who thereby enlarged its field of influence. Others subsequently raised objections to Nyman's work. In 1977 in the *Musical Quarterly,* for example, Christopher Ballantine still considered Reich an experimentalist rather than a minimalist. But shows of support also continued to surface. In 1976, in a review of Reich's writings in *Tempo,* Peter Dickinson defined the American composer as a minimalist, even though nothing in the composer's book would imply this. Reich, who had long disavowed the label *minimal,* seemed almost to accept it in an interview with Nyman in 1976; in any case, he did not contradict his interlocutor when the latter referred to his music as such (repr. in Nyman 2013, 330). Even Johnson, at the end of 1974, dropped his label *hypnotic*; he espoused New York minimalism after having maintained some years before that minimalism was above all Californian (repr. in Johnson 1991, 94).

14. Subscribing to an Idea

A NEW CURRENT AND MODERN MUSIC

A NEW CURRENT

On September 20, 1980, the eleventh Biennale de Paris opened. For more than a month, this art festival was punctuated by concerts presenting a *nouveau courant musical* (new musical current) that was developing in Britain, California, and France. The phrase was coined by musicologist Daniel Caux, then a producer for the public radio stations France Culture and France Musique. His articles had appeared in the newspaper *Combat* and the magazine *Jazz Hot;* he had also been the music columnist for the magazine *Chroniques de l'art vivant* and collaborated with the newspaper *Le Monde* and the label Shandar, which had released music by Sun Ra, Albert Ayler, and Cecil Taylor, as well as Young, Riley, and Reich. In fact Caux's commitment to American "new" music was not new. In the late 1960s he was already attentive to its developments. In an article for *L'art vivant,* Caux mentioned Riley's music and the French release of *In C* on Columbia Records (Caux 1969). *In C* was a "very simple" work, he wrote, capable of revealing "a fascinating modal world made up of groups and subgroups that endlessly break up and re-form" (29). Although he did not explicitly associate Riley, Young, and Reich together, Caux hoped to see "a wider distribution of their music" in France. The following summer he invited Young and Riley to perform alongside the jazz artists Albert Ayler and Sun Ra at the Nuits de la Fondation Maeght (see Caux 1970). The same year he joined with Aimé Maeght and Chantal D'Arcy to create the label Shandar. Caux wrote most of the liner notes and continued his work promoting the Americans' music: in 1970, Shandar released *Four Organs / Phase Patterns* by Reich; in 1972, *Persian Surgery Dervishes* by Riley; and in 1974, *Dream House 78'17"* by Young.

Meanwhile, in *L'art vivant,* Caux published a detailed biography of Riley, "one of the musicians most representative of the underground current in American new music" (1970), as well as a commentary on Reich's live electronic work and an interview with Riley, whose music he presented as being situated at the crossroads of East and West as well as of jazz (1971). Caux also devoted an issue of the journal to Young, including an essay on the composer, an interview, his compositions from 1960, and a testimonial by Cage (Caux 1972). Up to that point, however, nothing in Caux's writings explicitly linked the American composers. Riley had worked with Young and shared his interest in the East, Caux wrote (1971, 26), but his "evolving reiterations" (1970, 27) attested to an aesthetic progression of his own; Riley himself said as much (1971, 26). And although Reich used a "principle of repetition . . . [and] gradual expansion," no connection was made with the aesthetic of his colleagues (25). Even when Caux, Cage, and Young themselves discussed Young's music in the 1972 issue of *L'art vivant,* none of them related him to other aesthetics or composers: "No one before him had made the discovery of a music so eminently 'elementary,' nor will anyone after him be able to," wrote Caux (1972, 24). Indeed, Cage tended to confirm Young's isolation, or at least the lack of connection between his own work and that of Young; the latter's search for a music that would have a positive impact on humanity was not without interest, he asserted, but it turned out to be contrary to his own approach (26). Young himself denied the Cageian heritage (27), while also underscoring the uniqueness of his own work. At most he could be related to Scelsi, who shared his desire to create a "psychological state" (32). Thus none of the composers, including Young, saw any connection to the repetitive aesthetic in his music.

In over three years of Caux's reports, no link united the three American composers. In May 1973, however, when Caux devoted his music column in *L'art vivant* to Glass, he now treated the latter's close association with Young, Riley, and Reich as an established fact, even if he seemed unsure about the underlying nature of this association: "Contemporary music? Experimental music? Jazz music? Pop music? Although, in different ways, it would likely interest audiences from each of these musical categories, it seems difficult to classify the American 'New Music' illustrated by La Monte Young, Terry Riley, Steve Reich, and Philip Glass under any one of them, given their obvious distinctiveness" (1973, 25).

Up to then, Caux had mostly been inspired by the California journal *Source: Music of the Avant-Garde*, which regularly covered the works of the four composers but had never linked them. In 1973, the author gathered material from the fifth issue of the New York magazine *Avalanche*, to which Glass had given an interview in summer 1972 (Béar and Sharp 1972; Caux 1973, 25). Glass suggested that a similar aesthetic united the composers, an aesthetic from which he himself had recently escaped (28). The association seemed fitting to Caux, who up to that point had treated the American composers in isolation. Following Glass, however, who failed to develop the nature of the link between the protagonists, Caux was none too specific about it. He even suggested that for Glass "it is in no way a question of focusing attention on a static sound, as with Young; of improvising while submitting structures to the inspiration of the moment, as with Riley; or of unleashing a process of gradual phase shifting, as with Reich; but rather of creating a tonal music formed by repetitive figures played rhythmically in unison" (25). The link between the composers materializes instead on a structural level (fig. 2). "The goal of this diagram is only to visually convey the distinctiveness of each process," Caux writes (1973, 25). Indeed the point is to highlight the formal processes in order to connect their music, even if it means dropping all the other parameters that might distance them from one another.

In 1977, Caux contributed to the feature on American repetitive musicians in issue no. 26 of *Musique en jeu*.[1] He defended the notion that their music did not tend to numb the listener but instead facilitated active participation in listening. In Caux's writings at the time, the existence of an "American repetitive music" that broke with contemporary or avant-garde music was now clear, to the extent that he found it "pointless to fight against a 'label' that is already well established" (82). "Any listener who is

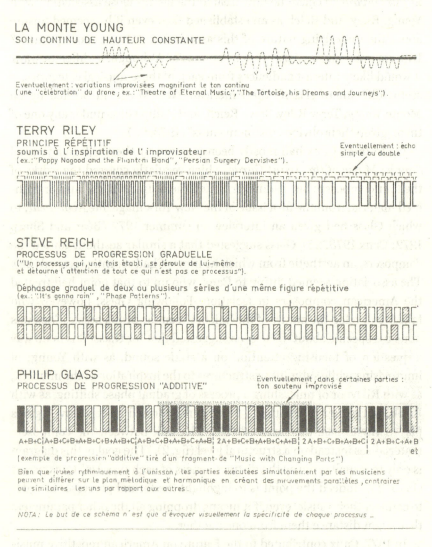

Figure 2. Diagram of the respective styles of Young, Riley, Reich, and Glass (Caux 1973, 25).

at all discerning can at once recognize this musical form," he claimed. Caux's "repetitive music" lay at the confluence of jazz and the East, with roots in neither Cageian indeterminacy nor serialism: "The idea was 'in the air.'" Incidentally, Yves Klein composed his *Symphonie mono-ton* in France in this same period (83). For Caux, "repetitive music" was above all "music in which it is a matter of listening to the sound, strictly speaking, rather than following a more or less literary thought that it is meant to illustrate" (82). In 1977, Caux remained faithful to Young's thinking. The last part of the article consisted of discussing his work, once again, in isolation from that of the other "repetitives"—such as Ashley—for whom Young served as a mentor.

MODERN MUSIC

What happened between 1978 and 1981 to make "modern music," as the British critic Paul Griffiths called it, change shape? Why did *Modern Music: From Debussy to Boulez* (Griffiths 1978) only briefly mention the music of Riley (166) and Reich (178–79)—without linking their music or relating it to that of Young, who is missing from the book—whereas three years later, *Modern Music: The Avant Garde since 1945*, by the same author (Griffiths 1981), connected Young, Riley, Reich, and even a newcomer, Glass? Why are their works from the 1960s or the early 1970s, which were considered in isolation in the 1978 book, gathered under the banner of minimalism in the 1981 volume? The answer, we discover on page 171, is that Nyman's *Experimental Music* transformed Griffiths's view of this music, which thus became the heir to Cageian indeterminacy.

Griffiths, who began writing for the *Musical Times* in the early 1970s while in his mid-twenties, belonged to a generation of critics active in the aftermath of the early struggles to win cultural recognition for Young, Riley, Reich, and Glass. Over the course of his numerous columns, Griffiths never opposed these composers' music, any more than he defended it; their place in the musical landscape seems to have raised no questions for this young journalist, who was to become "one of the most influential critics of his generation" (Williamson 2001). In any case, until the publication of *Modern Music: The Avant Garde since 1945* (Griffiths 1981), we find no effort in his texts to link the composers. The writing of "slow movements towards and away from a common pitch" is a characteristic shared as much by Luciano Berio (in *Agnus* [1970]) as by Terry Riley, György Ligeti, or Karlheinz Stockhausen (Griffiths 1971, 1190); "minimal" works have been produced by Morton Feldman, John Cage, La Monte Young, and Cathy Berberian (Griffiths 1972, 168); and processes to create "aural illusions" mark Ligeti's music (*Atmosphères* [1961]) as well as that of Stockhausen (*Stimmung* [1968]) and Reich (*Four Organs* [1970]) (see Griffiths 1978, 178–79).[2] Nothing either groups Young, Riley, Reich, and Glass together or sets them apart from each other.

In 1978, when Griffiths published *Modern Music: From Debussy to Boulez,* he drew especially on *Music since the First World War* by Arnold Whittall (1977). Whittall knew *Experimental Music* and Nyman's work, but he referred to it only briefly, to describe the "radical" aesthetic of Cage, ultimately preferring the label *systemic* to that of *minimalist* to discuss the music of Young, Riley, Reich, and Glass (211). Griffiths made no attempt to group the aesthetics together in this book. He discussed Reich and Riley separately, associating each of them with other schools and composers. And when Griffiths contributed to the first edition of *The New Grove Dictionary of Music and Musicians* in 1980, he followed Whittall's lead: the "minimalist music" entry refers readers directly to that for "systemic music," defined on the basis of Nyman's work and above all the work of Dennis (1974), whom Nyman himself ended up supporting (see chapter 13).

In 1981, however, it was a different story. Although the tenth chapter of *Modern Music: The Avant Garde since 1945* is titled "Indeterminacy: Changing the System" and again mentions the theories of Dennis (1974) and Parsons (1976), it contrasts sharply with Griffiths's previous writings. Now the author draws exclusively on Nyman; the "system change" refers on the one hand to minimal music and on the other to the link between music and politics (1981, 171–87).

Nyman's book *Experimental Music* and its minimalism, having become inescapable thanks to its successive adoptions, won Griffiths over in the end. In 1981 Young, whom he had ignored in 1978, was now "a central figure among contemporary American and English minimalists" (Griffiths, 1981, 176–77), while Riley's music, like Young's, employed "a small repertory of pitches and a high degree of repetition" (177), procedures later taken up by Reich and Glass. Exit Ligeti, Stockhausen, and the others: repetition and minimalism were the province of the four American composers alone (180–81).[3] The exclusion of Rzewski's *Moutons de Panurge* underscores this point. For Griffiths, that work was more political than repetitive; conversely, *Come Out* by Reich was more repetitive than political.[4] Griffiths's book met with enthusiastic support (see especially Nadeau 1981; Hayes 1982; and Hoffman 1982). The progress of minimalism was underway.

15. Disrupting the Status Quo

AMERICAN MINIMAL MUSIC

No matter how consistently composers of repetitive music
have spoken out against the intellectualism of the avant-
garde (which for Reich, includes Webern and Cage), they
cannot escape its influence.

(Mertens 1983, 87)

In 1980, numerous authors finally came to agree on the existence of a
minimalist current typified by the music of Young, Reich, Riley, and Glass.
These authors now rarely strayed from considerations that assumed the
fundamentally "repetitive" or "minimal" aspect of this music. Few still
alluded to the theatrical character of Young's music or approached the
music of Riley or Reich from the angle of electronics.[1] That the four composers' music was that of a single sound or iteration was now a proven
fact. And if these musicologists, critics, or composers had not entirely
settled the question of the genre's place in the history of music, that of its
underlying meaning, and that of the origins of the techniques imple-
mented by the four composers, all nonetheless seemed to agree on one
point: repetitive or minimal music had developed, and continued to
develop, as the antithesis of serialism and the modern music tradition of
continental Europe initiated by Arnold Schoenberg.

Also in 1980, however, the Belgian author Wim Mertens published a
book with an evocative title: *Amerikaanse repetitieve muziek: in het perspectief van de Westeuropese muziekrevolutie* (American repetitive music
through the perspective of the Western European music revolution). It
was the first monograph to trace the history of the music of Young, Reich,

Riley, and Glass. It also completely departed from what was being written elsewhere at the time. Here, this American music was presented as the last act of an evolution initiated in Europe by Arnold Schoenberg and Anton Webern. The theory was not only unique; it was provocative. How did Mertens manage to thoroughly reconfigure the musical roots of the four composers—the first, according to him, to have made systematic use of repetition? Moreover, how did he win favor with Nyman, who, rather surprisingly, wrote the preface, or with the British publisher Kahn & Averill, who brought the book out in translation three years later?[2] Finally, how did Mertens succeed in making his view of this slice of the contemporary music panorama a reality?

We approach these questions without attempting to demonstrate that Mertens was any more or any less "right" or "reasonable" than his colleagues and without considering the possible agreements between his analysis and others, since his was formulated in clear opposition to concurrent theories. We can best understand the paradoxes by pursuing the networks within which Mertens and his book developed, identifying the fundamental principles on which he built and the allies he enlisted, and shedding light on the subtle ways that he modified diverse theories and thus aroused the interest of others.

GENESIS

In the early 1970s, in the Flemish region of Belgium, Mertens was a young man who would soon study political science and then musicology at Ghent University. In Belgium, the music of those whom Mertens would call "repetitive" composers was still little known. At the most, some information might be gleaned from the French journal *Chroniques de l'art vivant*, which was known to certain Flemish musicians and musicologists (see Geysen 1974). In 1972, however, the musicologist Herman Sabbe, who would later become a specialist on the serialist current and the music of the composer Karel Goeyvaerts, a celebrated Belgian serialist (see especially Sabbe 1977 and Toop 1974), published an article titled "Ac' Art" in *Kunst- en Cultuuragenda*. There he recounted his discovery of Reich's music at the festival Musik der Zeit, organized by Westdeutscher Rundfunk.

This music and the fascinating attraction it exerted, he wrote, consisted of "collective realizations . . . in no case improvised . . . based on an obstinate technique that is extremely simple" (Sabbe 1972, 20). For Sabbe, this technique constituted above all an analogy with op art, with the musician working over a foundation of rudimentary elements that he brought into close relation with one another while also balancing their intensities, closing the structure, and opening the form. Like the viewer in op art, Reich's listener could choose to follow only certain details within the whole musical fabric (21). In his article on Reich's music, Sabbe thus coined the term *ac' art*, developing the visual analogy briefly mentioned by Caux in *Chroniques de l'art vivant* a year earlier (1971).[3] Like Caux, he made no link between Reich's music and any preexisting musical current, nor any other contemporary composers, American or European.

Some years later, however, when Sabbe again discussed Reich's music in the same journal (1979), his approach had changed. Gone were op and ac' art; Reich's music now had older, strictly musical, roots. His approach was one of "extreme simplification of musical resources," based on a "modular structure" (20) that had originated with Young in the late 1950s. This music, Sabbe wrote, was also that of Riley and Glass. It was sometimes called *minimal*. What explains the change in Sabbe's perspective on the same music—at least with regard to Reich—seven years later? Why did Sabbe now group the composers, whom he nonetheless described as "very different . . . from an aesthetic, technical, and ideological standpoint" (20)? In his article, Sabbe offered no explanation. Still, he made apparent the increasing solidification of the paradigm formulated by Nyman five years before, while also establishing it in Belgium. Indeed, the article leaves little doubt about the origin of the elements mentioned by Sabbe. His use of the label *minimalist;* his account of the genre's spread from the United States to Britain and then continental Europe, Young's founding role, and the movement's beginnings in 1958; and the repeated mention of Nyman himself all suggest that the latter's writings were what convinced Sabbe. Besides demonstrating the progressive validation of Nyman's paradigm, the article hints at the way in which, over the years, Sabbe would refashion the British critic's argument. He confirmed this already in 1979: minimalism went back to Young's serial period, and this minimalism spread to continental Europe in the late 1960s (20–21). By focusing on these movements, Sabbe magnified the European connection.

Not long before Sabbe began to subscribe to Nyman's views, in the mid-1970s, a series of Flemish composers in Belgium already saw the "repetitive" composers as potential allies in their attempt to establish their own aesthetic conceptions. One of these composers was Frans Geysen, a serialist who discovered minimal music thanks to Caux's work in France. In the early 1970s, Geysen was in the midst of his turn toward minimalism (Knockaert 2013). He wrote about it in 1974, in the magazine *Adem*: "I have received news about young American composers and descriptions of their music that have raised my spirits, since I feel a kinship between their aspirations and what I have been trying to describe as my objective" (Geysen 1974, 24).

At the time, the association of the four American composers wrought by Caux in 1973—following Glass's interview in *Avalanche*, in which he mentioned Young, Riley, and Reich to defend his own work (Béar and Sharp 1972)—incited the interest of the future "Belgian minimalist," even though he had "never listened to Young's music" (Geysen 1974, 25–26). The underlying system that would soon govern the exchanges among Nyman, Sabbe, and Mertens was already apparent: Geysen invoked Caux to buttress the theoretical bases of his own music (see Geysen 1974, 27–28); in so doing, he reinforced the Young-Riley-Reich-Glass connection.

AMERIKAANSE REPETITIEVE MUZIEK

In the end, the in-depth revision of Nyman's argument would come neither from Geysen nor Sabbe but rather from Mertens, at that time a second-year student at Ghent University. Mertens was also, perhaps even more so, a fan of the minimalist trend. He wrote a musicological memoir on the ateleological aspects of the genre (Mertens 1979), produced programs on Belgische-Televisieomroep on the subject, and even invited some of the American composers to perform in Belgium. In 1980, he helped to get Nyman's own music included in a compilation titled *From Brussels with Love* on the label Disques du Crépuscule. At the time, Nyman was not only a well-known champion of minimal music. He was also a renowned composer of minimal music, thanks mostly to the pieces he wrote for the filmmaker Peter Greenaway. Soon Disques du Crépuscule would release Mertens's own recordings; he too would write compositions that he called *minimalist*.

In 1980, Mertens published *Amerikaanse repetitieve muziek*, an analysis that presented the repetitive current "through the perspective of the Western European musical revolution." His demonstration was decisive: repetitive music was the final stage of the antidialectical movement created by the European avant-garde after Schoenberg (Mertens 1983, 87) and thus constituted a liberation from everyday reality (113). For Mertens, repetitive music was nothing less than an emancipation.

Some of the critics reviewing his book immediately highlighted what often seemed to them a weakness: his thesis lacked maturity; it was opaque.[4] The structure of the book itself, for example, did not follow his historico-teleological logic. Mertens opens with a long section on the history of the music of Young, Riley, Reich, and Glass (part 1); he then considers the developments that preceded the realization of their repetitive aesthetic (part 2) and ends with a series of ideological reflections, ranging from sociology to philosophy and aesthetics to psychology, while including other aspects of music history as well (part 3). The last two parts, announced as the crux of his argument, constitute less than a third of the book. In part 3, paradoxically, Mertens makes very little mention of the repetitive composers' music. Adornian theses on the evolution of the language of Western contemporary music, the "libidinal philosophy" of Gilles Deleuze and Jean-François Lyotard, and Freudian psychology are often subjects in their own right, considered in isolation from the connection promised by Mertens.

Because most of the book is focused on the four composers, Mertens tends to solidify the first part of Nyman's 1974 theory, on which he (like his teacher Sabbe) largely relied: "repetitive music" for Mertens is almost exclusively that of Young, Riley, Reich, and Glass. Unlike Nyman, however, who highlights his British colleagues, Mertens names no one after the American composers. This aspect of Mertens's work merits further attention.

Young, Riley, Reich, Glass: Revisiting Experimental Music

Although Mertens's discussion of the first half of the final chapter of *Experimental Music*—the section on the American minimalists (Nyman

1974, 139–57)—remains faithful to the source in many respects, it contains certain modifications. In Mertens's book, the connection among the four composers goes beyond a common style; a play of interpersonal influences also unites them. Up to this point, few authors had followed up on Johnson's idea that "there is a direct line of influence from Young, to Riley, to Steve Reich and Phil Glass" (1973, repr. in Johnson 1991, 56). Nyman himself, like many others, said no more than that Riley's music had developed from an element that was present only in a "passive" manner in *The Tortoise, His Dreams and Journeys* (1964–) or in *X for Henry Flynt* (1960): namely, repetition (Nyman 1974, 144).[5] Mertens, for his part, constructed a lineage from one composer to the next; in so doing he excluded any other network of influence or any other composer from the avant-garde or elsewhere. Mertens thus strengthened the supposed ties between the four composers and rendered their association even more factual. Nyman's argument (the first part, at least) becomes more substantial, especially since Mertens also brings in formal considerations.

These formal considerations, however "factual," likewise resulted from a series of adjustments to the hypotheses presented in writings that preceded his book. By defining the American composers' music as essentially "minimal" and "repetitive" (Mertens 1983, 11–12) and approaching it as such, Mertens excluded aspects that other authors sought to reveal. Consequently, many of the more recent developments in these composers' music—above all that of Young and Riley—fell outside his focus, by his own admission. It is no doubt also for this reason that Mertens did not follow the works of the two "originators" of the genre beyond the 1970s: their aesthetic was no longer of interest for his thesis on minimal music. Mertens says as much in his introduction: it is difficult to discuss repetition and minimalism with regard to whole sections of the four composers' work. On the one hand, in some respects the music of Riley, Reich, and Glass displays a rhythmic and harmonic complexity that corresponds little to the name of the genre; neither does the length of certain pieces (12). On the other hand, repetition is a feature found in many kinds of music, whether traditional or Eastern, and it is not systematically present in Young's music (16). Nonetheless, the repetitive reading, or rereading, of their works is the central thread that runs through the book.

Mertens does not merely construct a narrow lineage linking the four composers, nor does he simply group their music under the banner of repetition and minimalism. Anticipating the line of thought that he will pursue in the second part of the book, he also focuses on the ties between the repetitive composers and serialism, particularly with regard to Young and Riley. He reasons that if Young and then Riley distilled Webernian stasis and repetition in their own work, and if Reich and Glass followed their work, then minimalism is clearly rooted in the European classical tradition, and repetition may be the final development of modernity. All that Mertens needs to do now is show this last development to embody Deleuzian liberation rather than Adornian regression.

Mertens's approach to Young and Riley thus reveals a triple reworking—the (re)construction of the influences at play, the strictly minimalist focus, and the "serialization" of their earliest works—thereby laying the groundwork for the concept of a liberating music that is developed at the end of the book. Mertens divides Young's career into three phases: the first (1956–58) is serial and follows, through the use of drones, the static and in some respects "repetitive" work of Webern;[6] the second (1959–61), that of Fluxus, is transitional (Mertens 1983, 27);[7] and the third (1962–) is "repetitive." This last period, prefigured by *X for Henry Flynt* (1960), continues over the following years.[8] With this approach the influence of Cage (essentially during the liberating period of Fluxus),[9] that of theater, that of popular musics (an influence that, for Mertens, runs more from minimalism to popular music than in opposite direction), and that of Indian and traditional musics all go out the window. Indeterminacy and performance, among other subjects, are passed over in silence. The bases of Mertens's argument are established: Young started out with serialism and continued via repetition.

After having laid down the serial origins and repetitive foundations of Young's musical discourse (or at least having claimed to do so), Mertens draws a connection between Young and Riley. Both undertook experiments with sustained sounds when they worked with Halprin in 1959, he writes (1983, 21).[10] Riley subsequently focused on one of the "marginal" aspects of his colleague's works, particularly *X for Henry Flynt* and *Dorian Blues*: repetition. Riley, however, used it not as "a controlling mechanism," as in Young, but as "a means of forming his unusual material" (36).[11] According to Mertens, Riley simply replaced "the constant in Young's work with continuously-evolving repetition and multiplication techniques" (37).

From this reductive angle, Mertens considers Riley's works up to the years 1970–71, at which point he abandons him altogether. Riley's works, Mertens writes, are made up of tirelessly repeated cells that produce ever-new combinations. Whether by means of electronics, instruments, improvisations (for unlike Young, who "restricted compositional freedom," Riley is an improviser first and a composer second),[12] or the series (since Riley's modal language was influenced by Stockhausen),[13] it is repetition and its variations, inspired by Young, that form the basis of Riley's language (Mertens 1983, 36–37).[14] Reich, Mertens writes, subsequently "follow[ed] Riley's example" (1983, 48), although for his part, Reich leaves no place to chance. In Mertens, even more than in Nyman, the shadow of Cage fades away. Repetition pervades Reich's work almost without interruption, from the beginning of his career to the end of the 1970s, from electronic to instrumental music, from phase shifting to rhythmic construction as well as augmentation.

Mertens's reading of Reich's work, however, was hardly new. Many authors before him had noted the salience of repetition. Mertens, however, was pursuing a different process: in order to connect Young and Riley to Reich and to Glass, he had reconfigured the music of the first two and disengaged it from Cageian freedom. Already in 1980, this inversion of the genre's leading figures attested to a shift that would play out in the writings of many others: the displacement of minimalism's center of gravity, represented above all by Reich and Glass.

Thus, the first part of Mertens's argument consists of uniting the four composers through a line of descent and grouping them around repetition, while also disengaging them from other stylistic connections and from lineages other than that of serialism. In the end, this approach merely solidifies Nyman's thesis, although Mertens does not take up the idea of minimalism's British descendants. Nyman's work is only the first basis of his argument. The serial foundation and subsequent grouping around a "context of repetition" constitute the second. Mertens announces this from the outset: their repetition, unlike that used traditionally in Western music, is neither teleological nor narrative; it escapes the constraints imposed by the notion of evolution (1983, 17). This type of repetition, for Mertens, was what united the four composers and differentiated them from others. This specific type, too, was what placed minimalism at the end of the modernity, while also making it the final development of the Western musical canon.

The Origins and Ideology of Repetitive Music:
Adorno, Deleuze, Lyotard, and Freud

The thrust of Mertens's demonstration lay not only in his rereading and redeveloping the history minimalism as written by Nyman but also in the origins he gave to minimalism, as well as the ideology he attributed to the movement as a result. "As a result" because, although Mertens treated the supposed prehistory of the movement and its ideology separately, they are, in his discourse, intrinsically linked. "Repetitive music can be seen as the final stage of an anti-dialectic movement that has shaped European avant-garde music since Schoenberg" (Mertens 1983, 87). "The anti-dialectic tendency in 20th century music is a liberation from everyday reality. . . . This utopian attitude, which is the opposite of Marxist dialectics, forms the basis of the musical thinking of John Cage and the American repetitive composers" (113).

These few sentences embody the core of the argument. Once more, the argument does not appear from nowhere. Various reworkings enabled Mertens to establish the idea of a "liberating" minimalism integrated with the European avant-garde. Two maneuvers in particular synthesize this process. The first consists of rereading Theodor Adorno's theory of the antidialectical crisis so as to attach the "repetitives" to the end of the "Western European music revolution"; the second consists of abandoning Adorno and some of his "negative" conclusions in favor of a rereading of the "liberating" theory of Gilles Deleuze and of Jean-François Lyotard.

The breach that opened when Nyman hinted at the possibility of the serial origins of minimalism allowed Mertens to associate Young, Riley, Reich, and Glass with the revolution begun by Schoenberg. According to Mertens, the association derived above all from the basic mechanism of repetition and from the insertion of this mechanism into a specific context of the antidialectical movement postulated by Adorno decades earlier in his *Philosophy of New Music* (Adorno [1949] 2005). In 1980, Adorno was already required reading in musicological studies. His work had been translated, discussed, and developed in many writings, including those of Sabbe (1972b).[15] For Sabbe as for Mertens and many others, the notion that the twentieth century was in crisis was an indisputable fact. The works of Schoenberg, Webern, and, by extension, Stockhausen conveyed the uncertainties of humankind faced with the disintegration of the harmony of its existence: "The contradictions in society at large are mirrored in the contradictions of form and content, of idea and structure," Mertens writes (1983, 96). These contradictions explain the disappearance of the subject in music and the great quest for the autonomy of the work, which little by little becomes objective. As the expression of subjective feelings disappears, music gradually relates to nothing but itself. From Schoenberg to Stockhausen and even Cage, Western music has followed this direction over the course of the twentieth century. To uphold this conception, Mertens needs to make minimal music "objective," which requires him to further reframe the work of Young, Riley, Reich, and Glass. The emphasis on repetition in the first part of the book now takes on its full dimension: this basic mechanism is precisely and fundamentally opposed to the idea of a dramatic structure allowing the expression of subjectivity. Now, if the music of the four composers is repetitive, it moves neither backward nor forward; it "generat[es] the present at each moment," writes Mertens, quoting Ivanka Stoïanova (Mertens 1983, 89).[16] And since it is antiteleological, since it "evolves in place," in the instant, through continual "reprises" (Stoïanova 1977, 72), it relates to nothing other than itself. It is antidialectical.

The nature of musical process described by Reich with regard to part of his work (in which the content is only the process itself) is not without interest for Mertens's theory (Mertens 1983, 89). Its strictly "minimalist" character, however, does not quite serve his cause, given that it has little connection to a temporal conception of music. Indeed, the idea of minimalism itself was of slight interest to Mertens, who was looking to portray an antiteleological and subsequently antidialectical movement. For Mertens—paradoxically, in view of the title of his book—this aspect simply vanished. Logically, the same happened with the "superficial and defensive" idea that minimal music restored tonality (87). Likewise, the notion of its fundamentally Eastern nature demonstrated nothing more, in Mertens's view, than the ability of modern culture to annex a foreign culture (88).[17]

> The question that must now be considered is how this non-
> dialectical movement is to be evaluated, and what the
> ideological relevance of repetitive music is.
> (Mertens 1983, 109)

To integrate repetitive music into the modern landscape portrayed by Adorno, Mertens needed to adapt Adorno's philosophy of music and even, in the end, cut off from it. Doubtless he knew that Adorno characterized repetition, at least in the case of Stravinsky, as childlike or primitive (Adorno [1949] 2005). He also knew, as he himself confirmed, that Adorno saw "the absence of musical content . . . and the decay of the subject in and by capitalism . . . as a sign of defeat and regression" (Mertens 1983, 113). Mertens thus turned to Deleuze and to Lyotard, for whom the antidialectical tendency of the twentieth century was instead "a liberation from everyday reality" (113).

For Lyotard, Mertens asserts, the devaluation of sound material in serial music corresponds to the devaluation of "use-value" in favor of "exchange-value" in neocapitalist society (118). The loss of content in the work, as postulated by Lyotard, is nonetheless compensated for by an increase in libidinal intensity, which escapes the idea of exchange value; this intensity has "no finality or purpose" (118). Its increase appears especially in Cage's "new music." Thanks to Lyotard, the loss of content decried by Adorno can thus be evaluated positively, Mertens writes; it brings about an increase in libidinal intensity, which escapes capitalism and leads to its destruction (120).

Ultimately Mertens treated Adorno and the French philosophers the same way he did Young and Riley, on the one hand, and Reich and Glass, on the other: he leveraged the former to reach the latter. He provided no demonstration, however. The final pages of his book convey a notion of what would become "postmodernism" in Lyotard, with almost no ideological link to the repetitive composers—only a brief association of repetition in their music to repetition in the death instinct (Thanatos) and the libido (Eros) in Freud (123). "We maintain that this libidinal context has been recognized explicitly only by these American composers of repetitive music," Mertens writes, concluding that "in repetitive music, repetition does not refer to eros and to the ego, but to the libido and to the death instinct" (123). The repetition in the music of the American minimalists is not, in fact, "reproduction," Mertens declares, but "repetition of the identical in another guise." Its aim is not to represent the ego; its context precludes it. For Mertens, the American composers' repetition was impersonal and could thus be libidinal, and therefore liberating.

Attracting Nyman's Attention

How would Mertens's provocative propositions fare? In 1980, it was anyone's guess. However well constructed they might be, if no one picked up on them, the book would never leave the Flemish (and Dutch) musicological circles of its day. It would not achieve the status of truth. If Mertens wanted to see his typically European model of minimalism become true, others had to ratify it, seize on it, and further its thesis. That is precisely what happened with the first edition of *Amerikaanse repetitive muziek* in 1980: Nyman himself lent his support by writing the book's preface.

Although Mertens took a path diametrically opposed to that of the British critic, Nyman's book was his starting point. By stepping into the breach that Nyman opened, Mertens constructed his own thesis. *Amerikaanse repetitieve muziek*, translated as *American Minimal Music* when published in Britain and the United States three years later (Mertens 1983), helped solidify a dual "fact": the existence and the advent of a minimalist current made up of four American composers using repetitive processes in their music. Substantiated by Mertens, the biased Eurocentric fable (or a derivative of it) for which Ashley and Childs had reproached Nyman became real. Nyman translated the interests of Mertens, who in his own book transmitted the paradigm that the British critic had helped forge in *Experimental Music* ten years before. In so doing, Mertens also translated the interests of Nyman, who in turn wrote the preface to his work. Both intended to establish the idea of a scholarly and modern underpinning for a genre called *minimalism*, assuming its de facto entry into the canon. Moreover, both these authors were musicians who contributed their own compositions to this genre.

In his preface, Nyman could thus assert that minimalism had become an "established fact" and that it was "possible, indeed necessary, to put this music into a broader artistic, cultural, aesthetic, social, musical, and critical perspective"—specifically that outlined by Mertens, who viewed it as no longer in conflict with the European music tradition but rather in continuity with it (Mertens 1983, 8).

DAS EUROPÄISCHE MINIMAL-MUSIK-PROJEKT

For Mertens's thesis to gain credibility, others needed to take it up; it had to translate their interests as well. Thus, in the summer of 1980, a group of European authors and composers gathered for a vast enterprise called Das Europäische Minimal-Musik-Projekt (the European Minimal Music Project). It was launched by Michael Fahres, whom Mertens had just identified as one of the composers of European minimalism (Mertens 1983, 11). Fahres's goal was clear: to organize seminars, concerts, and master classes in an effort to defend and develop a European conception of minimalism that he shared, precisely, with other European authors and composers. The project also sought to establish a process of conservation, promotion, and research focused on an "international" conception of the genre. Minimalism, Farhes maintained, was a phenomenon that merited being documented; both its "wide impact" and its "international character" needed to be examined (Fahres 1982b).

Fahres assembled numerous allies around his project, which was financed by a fund established by the secretary general of the Council of Europe to promote German cultural influence throughout the world. He sent letters of intent worldwide to composers potentially interested in the project and compiled their responses (see Fahres 1982a, app. 4). Some sent their encouragement, others their objections: Nyman was "excited" by the project; Johnson wished it success. Riley indicated that he was not personally concerned with the clarification of the concept of minimal music. Stockhausen insisted that Nyman had produced merely his own fantasy: a minimalism that represented nothing. Ligeti declared that he was a "maximalist" and referred to Riley for minimalism, while Luc Ferrari could not identify with any of the terms proposed.

Composers supportive of a European conception of minimalism participated closely in the project: Dieter Schnebel, Hans Emons, and Klaus Ebbeke in Germany; Sabbe and Mertens in Belgium.[18] Mertens became one of the project's key participants. His conceptions doubtless opened paths for the possibility of a European minimalism; the project gave him the opportunity to see these conceptions develop while also spreading his name, particularly through the compilation of texts that was published in 1982.

This compilation included letters of support or opposition to the project, as well as a large section of biographies, documentary sources, discographies, and bibliographies concerning composers presented as "European minimalists," such as Fahres himself for Germany; Eliane Radigue for France; Louis Andriessen for the Netherlands; Frans Geysen, Goeyvaerts, and Mertens (with his group Soft Verdict) for Belgium; Bryars and Nyman for Britain; Giorgio Battistelli for Italy; and Arvo Pärt for the Soviet Union. It also included some twenty articles on minimalism. The main point was to give substance to a Continental conception of a genre that some saw as originating in the United States. Among the authors included in the collection of articles, Sabbe is surely the one who best illustrates these ambitions.

The same year that this set of documents came out—that is, three years after the publication of Sabbe's article "Stroop uit de Kosmos" (1979)—Sabbe's enterprise became a bit clearer, namely through his article "Vom Serialismus zum Minimalismus: der Werdegang eines Manierismus. Der Fall Goeyvaerts, 'Minimalist avant la lettre,'" published in *Neuland,* a German journal of new music (Sabbe 1982a).[19] The minimalism that he presented there was detached from its production context; it was no longer a concept forged by Nyman but rather a music that preceded its creation by the British critic. For Sabbe there was even a "minimalism avant la lettre," preceding the work of the American representatives of the genre. A path from serialism to minimalism indeed existed, Sabbe asserted. Nyman's historical approach, which partly rooted minimalism in the twelve-tone technique (Nyman 1974, 212) in order to elevate it to the pinnacle of modernity, had caught the Belgian author's attention. Sabbe adopted the same method to show that Belgium and the (former) serial music of the composer Goeyvaerts took part in an international minimalist movement that became, in Sabbe's account, as obvious as it was inevitable.[20]

Serialism within minimalism, minimalism avant la lettre, and Belgians as part of the musical current: the title of Sabbe's article said it all, as he racked up the evidence while also reworking it. He rarely mentioned the other pillar of the modernity constructed by Nyman: Cageian experimentalism.

Sabbe's emphasis on the serial roots of minimalism was even more pronounced in the article he wrote for the collected work titled *Das Europäische Minimal-Musik-Projekt* (Fahres 1982b). Sabbe's article left no lingering doubt about the dissemination of Nyman's thought and the support it had won among various authors and composers in continental Europe.[21] Saabe proposed a new reworking of the argument that consisted of linking serialism and minimalism: minimal elements were already present in Webern, according to the British critic (Nyman 1974, 212–13), but now we learn that Flemish composers, especially Geysen and Goeyvaerts, gave them prominence in their own compositions throughout the 1950s, long before the American composers did.

How did Sabbe manage to reconfigure minimalism so that in 1982 it no longer began in 1958 with Young (as he asserted in 1979) but in the early 1950s with Goeyvaerts? How was he able to place serialism at the center of the discourse and transform Belgian composers into the leading lights of one of the great movements of classical movement in his time? He did it by recruiting a new ally: sociology. The historical perspective—that used by Nyman to form a chain running from Cage to Glass—would not allow him to have Goeyvaerts or Geysen participate in the minimal movement. Goeyvaerts, in Belgium in the 1950s, could neither have been influenced by Cage or the four American composers nor have had any influence on their music. Out with Nyman, Cage, Fluxus, and the British minimalist; out with history. For Sabbe, minimalism gathered different "worldwide versions of the same worldview" (Sabbe 1982b, 1).

To present his sociological—and globalizing—reading of minimalism and to demonstrate the importance of the role played by Belgian composers in the construction of the genre, the Belgian musicologist nonetheless initially enlisted the aid of historical perspective. For Sabbe, Webernian serialism offered an essential reference point for the minimalism that would spread simultaneously in Europe and the United States. Webern's music contained a latent minimalism, Sabbe explained, reworking an argument of Nyman's in *Experimental Music* (Nyman 1974, 213). In Sabbe's view, in fact, "serial composition is based on a constant return (= repetitiveness) of a single sequence of elements (= minimalism in the strictest sense)," contrary to what many, including Boulez, had said in the 1950s and 1960s (Sabbe 1982b, 1).[22]

Webern thus merely emphasized the minimal nature of serialism in his own music (2). At the same time, Sabbe wrote, on two continents, Feldman and Goeyvaerts pursued Webnerian attempts to achieve a hypostasis of sound.[23] Goeyvaerts's piece *Nr. 4 met dode tonen* (with dead tones)] (1952) thus no longer quite fit with the serialism previously brought to light by Sabbe himself (Sabbe 1977) or by David Toop in *Perspectives of New Music* (Toop 1974). Instead it arose from a "unique process of gradual transformation" (Sabbe 1982b, 3). As such it became the missing link between Young and his European ancestors. For Sabbe in 1982, Webern and his successors, Feldman and Goeyvaerts, took the spotlight back from Nyman's Cage, whose experimentalism was now consigned to oblivion (4).[24]

Sabbe did not stop with the historical method or with the enlistment of Webern, Feldman, and Goeyvaerts to defend the idea that "minimalism was just as present in Europe as in the United States." He turned to sociology to assert that the genre was, moreover, a "typical phenomenon . . . of industrial society" (4), presenting different versions of the same worldview. He explained that if minimalism is described as atemporal (with no punctuation, duration, or expectation), ubiquitous (because it presents a unified reality), automatic (since the processes are self-replicating), and impersonal (given that the process shifts attention away from the subject), then it can symbolize a "loss of faith in historical progress, for no advancement any longer seems, in a global perspective, to be made in the interests of the group" (14).

This minimalism gained recognition at the end of the 1960s, at a time when it became extremely doubtful, Sabbe maintained, that the "industrialist" order of society as conceived in the 1950s could represent the natural order of things. The exhaustion of serialism, resulting from its disappointing open form and its closure in terms of content, gave rise to the genre (15). This serialism and this minimalism thus resemble the symbolic expression of a perverted rationalism whose aim is the technological control of nature and the technocratic control of society, where humanity is subject to (and not the subject of) thought and action (15).

Once again, this sociological conception of minimalism and this relation to the state of the world were not new. The author, who mentioned the work of Stoïanova in the notes to his article, was surely aware of the efforts of French philosophers and aestheticians to connect the genre to a school of thought that was gradually emerging in a series of writings: postmodernism.[25]

Throughout the texts of *Das Europäische Minimal-Musik-Projekt*, often suffused with Nyman's thought, the idea of the existence of a European minimalism is forcefully defended; Young, Reich, Riley, and Glass appear alongside their continental "counterparts" in the history of the genre's formation. Indeed, Young confirms the serial roots of his work (Fahres 1982c, 2) and his significant influence on the music of his minimalist successors (4–5). The *Projekt* relates minimalism to the music of Messiaen and Satie, as well as to the Notre Dame School, the *ars subtilior*, and Johann Sebastian Bach. It also includes discussions of the European appropriation and transformations of minimalism (Emons 1982) and the Continental composers involved: Goeyvaerts, obviously, but also Ligeti and Andriessen. Notwithstanding the magnitude of the project, its fate was akin to that of Ashley's *Music with Roots in the Aether*: only a few copies were printed, scattered today among a handful of European libraries.

16. Going beyond Modernity

JAMESON AND LYOTARD

FREDRIC JAMESON

> The force of the Adorno-Horkheimer analysis of the culture
> industry . . . lies in its demonstration of the unexpected and
> imperceptible introduction of commodity structure into the
> very form and content of the work of art itself. . . .
>
> What is unsatisfactory about the Frankfurt School
> position is not its negative and critical apparatus, but rather
> the positive value on which the latter depends, namely the
> valorization of traditional modernist high art as the locus of
> some genuinely critical and subversive, "autonomous"
> aesthetic production. Here Adorno's later work (as well as
> Marcuse's *The Aesthetic Dimension*) mark a retreat over the
> dialectically ambivalent assessment of a Schoenberg's
> achievement in *The Philosophy of Modern Music:* what has
> been omitted from the later judgments is precisely Adorno's
> fundamental discovery of the historicity, and in particular,
> the irreversible aging process, of the greatest modernist
> forms. But if this is so, then the great work of modern high

culture—whether it be Schoenberg, Beckett, or even Brecht
himself—cannot serve as a fixed point or eternal standard
against which to measure the "degraded" status of mass
culture: indeed, fragmentary and as yet undeveloped
tendencies in recent art production—hyper- or photo-
realism in visual art, "new music" of the type of Lamonte
Young, Terry Riley, or Phil Glass, post-modernist literary
texts like those of Pynchon—suggest an increasing
interpenetration of high and mass cultures.
(Jameson 1979, 132–33)

"Reification and Utopia in Mass Culture," published in 1979 by Fredric
Jameson in the first issue of *Social Text* (Jameson 1979), was one of the
groundbreaking texts that fundamentally reconfigured the now established (or nearly established) "modernity" of the music of Young and his
associates. In 1979, when authors such as Mertens were seizing on "repetitive music" to place it at the pinnacle of the music revolution begun by
Schoenberg, Jameson made Young, Riley, and Glass witnesses to the
advent of a new era: postmodernism. Recent approaches to their music by
American authors such as Robert Palmer and John Rockwell, who followed a long American tradition of presenting the popular as a distinctive
feature of the United States in contrast with the Old World, stimulated the
interest of various Marxist philosophers and sociologists seeking to fill
"the need for a renewed theoretical investigation of revolutionary possibilities existing in the advanced countries" in a time of the "bankruptcy of
liberalism" (Aronowitz et al. 1979, 3). "*Social Text* believes that the dialectical framework of the Marxian tradition is the only one in which these
issues can be adequately raised and discussed," the editors declared in the
first issue of the journal. For these editors—among them the literary critic
Jameson—"avant-garde literature or art must be understood in its dialectical relation to mass-audience culture rather than in terms of the stale
dichotomies between 'popular' and 'high' art" (5–6).

Although Jameson took up the idea of an "increasing interpenetration
of high and mass cultures" in the music of Young and his associates (1979,
133), he did not regard this development as favorably as the champions
of postmodernism did. Jameson was in fact not so much a theorist of the

postmodern as a critic of its underlying essence. For him, especially in a 1984 article for *New Left Review,* theories of the postmodern and the discourse on "the effacement in them of the older (essentially high-modernist) frontier between high culture and so-called mass or commercial culture" (54) were above all the result of the colonization of the cultural sphere by a "new" capitalism. Postmodernism was "the cultural logic of late capitalism," that historic moment where market and culture merge. "This whole global, yet American, postmodern culture is the internal and superstructural expression of a whole new wave of American military and economic domination throughout the world: in this sense, as throughout class history, the underside of culture is blood, torture, death and horror" (Jameson 1984, 57).

Although Jameson brought up Young, Riley, and Glass to create a portrait of his new world, he did not go into depth in his reading of their music. Nonetheless, in introducing his argument, he continually came back to the idea that Glass and Riley participated in the "synthesis of classical and 'popular' styles" (54): in his article in 1979, in some of his lectures, and in his article that appeared in *New Left Review* in 1984 and would prove to be one of the major texts on postmodernism and twentieth-century culture.[1] This idea, which until then had been only hinted at by various American music critics, would now be disseminated from one edition to the next, in numerous translations.

Jameson also did not go into depth about the composers' connection to the concept of repetition. For Jameson, as for Adorno before him (another Marxist and critic of capitalism), repetition was merely a characteristic of all the cultural productions of capitalism. In 1983, when the musicologist Richard Middleton addressed the question of repetition in popular music, he was not mistaken: the Marxists' view of repetition, be it modern or postmodern, was far from sympathetic (Middleton 1983). For Adorno, Stravinsky's repetitions were childlike or primitive, the figures of a regression standing in for progress (Adorno 1949). The German philosopher attributed musical "standardization" to popular music alone, with its sole practical and ideological function linked to a specific mode of production: "Listening to popular music is manipulated not only by its promoters but, as it were, by the inherent nature of this music itself, into a system of response mechanisms wholly antagonistic to the ideal of individuality in a free, liberal society. . . . The complicated in popular music never functions as 'itself' but only as a disguise or embellishment behind which the scheme can always be perceived" (Adorno [1941] 2000, para. 14).[2]

JEAN-FRANÇOIS LYOTARD

Some years before Jameson published his first readings of postmodernity, the philosopher Jean-François Lyotard was among the first in France to trace its outlines. In 1971, he submitted his thesis *Discourse, Figure* to Paris Nanterre University (Lyotard [1971] 2011). There he laid the foundations of "the practical critique of ideology," which led him to publish *The Postmodern Condition* in 1979. In this book he posed the postulate, subsequently taken up by many other authors, that postmodernity, or "incredulity toward metanarratives"—the totalizing or globalizing narratives that aim to encompass all of human history, experience, and knowledge—is as much an effect as a cause of progress in the sciences (Lyotard [1979] 1984, xxiii–xxiv). Like Jameson's argument five years later, that of Lyotard would meet with great success.[3]

Already in 1971, Lyotard strove to reinforce his argument on the state of the world by using the music of Luciano Berio as a case study. He published "'A Few Words to Sing': *Sequenza III*" with Dominique Avron in the second issue of a contemporary music journal closely associated with poststructuralist initiatives, *Musique en jeu* (Lyotard [1971] 2012).[4] There he asserted that *Sequenza III* for voice (1965) attests to the acceleration of the movement of musical "deconstruction" relating to capitalist recuperation. In Berio's piece the logic of the text is musical and that of the music is textual, he maintained; the work presents these two logics as irremediably divided, announcing the history of the breakdown of modernity that he would soon write.

Lyotard's ideological discourse was in no way veiled in his article in *Musique en jeu*. Yet his analysis was based neither on the collapse of cultural hierarchies nor on the repetitive nature of the music. In 1972, when he wrote "Plusieurs silences" about Cage in the same journal, he no longer concerned himself with these two subjects. In the same issue, however, two colleagues from his poststructuralist circle, Avron and Guy Rosolato, took up the issue of repetition.

In their articles neither sought, any more than Lyotard did, to combine repetition or "American repetitive music" with the fall of metanarratives. But following Lyotard, they looked at repetition—a repetition that is present, both affirmed, in all music—from a Freudian or Lacanian angle, attempting to give the concept a true depth of meaning. In so doing they also attributed a new richness to the musics—whether early or traditional—in which its role was more essential than in others, particularly modern music (Avron 1972, 107). For Avron as for Rosolato, cultural hierarchies tended to be leveled as a result of the rich psychoanalytic significations of repetition—engaging defense mechanisms or the death drive, the pleasure principle or even *jouissance*.[5]

Several years later, this singular approach to repetition again appeared in *Musique en jeu*, this time in an article by Stoïanova titled "Musique répétitive," in an issue devoted to the "American repetitive" composers. Captivated by their music—like Caux, who contributed an article on Young to the same issue (Caux 1972)—Stoïanova found in psychoanalysis a means to give more weight to the work of these composers. In their music, Stoïanova also found material to develop a psychoanalysis of musical language, as well as to help elaborate her poststructuralist approach (see Tack 1998, 777–78).

For Stoïanova, as for Avron and Rosolato before her, "all music is repetitive" (1977, 64). Far from being a sign of regression or the mark of cultural productions under capitalism, repetition "structures the flow of sound by cutting it up and gives power to memory by allowing the listener to 'recapitulate' what is heard, to project, in a spatial image after the fact, the spatio-temporal relations of the articulation" (65). For Stoïanova, as for her psychoanalytic predecessors, (musical) repetition furthermore brings pleasure in that it liberates the listener from the tension of goal-oriented listening. (Musical) repetition establishes and maintains a constant internal stability at all levels of the enunciation of sound. In this way, the repetitive enunciation conforms to the homeostatic conception of a pleasure principle that is identical to the constancy principle, or nearly so. At the same time, the homeostatic movement is also a backward movement, a return to the state of absolute rest: the death drive. The ambiguity of this repetition, Stoïanova writes, explains the polarized reception of the American composers' music, ranging from fascination to rejection (69).

For Stoïanova this "essential," structuring repetition, laden with rich psychoanalytic content, was especially present in the music of Young and his associates (65). Five years after the articles by Avron and Rosolato—and doubtless in part thanks to Caux's crusading work—repetition had changed teams: Stoïanova presented it as almost solely belonging to the American composers' music. For her, however, the way the composers used it differed from its use in "works of traditional music" (69). In the traditional works, repetition was narrative and explanatory, finalizing, directional, and functional. In the American composers it was nonnarrative, nondirectional, and antifunctional. "Repetition as practiced in American repetitive music—that of T. Riley, S. Reich, Ph. Glass—can be defined, in relation to other uses of repetition in music, as a *repetition that changes to assume the decentralizing and nondirectional movement of an iterative nonteleological enunciation*," Stoïanova wrote (66). The reader was now inexplicably led down the path of antiteleology. To conclude, Stoïanova even canceled what she had demonstrated earlier, namely the ambiguity of the reception of repetitive music; she now put the different tendencies aside and took another position:

> Devotees of classical, romantic, contemporary, serious, and avant-garde music . . . , the defenders of the great communicative mission of Western music are often the adversaries of the repetitive practice, because of its "exasperating monotony," its "tautological impoverishment," or its "sleep-inducing stagnation." These verbal formulas do no more than define the resistance toward repetitive music without explaining [that resistance]. They convey a reaction against the destruction of the great musical work that has always been experienced as a violation in "a world protected by its holiness."[6] (Stoïanova 1977, 74)

17. Opening the Borders

POPULAR MUSIC

"PLAY IT AGAIN SAM"

From his early research at the University of York in the late 1960s up to
the early 1980s, Richard Middleton championed the serious study of popular music. His doctoral thesis, published in 1972, analyzed the relations
between blues and pop music (Middleton 1972). His thesis director was
Mellers, the British researcher who, in *Music in a New Found Land*
(1964), regarded popular music as one of American music's distinctions,
which he would go on to research in its own right over the following years
(see chapter 4). Middleton followed and expanded the work begun by his
former teacher. In spring 1971, in the newly launched journal *Contact*,
"devoted to the discussion of twentieth century music of all kinds" (Potter
and Villars 1971, 1), he stated his intentions: pop music was well and truly
here, and it no longer made sense to neglect it as a field of study, especially
since such study proved fascinating (Middleton 1971, 10). Ten years later,
in accord with his ambition to make popular music a valid research subject, Middleton would found the journal *Popular Music* with Charles
Hamm. Among the supporters of the project were Howard S. Becker and
Mellers, who shared the interests of the journal's founders.

Already in the early 1970s, Middleton knew that many obstacles lay along the path to a recognition of popular music in the academic establishment, including its trivial or commercial nature. The fact that one had to turn to disciplines outside music—sociology, psychology, or anthropology—to give meaning to the genre was a further obstacle. Middleton also knew that to accomplish his mission he would have to fight against the thought of a pillar of music studies, Adorno, who had ceaselessly discredited popular genres some decades before. Thus in 1974, in his review of the English translation of Adorno's *Philosophy of New Music*, Middleton did not fail to underline the author's disdain for popular music genres, as well as his "absurd" views on jazz (Middleton 1974, 223). He was also aware that Adorno's criticism of popular music was based partly on what the latter saw as one of its basic characteristics: standardization.

In his 1983 article "'Play It Again Sam': Some Notes on the Productivity of Repetition in Popular Music," Middleton flatly refuted the arguments, not only of Adorno but also of Jameson, that associated repetition with a negative characterization of mass culture. Middleton's angle of approach remains unchanged from that found in his 1971 article: an "intralinguistic," formalist reading of the popular sheds light on nothing beyond the impoverishment of its language (Middleton 1983, 262). To turn the popular into a relevant field of study, one must look to the social sciences.[1] It was essentially by this means that Middleton promoted the value of the popular in "'Play It Again Sam.'" From Adorno and Jameson, Middleton accepted the well-established "fact" that popular music is repetitive, but he quickly dispelled any negative implication. Like Stoïanova some years before, Middleton used the work of French poststructuralists to point to the rich psychoanalytical content of repetition. Unlike in Stoïanova (or Mertens), however, repetition was in no way the exclusive province of the minimalists. Middleton thus led his reader down a single path: his own, that of the popular.

Indeed, in 1983, especially in Europe—after the work of Nyman (which Middleton discusses [1975]), Mertens, and several Continental authors—minimalism had clearly become a "serious" genre. When Mellers reviewed Mertens's book in 1984—and discovered the genre that the Belgian author was defending (Mellers 1984b)—he did not object to the author's classical historico-aesthetic construction. At most he mentioned, in terms of the Freudian argument—the same one Middleton employed in his 1983 article—Mertens's omission of the similarity in the ways that minimal and popular music functioned. In that 1983 piece, Middleton pays no attention to the former genre.[2] He makes no attempt to give value to the popular by using its supposed connection to serious music. For the author, the popular possesses its own value, inherent in its multiple significations.

Middleton therefore discusses only "popular repetition." By magnifying this repetition (he observes that it far surpasses the mere structural needs of capitalism) and making it a quality of the popular alone, he elevates the music to a prime research subject, just as Stoïanova or Mertens sought to do for minimalism. To achieve this, Middleton grants a little ground to the mass culture theorists, who established part of the "common sense" on repetitive popular music by associating it with "commercial manipulation" (Middleton 1983, 235, 261). But he immediately takes back this ground thanks to semiology: popular music is indeed repetitive (even if it is often wrongly considered so), but all music is self-reflexive (unlike language, which is denotative) and thus repetitive.

Having laid this basis, Middleton now needs only to give repetition its semantic richness: repetition is an object of pleasure or nonpleasure, but in all cases it has to do with the question of desire; it is linked to Barthesian *jouissance*; it is narcissistic, because it harks back to the first experience of sound, associated with the maternal heartbeat.[3] Once more, repetition is the pleasure principle and the death drive. It "opens up for us . . . a space within which specific manifestations of repetition-practice in popular music can be located as manifestations of a complex cultural game, into which play a variety of social and psychic forces" (266).

POPULAR MUSIC

> Here's how composer/instrumentalist La Monte Young plays
> the blues[:] . . . ."Each chord change is played for a day or
> two days. In other words, a day can represent a bar so that it
> takes twelve days to play a twelve-bar blues. . . . "
> (Palmer in 1975 article reprinted in Palmer 2009, 392–93)

> Steve Reich became the second composer of "trance music"
> to play at the Bottom Line within a month on Sunday,
> following Philip Glass's two nights there on Feb. 28 and
> March 1. This is a healthy trend, in that it not only means a
> new audience for two interesting musicians, but also
> suggests that a genuine fusion of styles and sensibilities may
> be taking place. By "genuine," one means the evolution of
> musical styles that have their own integrity, yet appeal to
> widely varying audiences, and even help bring those
> audiences together. In other words, it's the audience, not the
> music, that is "fused."
> (Rockwell 1979d)

> Philip Glass is perhaps the most popular "serious" composer
> today, an early minimalist who has now reached out to opera
> and rock.
> (Rockwell 1983c, 11)

In February 1975, when the classical character of Young's work received one of its first major validations thanks to Nyman, and when Nyman had just demonstrated the rooting of Young's music in the experimental tradition, Robert Palmer asserted in *Rolling Stone*, with the composer's statements to back him up, that this music was none other than the blues extended over several days. The piece discussed by Palmer and Young was not recent, however.[4] It was *Map of 49's Dream the Two Systems of Galactic Intervals Ornamental Lightyears Tracery*, a section of *The Tortoise, His Dreams and Journeys* from the mid-1960s. In March 1979, when Sabbe's article "Stroop uit de Kosmos" (1979) pursued the developments that Nyman had set in motion, the journalist John Rockwell asserted in the *New York Times* that the aesthetic of Reich and Glass was in many ways connected to that of rock (1979d). In summer 1983, when *American Minimal Music*, by Sabbe's former student Mertens, anchored minimalism in the European musical revolution initiated by Schoenberg, Rockwell reaffirmed his conceptions in his book *All American Music*. Rockwell discussed the same music, or at least the same composers, as Mertens. However rational and methodical their theories might be, they remained irreconcilable. How could the same subjects generate analyses so diametrically opposed? By considering the connections among the various exponents that evolved around these theories—Palmer and Rockwell, but also *Rolling Stone* and the *New York Times*, among many others—we can attempt an answer.

EAST/WEST, POPULAR/SERIOUS

To understand the dissonance between Nyman's and Palmer's views in 1975, as well as between those of Sabbe and Mertens in 1979 and 1983, on the one hand, and Rockwell, on the other, we need to go back to the 1970s. At that time Palmer was a young graduate of Little Rock University in Arkansas. He was the founder of the Memphis Country Blues Festival and a member of the rock group the Insect Trust. Palmer was a budding champion of popular musics and an occasional contributor to *Crawdaddy!*, a magazine founded in 1966 that claimed to be the first "to take rock and roll seriously" (Rockwell 1976). In 1971, rather fortuitously, Palmer went to Morocco for the magazine *Rolling Stone*, where he discovered the music of the master musicians of Jajouka:

> Like any budding beatnik growing up in the twilight zone between *On the Road* and Woodstock, I always made it a point to read anything by William Burroughs. I kept noticing cryptic allusions in Burroughs's work to Jajouka, a mountain village somewhere in Morocco, home of the Master Musicians. . . .
> Being a Stones fanatic, I was intrigued when I heard that Brian Jones had visited the village with Burroughs's longtime friend and frequent collaborator Brion Gysin. . . .
> In 1969 and 1970, Ed Ward had written glowing *Rolling Stone* reviews of two albums by the band I played with, Insect Trust. We met after a show, and when he became the magazine's record editor and found himself in a jam for a jazz reviewer, he remembered me. I had a journalism background, played sax and clarinet, claimed to know something about jazz, had long hair, and was under thirty. Obviously, I could be trusted. I began writing reviews, but Jajouka was still on my mind.
> By 1971, I was living in Manhattan. . . . We [Palmer, the journalist Michael Herr, and *Rolling Stone* cofounder Jann Wenner] were strolling down Seventh Avenue South, and a shop selling Oriental rugs captured our

attention. It reminded me of my imaginary Morocco, and I started barraging Jann with secondhand Jajouka lore. When I told him about hearing the Brian Jones recordings, Jann said: "I'll tell you what. You go over there and get that story, and I'll pay you five hundred dollars for it."[5] (1992 article reprinted in Palmer 2009, 331–32)

The discovery of the music of Jajouka made a great impression on the young Palmer. In his 1971 article, and over the following years, he continually mentioned Moroccan music and celebrated the mystical experiences to which it gives rise.[6] To name it, he appropriated the concept of "trance music." Initially this trance referred only to the music of the musicians of Jajouka: "Many of the groups that are holding together are connected with one or another of Morocco's musical brotherhoods, mysterious organizations whose origins, rituals, and other secrets are as inaccessible to outsiders as the sources of power that lie just under the surface in Jajouka. All anyone seems to know about these brotherhoods is that each has its own peculiar rhythm, and that each of these rhythms produces trance" (1971 article, reprinted in Palmer 2009, 345).

Soon, however, Palmer used his concept for other purposes. In his writings, trance quickly spread beyond the Maghreb and became the cornerstone of a discourse that sought to illuminate the interconnections between East and West—above all the latter's borrowings from the former—as well as the union of popular and serious music, at least from America. Indeed, from *Rolling Stone* and *Down Beat* to the *New York Times,* through monographs and teachings at Bowdoin College and Yale University, the same project underlay a large part of Palmer's work: the creation of a world in which cultural borders had been opened.[7]

Palmer's article "Trance Music: A Trend of the 1970's," from January 1975 in the *New York Times*, best attests to the author's quest to champion the experience of trance while also establishing the East/West and popular/serious connections that he so valued (Palmer 1975a). Trance, in that article, brings together an Indian raga singer, a Central Asian shaman, Moroccan brotherhoods, African American disco bands, John Coltrane, McCoy Tyner, Tangerine Dream, and also—perhaps especially—Young, Riley, Reich, and Glass (1). The varied uses of a rhythmic and modal repetition that induces relaxation, contemplation, or euphoria is what all these musicians share, Palmer asserts. Thus, Reich and his mesmerizing rhythms approach the rhythmic complexity of Moroccan music; the modal music of Young and

Riley resembles the "sonic massage" of Indian ragas (17). Repetition, high-lighted by Palmer on both sides of the musical panorama, becomes the bond in a world where geographical and hierarchical boundaries have collapsed. It shows "that this oldest non-chemical path to satori is becoming one of the most significant musical trends of the seventies" (Palmer 1975a, 17).

The efforts of several authors over the preceding years to unite the four composers around repetition, construed as an essential element of their music, clearly served Palmer's interests in the mid-1970s, as he sketched the formal outlines of trance music in similar terms. Two other efforts captured his attention even more. The first, as the composers gained acceptance in the music establishment, consisted of emphasizing the popular nature of their aesthetic, which cut across borders. The second, in another vein, approached their work from the hypnotic angle. Thus Palmer alternately drew on the works of John Rockwell and Tom Johnson, the respective representatives of these two views (see especially Palmer 2009, 402 and 393).

THE INSTITUTIONALIZATION OF POPULAR MUSIC

Palmer's January 1975 article incontestably illustrates the attempt he set in motion to level the musical hierarchies. It also shows how the *New York Times* and the cultural establishment more generally had come to support these new conceptions. At the time popular music and the move to take it seriously continued to gain ground in the American cultural establishment. Indeed, it seemed that after ethnic music—which opened the way to folk (see especially Pegg et al. 2001)—and after jazz, pop and rock also had to be taken into account.

Over the years, many had heard and then transmitted the views of authors such as Chase (1955), Ewen (1957), and Mellers (1964). Many pursued the idea that popular genres constituted one of the most authentic manifestations of a US style and therefore deserved widespread attention. Whether American or not, rock and pop became topics of analysis and discussion. In 1967, the literary theorist Richard Poirier even asserted that it was possible to "learn from the Beatles" (Poirier 1967); his article created a sensation in intellectual circles. It was reprinted two years later in an anthology with the evocative title *The Age of Rock: Sounds of the*

American Cultural Revolution (Eisen 1969), which collected essays on the genre by critics, music historians, and musicologists, including Mellers.

In 1971, in the journal *College Music Symposium,* the musicologist Charles Hamm called for "a needed change in attitude": by ignoring popular music, he warned, the field of musicology risked becoming less attractive to students, and the academic community risked losing prestige. Musicology must be revitalized by expanding it to include these musics and considering them suitable subjects of serious research (95). In 1981 he put this project into action, cofounding the journal *Popular Music* with Middleton, in which the latter would soon attempt to counter Adorno's inescapable criticism on standardization in popular music (Middleton 1983; see also chapter 16).

Meanwhile, the rock press was quickly developing. A year and a half after the founding of *Crawdaddy!* in 1966, *Rolling Stone* was launched in the United States. The high journalistic standards of its approach to rock had rarely been seen in the underground press. These standards, however, were not the only tactic that the defenders of popular music used to legitimate its validity. *The Age of Rock,* for example, presented rock as "a full-throated school that incorporates everything from blues to Indian classical raga, from Bach to Stockhausen and Cage" (Eisen 1969, xi). Indeed, its defenders quite often justified the merit of popular music based on its connections with serious music. The value of this music—or that of certain musicians such as Frank Zappa, by far the most cited in this regard—thereby only increased. The same connections also allowed popular music to break into the music establishment, which, with the passing years, could no longer ignore its existence. In this way the *New York Times*—which would hire Palmer as its first full-time popular music critic in 1981—gradually grew interested in popular genres. Conversely, the same confluence of interests led to Young's inclusion in *Rolling Stone* in 1975.

YOUNG'S BLUES

In 1975 Young, a composer of serious music who borrowed from the blues, offered *Rolling Stone* an opportunity to reaffirm the value of popular music, or at least to reveal a rarely noted correspondence between the two worlds. Robert Palmer relates his encounter with the composer:

> Here's how composer/instrumentalist La Monte Young plays the blues. He finds a space in a museum or gallery, moves in slide projectors, electronic sine-wave generators, microphones, as many Altec Voice of the Theater speakers as possible, and two or more instrumentalists. He tunes one of the generators to 180 cycles per second, hooks it up to a bank of speakers, and turns it on. . . . Once the generator is humming away at a *pure* 180 cycles per second, . . . chords can be built up with the help of additional generators, other instruments, and amplified voices. *And*—pay attention, now—the result can be a form of blues "in which each chord change is played for a day or two days. In other words, a day can represent a bar so that it takes twelve days to play a twelve-bar blues." (1975 article reprinted in Palmer 2009, 392–93)

In this article, Palmer seeks once again to cross stylistic borders and level cultural hierarchies. He also attempts to establish a new East-West connection: "Drones, introduced via Indian music, were big during the sixties. John Coltrane's improvisations took advantage of these one-note or one-chord continuums, as did Canned Heat's boogie" (394). For Palmer, Cage has disappeared from Young's music; instead Indian music, in particular its natural harmony, along with a pronounced interest in the "psychophysics of sound," explains his work.[8]

When Palmer turned to Riley's work in *Down Beat* in November of the same year, he again offered an Eastern- and popular-oriented reading of the composer's work: Riley was a "doctor of improvised surgery" on whom Eastern music had had "a considerable impact." His career had "responded to developments in jazz in several illuminating ways." His *In C* (1964), a "blueprint for collective improvisation," had influenced numerous musicians of such varied backgrounds as Reich and Glass, Soft Machine and Brian Eno (1975, reprinted in Palmer 2009, 401). In his interview with Riley, Palmer again highlighted hypnosis inherited from the East and improvisation stemming from jazz. In his interview with Glass three years later in the *New York Times* (1978), he did the same. At the time, for Palmer, the aesthetic of the group Young-Riley-Reich-Glass still bore the label "trance music," although elsewhere he called it "minimalism."[9] He portrayed Glass as an avant-garde composer in jeans and loafers who exerted a notable influence on the world of pop and who also conversed with its musicians (13). In his liner notes for Glass's *Einstein on the Beach*, Palmer announced, once again, that "the era of the serious composer as performing musician and pop hero is already upon us" (1979; Palmer 2009, 409).

In April 1979, in the *New York Times*, Palmer repeated what he had long maintained: "Today non-Western music has colored various strata of our popular music, deeply and decisively affected the structure and substance of modern jazz, and become the single most important influence on several of our most widely admired and imitated composers" (Palmer 2009, 320). The group Young-Riley-Reich-Glass once again came to the aid of Palmer's theory. They were "the most important and influential American composers to have emerged from the era of the global village"; "becoming involved in non-Western music was the turning point in their careers" (Palmer 2009, 319). In 1981 in the *Atlantic Monthly*, in an article on Young's career, Palmer once again presented Young as the initiator of a school of music that highlighted simplicity, stasis, and repetition rather than the traditional Western values of complexity and development. Young was the composer who had influenced the work of Glass, Reich, and Riley (Palmer 1981, 48–49), and he was also the one who had seen his ideas infused into rock, particularly with the Velvet Underground, whose sound and style he shaped (54). As Eno confirmed, "La Monte Young is the daddy of us all" (quoted in Palmer 1981, 49).

"MOTORBOATING"

Palmer could not transform minimalism by his own writing alone. He needed to turn elsewhere for arguments on which to build. The appearance of a new paradigm on cultural hierarchies, which he himself reinforced, was one such resource. He also needed to find pulpits from which to preach his faith, such as an influential journal or magazine. And he needed to locate allies with whom he could share his ideas on music. John Rockwell, a former student of cultural history at the University of California at Berkeley who was a journalist at the *New York Times*, would become such an ally. Before Palmer, Rockwell had campaigned in that newspaper for recognition of the repetitive composers. Prior to that, in the course of the 1960s, the *New York Times* had shown little or no interest in them. Its chief critics turned their attention mostly to the establishment music scene of upper Manhattan. If they mentioned the music of Young, Riley, Reich, or Glass, it was with thinly veiled sarcasm, very often without connecting their respective aesthetics. To better appreciate Rockwell's contribution, let us first explore the work of the critics who preceded him.

In 1961 Eric Salzman, the first *New York Times* critic to review Young's arrival on the local avant-garde scene, mocked the "remarkable achievement" of Toshi Ichiyanagi, who succeeded in delivering "566 repeated elbow smashes" on a piano during one of his performances of *X for Henry Flynt* (Salzman 1961). In the wake of Salzman, Theodore Strongin wryly remarked on Young's work and that of his repetitive colleagues: the iterations of *Come Out* by Reich, he found, were so hypnotic that they lost "the strong indignation of protest" (Strongin 1967, 36);[10] Young's drones seemed "to be originating in one's own head or other part of the anatomy" (Strongin 1968a); Riley's music failed the test of recording and would "groove" more as a live experience (Strongin 1968b). Grace Glueck adopted a similar tone: she saw a link between "minimal art" and Reich's work, but the composer's figures were more "sound effects" than music (Glueck 1967). Harold Schonberg (who received the Pulitzer Prize for Criticism in 1970) essentially agreed: Reich's work was above all "an exercise in acoustics" (Schonberg 1973a). He also characterized Riley's approach as "anti-art" (Schonberg 1969c); Riley's work, like that of Young (with whom he had shared the stage one night at the Carnegie Recital Hall), mostly evoked "motorboating . . . a loud putt-putt sound [that] . . . Young dotes on" (Schonberg 1969b).

In the writings of the *New York Times* critics, the connections between the future minimalists were often unclear. In December 1969, Strongin noted that Reich's concept of gradual process could be applied to Riley's music, but he associated the two composers with Jacques Lasry (Strongin 1969). When critics did venture a connection between the composers, they often did so timidly, and they regularly excluded Young. Riley and Reich were their main focus of attention. Glass interested them no more than Young; his work was "artistically limited enough to be merely trivial" (R. Jones 1969).

Nonetheless, one critic took a somewhat different view of these composers' music: Donal Henahan, who would become the music editor for the *New York Times* in 1980. He too covered their music, but without the disdain of his colleagues. Moreover, although the link between the future minimalists escaped him at first, he later saw it clearly: in 1969, he called both Riley's and Reich's work "hypnotic" (Henahan 1969c).[11] In the same vein, one of Henahan's colleagues, Peter G. Davis, proposed the existence of a "neo-primitive school" encompassing the two composers as well as Glass (P. Davis 1970). Two years later, Rockwell would arrive at the *New York Times*.

BLANK ART? TRANCE MUSIC? MINIMALISM?

From 1970 to 1972, Rockwell wrote on classical music for the *Los Angeles Times*. There he voiced his enthusiasm for the aesthetic of the repetitive composers. Riley and Reich, he wrote in 1970, united around a simplicity that had been accepted in other arts by both audiences and critics.[12] Their simplicity ran counter to the notion that music should be "a sort of occult mystery," in which "techniques and rituals are jealously guarded by a musician-priest caste" (Rockwell 1970c).

In the *Los Angeles Times,* Riley and Reich were not yet either minimal or hypnotic composers. Moreover, their music did not seem to be fundamentally connected, nor was Young's music associated with them. Not until February 1972 would Rockwell affirm that Young's aesthetic had been, if not an influence on, "at least a confluence with" that of Riley, Reich, and even Glass (Rockwell 1972a, 41). Some months later, he confirmed the links between Glass and the two others: all three represented the latest and most intriguing manifestations of the avant-garde (Rockwell 1972b, 48).

Rockwell's writings in New York strengthened the link between Young, Riley, Reich, and Glass. There he was not the only one to support the idea of their connection. At the same time as Rockwell, Alan Rich, writing for the *New York Magazine,* fell into step with the defenders of this conception. Previously he had related the hypnotic character of Riley's *In C* to Indian music or to that of Stockhausen (Rich 1969), and he had attributed the incessant repetitions of Reich's music merely to "his own imagination" (Rich 1970, 54). In 1972, however, he viewed the two composers, along with Glass and Young, as sharing in an aesthetic of "slow-moving, hypnotically monotonous music" (1972b, 59; see also 1972a).

During the same period, Rockwell was lavishing praise on those same composers, who started to form, in his own writings, a small group. In the *New York Times*, he asserted that Riley's *In C* marked the beginning of the American avant-garde's fascination with hypnotic repetition (Rockwell 1973b; 1973c) and that Reich and Glass were at the center of a serious aesthetic, uniting the intelligentsia with a wide audience whose enthusiasm spread to Europe.[13] Indeed, Rockwell's articles highlighted the music's deep bond with the people. Through improvisation and rhythmic energy, it reconciled classical and popular genres (see especially Rockwell 1974e).

In the mid-1970s, Palmer's conceptions seemed particularly well suited to the aims of Rockwell, who was now the chief music critic at the *New York Times*. Both strove to narrow the divide between "serious music" and the musical traditions that had previously been ignored. Rockwell borrowed Palmer's concept of trance—a music that was "harmonically static and built by the linkage of short, repeatable melodic and rhythmic modules" (Rockwell 1975a)—to illuminate a connection between the serious music of the four composers and pop or rock, genres whose development he was chronicling in the *New York Times*.

Throughout his career, the relations between so-called art and the popular remained one of the cornerstones of Rockwell's discourse. As he continually pointed out, Reich and Glass not only managed to interest wide audiences, but also influenced rock and pop. Glass attracted the attention of pop audiences thanks to his pulsing, hypnotic music (Rockwell 1977b). His opera *Einstein on the Beach* could appeal to a rock and experimental jazz audience (Rockwell 1979c), while Reich had the ability to reach fans of progressive jazz and art rock (Rockwell 1978a; 1978c; 1979d). Reich and Glass were thus the pivotal figures in an argument in which Rockwell never concealed his dual motive of assailing stylistic hierarchies and defending rock.[14] The union of these two worlds, however, was not effectively demonstrated. In his writings, Rockwell never developed the nature of the minimalists' influence on popular music. He merely recited certain common characteristics: the music is played at high volume; it is based on drones; it is hypnotic; it evokes the East through its rhythms and its meditative calm (Rockwell 1975b). But we never find out how the fusion and borrowing operate.

Moreover, like the few other authors who defended the idea of a connection between these styles, Rockwell maintained that the influence essentially flowed from classical to popular music: the latter adopted some of the former's aesthetic underpinning. This adoption helped give both musics a place and a value. Rockwell never missed an opportunity to bring the two audiences together in his writing, nor did he hesitate to put up smokescreens. He would go so far as to have Reich appear in the pop section of the *New York Times* without justifying his presence there, or to include Glass in the list of runners-up for the ten best pop albums of 1977 with no explanation (Rockwell 1977g). Rockwell used the minimalists to promote a new cultural order in which the audience—no longer made up of only the elite (but still not including the masses)—was finally taken into account (Rockwell 1980b, 19).

The choice of a name for this music mattered little to him. Although he initially opted for Palmer's *trance music* (Rockwell 1977f; 1978b; 1979a; 1979d; 1979e), he sometimes called it *blank art*. At the end of the 1970s, the term *minimal music* seemed sufficiently widespread for him to finally abandon the two earlier names (Rockwell 1981a; 1981b; 1982). This minimalism represented, for Rockwell and many others at the time, an avant-garde movement whose well-known representatives were Riley, Reich, and Glass (Rockwell 1982). Young, the composer who "helped" the minimalists make a place for themselves in the establishment, no longer appeared with his drones in the writings of this critic, whose focus was repetition.[15]

ALL AMERICAN MUSIC

In 1983 Rockwell published a monograph titled *All American Music*. There he sought to present "new American music as it really is" (Rockwell 1983c, back flap). In the acknowledged tradition of Mellers's *Music in a New Found Land*, also published by Knopf (1965), or Hitchcock's *Music in the United States* (1969) (Rockwell 1983c, 3), which presented the mixture of classical and popular styles as a distinctive American feature, *All American Music* aimed to "demonstrat[e] not only the possibility but the necessity of dealing with artists as seemingly unrelated as Elliott Carter and David Byrne of the Talking Heads with the same passion and respect" (Rockwell 1983c, back flap). Rockwell's mission was to shatter the "cultural prejudices" that long excluded experimental, popular, and Eastern music from the subjects treated by critics (7). In line with this effort, "the Orient, the visual arts, and the evolution of minimalism" (as the chapter on Glass is titled) hold a prominent place in the book.

All American Music synthesizes Rockwell's writings that appeared in both the *Los Angeles* and *New York Times* over the course of the 1970s. The author announces from the start the "resolution" of a conflict in which he himself has taken part: that between popular and serious music (Rockwell 1983c, 3). What characterizes the music of the United States is precisely, Rockwell asserts, the dialogue between "cultivated" and "vernacular." And what connects Rockwell to "a growing group of musicians, music-lovers and academics" (12) is an interest for music that impacts "society at large" (7). Rockwell is furthermore interested in artists who are determined to remain independent, who have moved beyond the expectations of a cultivated tradition, whether in a popular or academic mode. These artists are, in that regard, typically American (8–9). The émigré Ernst Krenek, Elliott Carter, Babbitt, and Cage are thus seen as precursors with roots in populism, experimentalism, and the prewar Franco-German tradition; David Del Tredici, Rzewski, and Ashley continue the experimental tradition of Cage; Glass and Laurie Anderson fall within minimalism and performance. These last two have mingled with rock; they integrate into this panorama proposed by Rockwell that extends even to the "transcendental primitivism" of Neil Young and the "symphonic dreams" of Ornette Coleman.

Rockwell thus makes a clear distinction between minimalism, Cage, and his successors David Del Tredici, Rzewski, and Ashley. Cage's writings freed many composers—such as Philip Glass (119)—from the rules that had formerly stymied composition. Rzewski and Ashley, however, have little to do with minimalism. Rzewski's *Les Moutons de Panurge* (1969), in spite of its formal similarities with the genre, constitutes a "political" work that is not addressed to the same audience as the works of the minimalists (85). Ashley indeed "emerged from minimalism" (103) and produced works in that vein, such as *She Was a Visitor* (1967). Other pieces, however, such as *Perfect Lives* (1978–83), are, from the perspective of the static and repetitive work of Young, Reich, or Glass, "positively maximalist" (104). Thus Cage, Rzewski, and Ashley are eliminated from the minimalist environment in which the central figure is Glass. Rockwell thoroughly refashions the genre to make it correspond to his interests.

Having supported the idea of these composers' independence from tradition, Rockwell writes that Glass constructed his style more or less on his own (119). In *All American Music*, Reich's link to Young is almost entirely absent, while Riley and Reich are merely "precedents" (113–14). Glass's music has its origins in the work of his teacher Nadia Boulanger, in Indian music, and in the minimal painting and music scene of lower Manhattan in the 1960s.

But the Glass who interests Rockwell is the one who evolved toward tonality (118) as well as toward rock. The composer introduced the notion of the group in new music (121); he formed the band Polyrock and influenced musicians such as Glenn Branca and Rhys Chatham (121), Laurie Anderson (127–29), and the Talking Heads (241). Glass, Rockwell argues, reached rock audiences (120) with a seemingly simple music that is rhythmically complex (119). Glass succeeded in making serious music appeal to the general public. For Rockwell, this Glass was the perfect instrument for the construction of a new world without stylistic barriers.

18. **1984**

In the second half of the twentieth century, what did American music consist of? We have considered this question at three different points on our path to study "minimalism in the making": in 1960, right before Young's name appeared for the first time in the music literature of his day (chapter 1); in 1967, a year after Cardew asserted that Young was one of the greatest composers of his time (chapter 4); and in 1975, shortly after Nyman portrayed Young as the father of an essential movement of modern music (chapter 10). In 1960, 1967, and 1975, the answer to the same question differed, particularly with regard to Young's place, as well as that of Riley, Reich, and Glass. The essence of their music varied according to individuals and interests, as well as aesthetic and geographical considerations. Numerous conceptions, sometimes contradictory, defined each composer's music. In the early 1980s, as we have seen, Nyman's historiographical construction often supplanted all others. Article after article, book after book acknowledged the existence of minimalism and granted it official recognition. The truth of this idea was so frequently espoused that it became difficult, at the time, to see the music of the four composers as anything else.

A GROWING CONSENSUS

Three statements in particular made such an impact that they acquired an almost "factual" status in the mid-1980s. The first underlined the deep connections among the musics of Young, Reich, Riley, and Glass. The second concerned the unification of their aesthetics under the label *minimalist music*. The third pointed to the fundamentally classical, even "canonical," character of these composers' works. Whereas in 1975 the idea that their works had reached the pinnacle of contemporary music was true for only a few authors, ten years later it had essentially become a fact.

In the early 1980s, the paradigm of the connection between Young, Riley, Reich, and Glass had supplanted most of the other associations established by various authors since the early 1960s. Now there was almost no mention of what linked Young to Cardew, Riley to David Behrman, or Reich to Rzweski. Likewise, very little was said of the link presented by Nyman in 1974 and regularly reaffirmed by critics between the British minimalists and the four American composers (see especially Nyman 1980). Instead, it was the American part of Nyman's thesis that was frequently taken up to introduce the local or national developments of this music. The notion of an aesthetic uniting only these four composers was common among authors of the day such as Joan LaBarbara (1974), Roger Reynolds (1975), Dieter Schnebel (1978), and Cage himself, who in 1979 mentioned the composers' shared concept of "periodicity."[1]

This association, still fragile and imprecise in the mid-1970s, would become factual ten years later. Even though some authors did not explicitly subscribe to the idea of minimalism, many others manifestly rallied behind the designation for this group of composers. In 1976, when Dickinson reviewed Reich's *Writings about Music* in *Tempo*, even though the American composer had denied ties to any tradition at all, the British critic described his music as minimal and connected it with the work of Young, Riley, and Glass (Dickinson 1976, 43). A 1982 article by Tom Johnson attested even more clearly to the broad consensus that had formed around the concept of minimalism. In "The Original Minimalists" he wrote, "It is commonly accepted in Europe, and widely known here, that the originators of minimalism are Terry Riley, Steve Reich, and Phil Glass. I read this again in *Newsweek* only a few weeks ago. . . . Phrases like 'the original minimalists' have become so common that this is now widely accepted as a truism" (Johnson 1982, 68).

For all that Johnson insisted, in 1982, that the label could be applied to the music of Jennings, Maryanne Amacher, Ashley, and Behrman and that the music of Reich and Glass could not be reduced to this conception, his objections seemed to come too late to make a difference. One year later, Young himself acknowledged that he had initiated minimalism and that certain of his works embodied it.[2] The concept had become sufficiently solid that certain composers who had long been reticent ended up accepting it, at least in part.

Young was simply another new ally. Now some even believed that the minimalists, who had been derided or ignored several years before, had in fact produced the most important music of their time. The appearance of the four composers' names in music dictionaries and encyclopedias attests to this shift: *Harvard Concise Dictionary of Music* (Randel 1978), *The Concise Oxford Dictionary of Music* (Kennedy 1980), and the *Dictionary of Music* edited by Alan Isaacs and Elizabeth Martin (Isaacs and Martin 1983) all devoted entries to them. Although these works discussed neither the connection between the composers nor minimalism as a movement, other books placed minimalism at the center of recent history. In 1984, people may not have known whether the music of Young, Riley, Reich, and Glass developed in an experimental or a serial context, or whether it was in constant conversation with the popular; what they did know, however, was that it constituted one of the most important aesthetic developments of the second part of the twentieth century. That fact appeared not only in *The New Grove Dictionary of Music and Musicians* (Chase et al. 1980, 434–35); it also figured in the *Algemene Muziek Encyclopedie* (Robijns and Zijlstra 1983), *La nuova enciclopedia della musica Garzanti* (Marengo 1983), and the *Dizionario enciclopedico universale della musica e dei musicisti* (Basso 1984). Minimalism was well on its way into the canon of serious music.

DISPARITIES AND CONTROVERSIES

Even so, the controversies around the four composers' music and its status had not yet disappeared. In 1975, for example, Robert Erickson devoted an entire chapter to drones in *Sound Structure in Music,* without touching on Young's music or that of his three "successors." In 1977, Christopher Ballantine discussed the work of Young and Reich as experimental music but did not mention minimalism of any kind. For Elliott Schwartz in 1978 and Jon Appleton in 1979, Reich was still a composer of electronic music. For Peter Frank in 1979, Young was still one of the members of Fluxus. In 1980–81, for Conrad Cummings and David Hicks, Young had initiated a long tradition of electronic music (106). Moreover, some continued to ignore the music of Young, Riley, Reich, and Glass; for example, Ronald Davis, in *A History of Music in American Life* (1981), made no mention of them. For some authors, such as Joan La Barbara, the term *minimalism* and its representatives seemed questionable (1980, 12). In 1981, Donal Henahan was still not convinced by the repetitive aesthetic. For him Glass's music was quite simply a "going-nowhere music" (1). In the 1984 *New Oxford Companion to Music* (Arnold 1984), one still found no minimalism in the United States, and hardly any minimalists. For some, "pluralism" was what defined American contemporary music, as dominated by the figures of Elliott Carter, George Crumb, and Steve Reich (Crawford 1984, 1889).

As if the persistent controversies and resistance were not enough to undermine the hard-won certainties regarding minimal music, the essence of that music remained a bone of contention. In 1980 Mertens's *Amerikaanse repetitieve muziek,* the first monograph devoted to minimalism, showed how solidly Nyman's paradigm had become established. Although largely inspired by the British critic's thinking, however, Mertens's book—as well as some of his later developments—reversed Nyman's perspective, which had consistently opposed experimentalism to serialism. For Mertens, minimalism was born of the musical revolution initiated by Schoenberg and Webern. In 1983, the year that Mertens's book came out in English translation, Rockwell published *All American Music.* Minimalism was further shaken up: whereas Nyman and Mertens concurred at least on the classical roots of the repetitive composers' music, Rockwell highlighted its popular connections. Just as Mertens had his own followers—mostly from continental Europe—Rockwell found many champions of his approach in the United States. Thus, similar proposals appeared in Palmer's writing as well as in the writings of Jameson (1979),

Kristin McKenna (1979), Robert Coe (1981), Joel Rothstein (1981), Marc Kirkeby (1982), and David Garland (1983).

In 1984, some months after the publication of both Mertens's book (in English) and Rockwell's, the cards were reshuffled. Some, clinging to the certainties passed down from Nyman and proven over the second half of the 1970s, considered minimalism to be fundamentally Cageian. Others, especially European authors, believed that the movement was rooted in serialism. Still others saw a real connection between minimalism and popular music. In 1984, however, no one could tell which of these conceptions would ultimately prevail.

19. Confirming an Established Fact

PERSPECTIVES OF NEW MUSIC

In the mid-1980s, the idea that the music of Young, Riley, Reich, and Glass was minimal greatly solidified. The less robust notion that placed their work at the pinnacle of art music had just received a shock. After the critical work of Rockwell and his disciples, it had now become conceivable that this music could above all be linked to popular repertories, which were winning recognition for the first time within the music establishment. Once more, uncertainty clouded the origins and true nature of the four composers' music.

By about ten years later, however, it seemed that these questions had been resolved: articles on minimalism appeared in 1992 and again in 1993 in *Perspectives of New Music*, one of the most scholarly musicological journals, which up to then had never paid any attention to the four composers' music. The serious character of the genre was confirmed. The supposed popular roots of minimalism had perhaps been a fiction. What is more, minimalism was now taking on a new form. It lent itself to musical analysis (in spite of Reich's claims) and was also teleological (in spite of Mertens's). The term designated an aesthetic in which music and the visual arts were fundamentally linked. What recent event might explain this new change in minimalism? Once again, the focus was on the composers' works from the 1960s and 1970s.

By following a series of participants over the course of the various alliances they formed and the subtle modifications they made to preestablished concepts, we can best understand this transfiguration and the paradoxes it generated. It seems once more that the explanation for the metamorphosis of minimalism lies not so much in the music itself as in the discourse around it. To illustrate this point, we look first at how *Perspectives of New Music* and the defenders of musical analysis gradually rallied around an ever-more solid minimalism. Then we consider how the journal itself refashioned minimalism, and finally how the relation uniting the musical genre with its visual arts counterpart returned in the literature on the subject.

MINIMALISM'S INCURSION INTO *PERSPECTIVES OF NEW MUSIC*

In 1992 and 1993, new forums devoted to feminism, critical theory, the minimalists, and Cage appeared in the journal *Perspectives of New Music* (30, no. 2; 31, nos. 1 and 2). Founded thirty years before, the journal had up to that point been known for its interest in formal analysis and its unconditional support of the Princeton serialists, with Babbitt at the forefront.[1] Why did it change its focus in the early 1990s, and why did the music of Young, Riley, Reich, and Glass, whom it had simply ignored until then, belatedly appear in its pages?[2]

The Princeton School

The first issue of *Perspectives of New Music* came out in autumn 1962. Financed by the Fromm Music Foundation (the philanthropist Paul Fromm was a well-known patron of the twelve-tone composer Ben Weber), the journal was published by Princeton University Press at the instigation of the composer and theorist Arthur Berger (whose style was known for combining neoclassical diatonicism with the twelve-tone technique; see Perkins 1966) and his former student Benjamin Boretz. According to the editors, the journal was created to raise awareness among composers and members of the musical community about "the development of ideas that determine the nature of musical phenomena today as well as their future course" (Berger and Boretz 1962, 4). The journal aimed to make up for the lack of representation for young American composers (5), but to some its main distinction was a certain cronyism. That, at least, was the criticism made by the musicologist Joseph Kerman in the journal in 1963, in response to an article by the pianist Charles Rosen the year before, in the journal's first issue.

In 1962, Rosen launched a virulent diatribe against "the present state of music" and all its participants—"composers, performers, musicologists, and public alike" (Rosen 1962, 80). Performers were refusing to play contemporary works; composers had turned toward extreme complexity and then to electronic music, which banished both performers and the public; musicologists were continuing to teach music history without asking themselves about the relevance the discipline might have today; critics and the public were finding no consensus: such is the panorama that Rosen presented on the music of his day. It was a matter, he wrote, of finding a common ground. This he proposed to do by following only the composer's point of view. It was up to the composer to help us decide what to study and what to leave aside, Rosen asserted; musicology and interpretation must be subordinate to composition (80–82). As a result, an analytical—and not historical—approach to the work should be favored (86).

Kerman, a graduate of Princeton on the faculty at Berkeley, did not fail to grasp the "ideological" tenor of Rosen's essay (Kerman 1963, 153); Rosen, too, was a Princeton graduate as well as Elliott Carter's pianist of choice. Kerman indeed knew to whom Rosen addressed his exhortation and from which pulpit he was preaching: "the composers" whose direction Rosen thought others should follow, he argued, were none other than those of the "Princeton School," who largely constituted the journal's editorial committee (152). *Perspectives of New Music* is not published for Roy Harris, Gian-Carlo Menotti, Alan Hovhaness, Hunter Johnson, Peggy Glanville-Hicks, Meyer Kupferman, or La Monte Young," Kerman continued. By advising the reader to follow the composer's voice, Rosen was doing nothing more than attributing "standards of musical significance" to this school—and to the composers in whose name he was speaking (155). In the past, Kerman had already assailed the American music intelligentsia and the patriotic nepotism that it could display, aided in particular by record companies such as Columbia (see especially Kerman 1958 and 1961). In 1963, he launched a similar attack on *Perspectives of New Music*: that journal, while claiming assuredly to present "the development of ideas that determine the nature of musical phenomena today," above all demonstrated, in Kerman's critique, the cronyism that corrupted the music establishment.

At the same time, the composer and musicologist Barney Childs likewise deplored some of the directions taken by the journal and by the defenders of pure musical analysis. Owing to an overly traditional or universal approach to music, he asserted, certain works ended up simply being excluded from musical literature (Childs 1966, 436). For Childs, such works did not lend themselves to the rhythmic and metrical analysis grids generally used. A pause, for example, could constitute—in indeterminate music and even more so in Cage's *4'33"*—a continuum of its own, even the structure of the work itself. The same was true of the pulse: a single pulse could be considered the actual work, as in the case of *Two Sounds* and *Composition 1960 #7* by Young (437).[3] To understand these pieces, then, the analyst should not be looking for rhythmic or metrical cells but rather consider the work in terms of its unique overall temporal structure. Published in *Texas Studies in Literature and Language*, Childs's critique, and his attempt to counter the rhythmic conceptions that left the work of Cage or Young in the dark, received no response. Nor was there any follow-up in *Perspectives of New Music*.

Over the following years, *Perspectives of New Music* proved Kerman right with regard to Young and his minimalist successors, consistently ignored by the journal. In 1971, Benjamin Boretz and Edward T. Cone edited *Perspectives on American Composers*, a selection of texts drawn from *Perspectives of New Music*, including essays by Edgard Varèse, Milton Babbitt, and Roger Sessions. None of the composers whom Kerman cited was represented. *Perspectives of New Music* continued to symbolize this "highly specialized theory journal for contemporary music," as Fromm himself—who dropped his financial support for the journal in 1972— regretted (quoted in Berry 2006, 21n49).[4] Boretz and Berger would later recognize the "clannish" nature of the journal, essentially dedicated to the study of Princetonian serial music by means of the pure musical analysis that it helped promote in the postwar United States (see Berger, Boretz, and Tichenor 1987, 597–98).[5]

Who Cares If You Listen

Over the decades, however, the landscape in which the journal evolved had transformed. In the years following the publication of his book *Contemplating Music* (1985), Kerman became for many the initiator of a new musicology, or postmodern musicology, that opened the doors to critical and interdisciplinary approaches (particularly psychological and sociological), to feminism, and to gender studies, thus turning its back on the idea of the autonomy or organicity of the work and on traditional positivistic musicology.[6] Now the criticisms that Kerman once again leveled at *Perspectives of New Music* no longer passed unnoticed (1985, 101–5). He denounced the journal's sole concern with pure analysis as a sectarian attitude on the part of the Princetonians' leader; essays such as "Who Cares If You Listen?" by Babbitt became for some, such as Susan McClary (1989), the symbol of an outmoded elitism from which it was time to move on. Boretz, who edited the journal until 1983, addressed this polemic years later: in his article on the history of *Perspectives of New Music* (2012), he introduced his remarks by answering the numerous criticisms received over the years. The 1992 and 1993 volumes of *Perspectives of New Music*—with their forums on feminist and critical theory of music—attest to a rally around a new conception of the cultural landscape, or at least around a position that could only align with postmodern thought, which had become inescapable.

Those two volumes also show the editors covering repertories and figures formerly ignored by "modernity": Cage and minimalism, to which two forums are dedicated. The serious music canon of the second half of the twentieth century had indeed evolved over the years; it was no longer possible to turn a blind eye to the music of Young, Riley, Reich, and Glass. In the journal's pages in 1990, Boulez, who had long ignored the existence of minimalism and later heaped criticism on it, continued to call it "primitivistic" and consider its "attempt at radical simplification . . . inadequate."[7] He nonetheless conceded that this attempt was "not uninteresting" and, moreover, that it represented one of the two great musical currents of his day, the other being neoromanticism (Boulez, Menger, and Bernard 1990, 12).[8] Finally, during this period the editorial board had changed. Now it included Jonathan Kramer, whose chief legacy would be his postmodern musical and theoretical work; the experimentalist Larry Polansky; and even Pauline Oliveros, who was regularly associated with the American aesthetic of static music. All were probably far more inclined than their predecessors to validate the existence of a minimal current.

The recent transformation of *Perspectives of New Music* and its consideration of minimalism thus substantiated the newly gained ground for both postmodernism and minimalism as legitimate categories to define the contemporary cultural landscape in the early 1990s. In order to enter the journal, however, this minimalism would also be refashioned, as the article by Richard Cohn that opened the forum on minimalists attests.[9]

PERSPECTIVES OF NEW MUSIC'S INCURSION INTO MINIMALISM

Under the form(s) it had previously been given, minimalism could not make its entrance into *Perspectives of New Music* merely on the strength of its gradual establishment or its association with a postmodernism then in full flower. For it to appear, it had to be adapted to the journal, in the same way that the journal had adapted itself to minimalism; it had to become reducible to formal analysis. In the first article in *Perspectives of New Music*'s forum on minimalism, "Transpositional Combination of Beat-Class Sets in Steve Reich's Phase-Shifting Music" by Richard Cohn (1992), the author's main goal was to establish minimalism's openness to analysis. To understand this work, we first need to understand why minimalism had resisted musical analysis until then.

Minimalism before Analysis

Prior to Cohn's article, minimalism had rarely been the subject of musical analyses as such. Apart from the attempts of Brian Dennis (1974), Paul Epstein (1986), and Robert Morris (1988), the genre long suffered from disinterest on the part of the defenders of the analytical approach. Minimalism was thus ignored by *Perspectives of New Music* not only because it had been created outside of Princeton or on the margins of serialism, but also because it was seen by some as irreducible to the discipline of analysis. Three characteristics attributed to this music explain that particular quality: its simplicity, its ateleological nature, and its non-European origins.

The first is partly due to Reich's own statements; in the 1960s–70s, he was among the first to discuss the absence of structural cues in his music. According to Reich, this music contained no hidden structure, no mystery. There was nothing more to discover than could be heard; indeed, this was what distinguished his own music from that of Cage or the serialists.[10] Even though Reich's discourse would evolve, authors such as Dan Warburton (1988, 135–36), following his lead, echoed and disseminated this postulate: minimal music truly was of an astounding simplicity. The second characteristic owes to authors such as Stoïanova (1977), Mertens (1983), and Kramer (1988). In their writing, they conveyed the idea that the music of the minimalists was ateleological, "vertical," with no beginning or end, devoid of progression or event; it was "going-nowhere music," as Donal Henahan claimed in 1981. Finally, the third characteristic also arose in the wake of writings by Reich and his minimalist colleagues: minimalism was hardly rooted in the European classical music tradition, apart from early or baroque music. That was partly Tim Page's theory (p. 1981), as well as that of Robert K. Schwarz in *Perspectives of New Music* some years earlier (Schwarz 1980–81 and 1981–82).

How, indeed, was one to analyze this transparent music, which failed to unfold in time and employed none of the techniques for which the Western serious music tradition had developed its tools? It then seemed an almost impossible task. So the formalists banished minimalism, Cohn asserted in his article. But he would reverse that trend.

Minimalism and Analysis

By adopting a "formal language," Cohn (1992, 148) sought to demonstrate that Reich's minimal music held mysteries that the analyst must reveal, that it unfolded over time, and that it was under the sway not so much of non-Western music as of the Second Viennese School, regardless of what the composer said. Drawing on a "technology" (149) long employed in *Perspectives of New Music*, by inviting numerous allies from among the journal's collaborators and reshaping Reich's musical language, the musicologist set out to "prove" what Reich's music really was. Rather than retrace in detail the long and complex path that Cohn forged to lead readers to his indisputable truth, we will highlight here the main lines and principal developments of his argument that are relevant to our focus.

The first elements on which Cohn relies to give weight to his theories are methodological. He calls up a group of procedures developed in the "twelve-pitch-class universe" (149) by theorists as renowned as Babbitt, Boretz, John Rahn, and David Lewin (174). The argument follows the methodological tradition of musical set theory, with its collections of pitches that are related via the concepts of inclusion, complementation, and transformation. This dense theory was widely known and validated in numerous works.[11] Before beginning his demonstration, Cohn allies it with an array of tools that have proven their worth; thus anyone who might oppose him must first oppose them, even before broaching his own theory.

This technology and these technologists, however, are but one reinforcement among others to establish Cohn's theory, which illustrates minimalism's adaptability to analysis. To that end, the author produces a series of transformations of Reich's musical language. Through successive reductions of Reich's musical writing, he directs readers down a single path, closing off all possible secondary routes.

Cohn considers only two works, *Violin Phase* (1967) and *Phase Patterns* (1970), and he focuses solely on their scores. He identifies rhythm as the main material of the composition, cuts up metric cycles, and segments regions and sequences. He transposes the principle of pitch class and pitch-class sets to the rhythm; then he transposes, "*mutatis mutandis*," cycles and cells into "beat-class sets" (149), those numerical combinations borrowed from set theory. Cohn defines vectors, cardinalities, and attack points. He runs his combinations through common "theorems" (154). In other words, he proceeds from one reduction to the next in order to show the music as it really is, as in the numerous figures he presents over the course of his demonstration. The reader need only observe his diagrams, constructed with a vast apparatus, to find Reich's music reduced to its essence.

Regions	Low C#	High E/ double-stop	Low + high
0,0	2–5	4–23	6–32
0,11	4–8	8–6	11–1
0,10	4–23	6–32	8–23
0,9	4–26	7–35	9–9
0,8	4–20	8–23	10–5
	4–20		
0,8,7	5–20	9–9	11–1
0,8,6	6–18	10–5	12–1
0,8,5	5–27	8–23	10–5
0,8,4	6–20	12–1	12–1

Figure 3. Beat-class sets in Reich's *Violin Phase* (Cohn 1992, 166).

His dissections of the music progressively establish symmetries; iso-morphisms and similarities appear within the pieces—among pitches, attacks, and rhythms—as well as between the pieces themselves, with numbers as "proof" (fig. 3). What do these similarities within Reich's pro-cesses mean? Cohn's reworking of the music via successive reductions pro-poses an answer to precisely this question: they reveal the processes of integration carried out by the composer and weaken the possibility that the works' properties could be fortuitous (164). Cohn's analysis further displays the arrangement of frequencies into long-range patterns to show that the work has a goal, a teleology. In every case, the author writes, the simple use of a "process" attests to a development in time (169). Moreover, the use of canons or "combinatorial tetrachords" confirms the impossibil-ity of Reich's complete departure from the Second Viennese School, in particular from Webern's music (171). Finally, the influence of African music, according to this analysis, was no more or less present before than after the composer's trip to Ghana (167).

Cohn thus untangles many of the mysteries inaccessible to the ear or via a basic description of Reich's musical language. He proves that mini-mal music is no less reducible to musical analysis than any other genre. In so doing, he reaffirms the importance of analysis and of the serialists, their methods, and the Second Viennese School, from which Reich cannot escape. The composer, Cohn asserts, did not abolish the old modes of hearing; he simply displaced them (171). Nonetheless, Reich's music, which has served to raise pure analysis to the pinnacle of musicology, also benefits from this exercise: it has taken on a "complexity" (168), or at least a depth, that it lacked before.

In spite of all Cohn's efforts to demonstrate the substance of Reich's music, in spite of an argument based on the most technical form of musical science, the musicologist never proved what Reich's music actually was. Instead he carried out a series of manipulations (transpositions or translations, slicing and dicing every which way) on what would perhaps become "Reich's music," insofar as others followed suit. The author suggested as much himself: he had merely outlined one possible path among others (157, 163).

Minimalism after Analysis

The analytical depth that Cohn attributed to minimalism appeared to have proved its mettle—at least sufficiently for Kyle Gann to announce in the journal's second minimalist forum, with no justification whatsoever, that "Young's *The Well-Tuned Piano* may be the most important American piano work since Charles Ives's *Concord* Sonata" (1993, 134). In his article Gann granted this piece the same analytical depth as Ives's. Although, as he himself pointed out, the work was largely improvised and varied from one performance to the next, he assigned it a key, themes, sequences, cadences, patterns, events, sections, and even harmonic progressions. Gann's ally was no doubt influential enough to enable him to propose this reading: Young himself provided materials and offered suggestions.

Unlike Cohn, Gann did not redefine minimalism in depth; his goal was to offer "a prolegomena [*sic*]" for further studies (160). No doubt his chief aim was to demonstrate, once more, the importance of analysis and to associate minimalism with this methodological tradition. By then, that aim was almost needless; Cohn had already accomplished that task. Indeed, in 1994 Cohn would win the Outstanding Publication Award from the Society for Music Theory for his article on Reich's music.

THE RELATION TO VISUAL ARTS

> It *is* true that certain earlier works of minimal painting and
> sculpture have already taken on a kind of "historical"
> stature—that they are now regarded as integral to the recent
> history of art even by those who originally questioned the
> validity of minimalism. No parallel canonization of even a
> provisional sort seems to have taken place in music, for even
> the earliest minimal pieces are still regarded as controversial
> in many quarters.
> (Bernard 1993, 125)

Among the transfigurations of minimalism that took place in the 1992
and 1993 issues of *Perspectives of New Music*, that conveyed by Jonathan
Bernard's article was highly significant. In "The Minimalist Aesthetic in
the Plastic Arts and in Music" (1993), minimal music is nothing less than
an "aesthetic," as the title indicates, as essential to the visual arts as to
music. How did minimalism ascend to the rank of an interdisciplinary
aesthetic? Once again, observing the networks of alliances and the various
processes within the establishment—its interdisciplinary approaches, first
of all, and then its concept of minimal art—makes it possible to understand this development.

Interdisciplinarity

In 1993, Bernard's idea of connecting minimal music to the visual and
performing arts was not new. In the mid-1960s, numerous theorists
sought to associate Young's work with performance art or with the Theatre of Mixed Means, as attested in particular by Kostelanetz's work.
Others, like John Perreault, even tried to connect the four composers'
work to the developments in minimal art. Although the idea of abolishing
borders had its followers, it was soon forgotten. Over the 1970s and 1980s,
the establishment of a "pure" musical minimalism had rallied so much
support that it became difficult to propose the relation to the visual arts,
as either an alternative or an adjunct reading.

This shift can be seen in the later writings of some authors who went
from an interdisciplinary conception of the four composers' work to a

strictly musical one. In 1979, after having read Nyman, Sabbe abandoned the pictorial analogy and began to consider repetitive music in a narrow sense. Likewise, certain theories linking music with other arts were abandoned over the years. After 1968, Kostelanetz continued to chronicle the activity of the New York avant-garde, but he gradually gave up his concept of the Theatre of Mixed Means. The visual or theatrical relation faded in favor of a nonrelation. Hitchcock tried to reactivate the connection during the 1980s in a paper he presented at the College Art Association conference, but he did not publish it afterward.[12] The relation between visual arts and music remained suppressed for years. Meanwhile, however, interdisciplinarity developed in other areas. Following Kerman, a musicology that would be known as postmodern turned to other related disciplines to enrich its investigations. Partly for that reason, the visual arts connection could be revived in the early 1990s. It had finally become possible—some decades after the work of figures such as Kostelanetz, and probably in part thanks to them—to approach music without ridding it of all its nonmusical components.

Minimal Art

The advent of interdisciplinarity alone does not explain the belated renewal of interest in an approach uniting minimal art and minimal music. In the early 1990s, minimal art too became established apart from any relation to music. A struggle for its recognition took place over the last third of the twentieth century, waged by authors such as Richard Wollheim (1965), Barbara Rose (1965), and Gregory Battcock (1968) in the 1960s; Rosalind Krauss (1977) and Robert Pincus-Witten (1977) in the 1970s; and Barbara Haskell (1984) and Kenneth Baker (1988) in the 1980s. It also mobilized artists such as Ad Reinhardt, Donald Judd, and Robert Morris and galleries, exhibition halls, institutions, and even universities such as Harvard, which invited Frank Stella to discuss his work in 1984 and then published his lectures (Stella 1986). Finally, Edward Strickland (1993, 17–118) and Jonathan Bernard (1993) would confirm this establishment of minimal art. For the latter, "Earlier works of minimal painting and sculpture have already taken on a kind of 'historical' stature" (125). Moreover, the connection with minimal music, "revealed" by some authors years before and subsequently consigned to oblivion, would finally reappear thanks to Bernard's new work.

20. Furthering the Fight

NEW SOUNDS

After the minimalist forums appeared in *Perspectives of New Music*, it became difficult to question the essentially serious nature of the music of Young, Riley, Reich, and Glass or to deny their works' importance in the musical landscape. The Easternized or popularized conceptions of the genre proposed some years earlier by authors such as Rockwell and Palmer might have been mere fictions after all. That, in any case, was how Elaine Barkin, one of the coeditors of the analytical journal, viewed Rockwell's *All American Music*:

> "A tale of traditional, cultivated music opening itself up to the diversity of the true American experience [of] new American music as it really is . . . ," a loaded tale unwinding along a trail of Mr. R's own invention, whose starting point is cultivated Old World; a tale-trail which, by inbreeding, outbreeding, fusing, synthesizing, [and] hybridizing . . . re/un-covers its New World American Way, overruns those cultivated ancestors and their heirs "who enriched our music but also suppressed the nascent evolution of a truly American culture," and reappraises compositional attitudes "that impeded the evolution of a truly American music," a musiculture whose real time has—apparently—come, is now. (Barkin 1983-84, 533)

From reading *Perspectives of New Music*, one would think that the critic's book was no more than a fable—a dangerous one, at that—dedicated to "consumerism, consumers, their goods and fashions" (542).[1] Rockwell omitted the fact that musical categories—serious and popular—not only were necessary but also would survive, Barkin affirmed (537). Rockwell bisected culture by placing simplicity on a pedestal to the detriment of complexity, supposing that this complexity was a quality defined outside of any context (540); he "tracked" intra-American crossover currents and extra-American connections. His book ultimately had little to do with "the best minds" of his time (544).

However fictional Rockwell's stories may have been for Barkin and for *Perspectives of New Music* in 1983, they nonetheless seem to have acquired factual status some years later. In 1993, the year in which the second minimalist forum appeared in the journal, the musicologist Edward Strickland published *Minimalism: Origins* (1993). This book not only attests to the existence of minimalism—now certified by *Perspectives of New Music*—but also tends to confirm the validity of Rockwell's angle of approach. For Strickland, the minimalists were indeed popular serious composers: they had gathered a wide audience around their music, as Rockwell maintained—but that was not all. Whereas the *New York Times* critic had above all defended the idea that "it's the audience, not the music, that is 'fused'" (Rockwell 1979d, 6), Strickland argued that jazz, blues, and rock could be found within the four composers' music itself. A new paradox appears: the popular is no longer situated downstream from minimalism but directly inside it.

To understand the coexistence of a serious minimalism and a popular minimalism, as well as the new paradox that emerged, we need to look once more to those earlier years.

ALL AMERICAN MUSIC AFTER *ALL AMERICAN MUSIC*

In summer 1983, Hitchcock was among the first to defend Rockwell's book. He presented *All American Music* as a "bold, coherent, and comprehensive" work that clarified the contemporary American musical landscape, a book that deserved a place among the "classics" of literature on American music (Hitchcock 1983, 336). Similarly, Mellers, whom Rockwell cited as his other major influence (Rockwell 1983c, 3), wrote in the *Musical Times* that the book was "a probing account of the tangled inter-relationships of American tradition and experiment" (Mellers 1984b, 207). Rockwell, the historian of culture who wove the connection between East and West, even attracted the attention of the journal *Ethnomusicology*, where a reviewer described *All American Music* as "the best book yet on recent cultivated music in the United States" (Radano 1984, 149).

If the reviews of the hybrid landscape outlined by Rockwell were particularly enthusiastic, it is partly because the author was able to capture the interest of various authors who shared his views on the contemporary scene.[2] It is also because, as we have seen, the popular was gradually making a prime place for itself within the music establishment. Thus, the book *Music in the New World* by Charles Hamm (1983), another leading scholar, was also regularly discussed during 1983 and 1984. Hamm paid little attention to minimalism, merely reproducing the usual formal descriptions borrowed from Nyman (1974) and Salzman (1974a), among others (e.g., Hamm 1983, 669). For him, those composers were part of an avant-garde with no apparent connection to the popular repertories that were his main focus. Having exhorted universities to turn their attention toward popular musicians (Hamm 1971), the former president of the American Musicological Society now rallied definitively to that cause in a book that was widely acclaimed by critics. Like Rockwell before him, Hamm joined the growing ranks of partisans of a popular view of twentieth-century music. Hitchcock affirmed their commonalities: "The two view similarly the essence of American music" (1983, 334). Over the course of their cultural histories, both rejected an exclusive and elitist concern for serious arts alone.

Much like Hamm in his own field, Rockwell would continue to pursue this work after his monograph was published. Over the 1980s and 1990s, until he was named director of the Lincoln Center Festival in 1994, Rockwell worked to (re)construct the contemporary musical landscape in the *New York Times* and in the process contributed to expanding minimalism's reach, particularly in popular circles (see especially Rockwell 1986). He helped establish Louis Andriessen, Paul Lansky, Lee Hyla (Rockwell 1984), and John Adams (Rockwell 1985a) as the next generation of minimalists. In the course of the 1980s, Rockwell espoused the concept forged by Nyman once and for all, even though, according to Rockwell, it reflected the reality of the music he described very little. For Rockwell, the minimalists—Riley (after *In C*), Reich, and Glass, with their music of strong rhythmic energy and "shifting patterns" (Rockwell 1986)—had in fact been labeled minimalist "by accident" (1985a; 1985b). The "true" minimalists were instead Cage, Feldman, Lucier, and Young (Rockwell 1985a; 1986). Nonetheless, the repetitive trio was so firmly associated with the label *minimalist* that Rockwell, in turn, could only use it himself.

POP EXPERIMENTALISM

Like Rockwell, the defenders of a popular conception of minimalism were regularly confronted with the question of categorization. If the boundaries between popular and serious music were collapsing, it would make sense to eliminate the categories reproducing the former separation of these spheres. Scholars and critics often pointed to a much too serious minimalism as a genre evoking these categories to be demolished. But the concept had now become so solid that it was almost impossible to obliterate it, as attested in two books from the mid-1980s that sought to shed light on the stylistic connections dear to many authors of the day: *Recombinant Do Re Mi*, by Billy Bergman and Richard Horn (1985),[3] and *New Sounds*, by John Schaefer (1987). Both books indirectly demonstrate the realization of the serious paradigm of minimalism, which, though barely formed, was nonetheless subject to new attacks and transformations.

In *Recombinant Do Re Mi*, we read that categories such as minimalism "tend to dissolve once the music's many facets are taken into account." By Glass's own admission, "there are no hierarchies anymore" (Bergman and Horn 1985, xii). The response to serialism—since it was in opposition to serialism that the minimalists elaborated their language—was not found within serialism itself, but rather outside of it: "And it's the driving, danceable rhythm of rock—the modern day passacaglia and sarabande—that young composers such as Glass and Reich found missing in serial music" (xv–vxii). Reich—who up to then, like Glass, had said little about rock—joined the conversation as well: "I benefited from the rock world. . . . I'm not going to pin down what I got, but I got a lot, and I'm glad if I can give something back" (xii).

Bergman and Horn's proposal went even further than Rockwell's: Over the preceding years, serious experimental music and rock had clearly interacted, producing a crossover between the two spheres. Now "experimental pop" prevailed, encompassing the world of rock as much as that of art music (xi). The foundation for the crossover that the two authors invoked in their book had its origins in a succession of earlier writings. Now they needed only to perform a simple equation: in the 1960s and 1970s, minimalists and rock musicians alike turned their attention to (and drew their inspiration from) the East, and this non-Western orientation was what brought them together.

Rockwell's thought particularly resonated with defenders of popular music and of composers who had no use for cultural hierarchies, such as Bergman and Horn. It also attracted the attention of a producer of eclectic radio shows at WNYC-FM, John Schaefer. Published in 1987 by Harper & Row, Schaefer's book *New Sounds* reinforced the theories of the *New York Times* critic. For Schaefer as for Rockwell, music categories had become useless. The concept of minimalism was simply "an accident of musical history" (Schaefer 1987, xii). A certain modern music, the author asserts, evolves in a gray area between classical and rock, ethnic and jazz, Eastern and Western, electronic and acoustic. It is merely "for convenience's sake" that these labels are retained to define the music of Young, Reich, Riley, and Glass (64). For Schaefer, the borders of the concept of minimalism are indeed difficult to stabilize. Satie's *Vexations*, Ravel's *Boléro*, or even— perhaps especially, as for Rockwell—Cage's *4'33"* can all be considered minimalist (65, 66). By his own admission, however, Schaefer cannot manage to cast off the designation *minimalist*. And although he makes numerous allusions in his book to the minimalists' popularity and their influence on popular music (see especially 70, 81, and 241–64), we learn nothing of how Reich and Glass came to rock beyond their having founded groups and gone on tours. In 1987, although Schaefer revised minimalism somewhat, he mostly reinforced its serious foundation.

TOWARD A POPULAR MINIMALISM

In the late 1980s, Salzman also rallied to the conceptions defended by Rockwell and his colleagues. In 1988, he published the third edition of

Twentieth-Century Music. There minimalism has evolved: lacking any connection to the popular in 1974, it is now linked with it. Rockwell has clearly made his mark; in fact, the author cites him. But whereas some of the authors who drew on *All American Music* saw a palpable influence of rock on minimalism, Salzman presents the relation differently, particularly in the case of Glass: "in fact the opposite is true; [Glass] had a major influence on pop music in the late rock era" (1988, 220). He inspired Eno and the Talking Heads. Once again, the form and the nature of these borrowings are not described. Not until 1993—with the continued rise of the defenders of the popular—would that demonstration be made, and indeed sanctioned by a scholarly publisher. That year Strickland published *Minimalism: Origins* with Indiana University Press. Once more, the demonstration built on previous readings. It did not reveal what was already within minimal music that had eluded many authors; instead, it constituted the end result of a vast yet subtle remodeling of the facts that preceded it.

Fanfare *and* American Composers

This remodeling had largely been undertaken by Strickland himself since the early 1980s, when he joined the magazine *Fanfare,* which reviewed new classical and jazz records. At the time, the minimalist paradigm did not yet reign supreme over the American cultural sphere. Indeed, in 1980, Strickland applied the term "modularists" to Riley, Reich, and Glass (1980), whose association was already almost a fact. In just four years, shortly after the publication of Mertens's and Rockwell's books, Strickland definitively dropped the term: "I've conceded defeat to *vox populi vox Dei*," he explained (Strickland 1984). In subsequent writings, Strickland no longer used any term other than *minimalist* to designate the music of the four composers.

Nor would he deny, over the years, his admiration for their work, particularly that from the beginning of their careers (see especially Strickland 1986a; 1987). When he tried to define their music, the classical connection was what he first highlighted. In 1980, for example, he described Riley's ragas as having the same trance qualities as Stockhausen's *Stimmung* or Bach's timeless counterpoint (1980). In the popular register, he wrote, these ragas evoked at most, and in some respects only rhythmically,

In a Silent Way by Miles Davis. Indeed, in *Fanfare* it is rare to find the approach that aims to link minimalism with popular music. In 1991, however, when Strickland, a jazz lover, published his first book, a collection of interviews titled *American Composers* (1991), his perspective changed.[4]

There contemporary American music, and especially minimalism—"the first indigenous classical style created and shared by Americans" (1)—is largely characterized by its borrowings from jazz. The music of Young, Riley, Reich, and Glass incorporates its rhythmic and metrical principles, turns to improvisation as a creative underpinning, and adopts modal jazz's rejection of harmonic progressions (3, 4). This music even encompasses the dynamic of rock, its amplification or its group formation, not to mention the borrowing from Eastern music—a direction that enabled the Americans to shed the European influence, particularly of serial music (6, 8).

Strickland's conceptions are far from arbitrary; to elaborate them, he relies on the works of Chase, Ewen, Hamm, Hitchcock, and Rockwell (9). But the singularity of Strickland's new perspective does not come from their books. Those authors were interested in minimalism, but all except Rockwell maintained its distinction from the popular. Strickland, however, affirms the connection, as the composers themselves attest to their roots in jazz or rock. Indeed, by 1991 popular genres had become so interesting to the minimalists that they themselves came to modify the definition of their own music. And Strickland, who had never masked his interest in the popular, followed suit.

The interviews with minimalists in *American Composers* are brimming with references to popular music, which Strickland does not fail to underline.[5] Between the lines of the book, a new conception of minimalism is being forged. Reich once again affirms this influence: "Kenny Clarke had a sense of time that propelled the entire band, a buoyant, permanent uplift I found riveting and wanted to imitate and in many ways still do. . . . The jazz influence that's all over my work is not so specific, but without the rhythmic and melodic gesture of jazz, its flexibility and nuance, my work is *unthinkable*" (Strickland 1991, 38). The combinations and permutations of sets of tones within modes inspired by jazz were translated into the "clouds" of *The Well-Tuned Piano*, Young asserts (63–64). "What I liked in La Monte and in jazz I distilled down to that simple form" (i.e., repetition), Riley maintains. He cites his strongest influences as Middle

Eastern devotional music, along with "jazz and Indian classical music and Persian music" (111, 119).

The influence of the popular, particularly jazz, is not, however, the only novelty we find in *American Composers*. The book also shows how a wide range of composers had rallied to the idea of minimalism, which by then had become too solid to dispute, as Strickland also never fails to emphasize (see especially 45, 60, 110–11). The proven existence of minimalism is, in fact, the subject of Strickland's 1993 book, in which he retraces its origins.

Origins

What does Strickland retain in *Minimalism: Origins* (1993) of his previous portrayals of minimalism and the postwar musical landscape? What does he add or subtract, and how does he adapt them? The book is based on a series of "proven" facts, including the conceptions that Rockwell developed in his own writings. But after having obtained, in *American Composers*, "confirmation" from the composers themselves that popular music permeated minimalism, Strickland develops a new conception of the music of Young, Riley, Reich, and Glass.

Various previously established elements are changed in Strickland's new book, beginning with the very existence of minimal music, as seen in the book's opening line: "The death of Minimalism is announced periodically, which may be the surest testimonial to its staying power" (1). This movement, as we now read everywhere, is authentically American (3), created by the four composers Young, Reich, Riley, and Glass. They and their works are the subject of Strickland's book. He thus reinforces the links between the four: Glass was directly influenced by Young and perhaps by Riley, in addition to Reich (Strickland 1993, 204, 211). He furthermore disentangles these links from the rhizomes that connect the composers to other people and currents in the past.

But not all arguments are laid to rest, as Strickland (1993) himself points out. The logic of the passage from drone to repetition, from Young to Riley, or simply the context and meaning of repetition in the music of one or the other continues to be debated (145–46). For the author, the true roots of repetition in Riley lie in tape music (146). Another issue that arises is the particularly long-standing opposition between serialism and Cageian experimentalism as the origin of the movement. Strickland situates minimalism more on the Cageian side of the serious music orientation with which the movement was often associated. Contrary to Mertens or Cohn, Strickland asserts that minimalism broke from serialism (120, 126), whereas it could never have developed without the precedent of Cage (160–61).

The originality of Strickland's thesis, however, is rooted not so much in these ideas as in his tendency to reinforce the link between the musical movement and other disciplines by devoting long sections of the book to minimalism's "equivalents" in dance, cinema, literature, and particularly the visual arts, as Bernard (1993) did shortly before.[6] Strickland also emphasizes minimalism's connection to the popular by reformulating certain of the movement's stylistic foundations. Examples abound: growing up, Riley was exposed much more to popular than to classical music (133); the four minimalists are former jazz musicians (150), modal jazz having been one of the most important influences on the development of minimalism, soon joined by "the rhythmic propulsion of rock" (150); Riley's *In C*, which does not specify instrumentation, departs from "the academic fetishism of the score"; *In C* furthermore adopts a structure "overtly influenced by modal jazz" (177, 180); Reich's *Music for Three Pianos and Tape* contains chords derived from jazz (184); Glass was influenced by Coltrane, just as his three colleagues were (203); and so on. Minimal music has enjoyed great popularity and influenced popular culture, but above all it is fundamentally popular, regardless of what the contributors to *Perspectives of New Music* say.

21. 1994

THE ARRIVAL OF MINIMALISM

What was American music in the second half of the twentieth century? What was minimalism? How would these questions be answered in 1994, a few months after the appearance of the minimalist forums in *Perspectives of New Music* and of Strickland's book *Minimalism: Origins*? Let us first consider the responses to the same questions ten years earlier, in 1984. At that time, a fundamental link between Young, Reich, Riley, and Glass began to be recognized. In the end, what might have formerly differentiated them from each other or connected them to other music figures or genres was now forgotten. Likewise, the issues around the label for their music fell away. In 1984, after almost a decade of hesitations and support for various alternatives, it was now rare to find composers who still opposed the label *minimal* being applied to their music. What is more, the four minimalists, long denigrated in the 1960s and 1970s, now began to claim an important place within the serious music tradition of their day. At the time, only Rockwell and a few others cast doubt on the conception that theirs was a strictly serious music. According to Rockwell, Young, Riley, Reich, and Glass were indeed serious composers, but they were now much more popular than it had long seemed.

Ten years later, in 1994, the question of whether minimalism was a serious or popular genre had not yet been decided. The controversy was even more intense than before, depending on whether one followed *Perspectives of New Music* or Strickland. The nature of minimalism, as well as its place within the American music of the second half of the twentieth century, was still being clarified.

In 1994, minimalism was obviously no longer a doubtful concept upheld only by Nyman and a few others; it had indeed become the repetitive music of the four composers. Furthermore, even though its cultural preeminence was still occasionally questioned, most of the authors who had previously omitted minimalism while covering the developments of American music now took it into consideration. The almost pervasive rally around a "triumphant" minimalism was thus one of the main movements that can be observed from the middle of the 1980s, along with the development of schools of thought around the serious-or-popular question mentioned above.

The International Cyclopedia of Music and Musicians, edited by Oscar Thompson, attests to this change. In the 1975 edition, minimalism is absent; in the "addenda" of 1985, it is now a form of repetitive composition that originated in the United States (Thompson 1985, 2576). Minimalism's overdue appearance in the encyclopedia results not so much from the music having changed since 1975—something the definition does not imply—as from the fruitful struggle for recognition of the movement. In either case, American music has changed. The same scenario plays out in the successive editions of *Grove*: whereas the 1980 edition of *New Grove* has no entry for minimalism,[1] one appears in the 1986 *Grove Dictionary of American Music* (Dreier 1986, 3:240–42), as well as in the 1988 *Grove Concise Dictionary of Music* (Sadie 1988, 490). In the latter, minimalism is now reified to such an extent that its origins go back to the music of Satie, almost a century before the term was created by Nyman. There is not much new to learn about this music; minimalism gradually freezes at the turn of the 1980s.

The International Cyclopedia of Music and Musicians and *Grove* are but two examples among many. In the 1978 edition of *Harvard Dictionary of Music,* minimalism, like the connection between the four composers, barely exists (Randel 1978); in the 1986 edition, it figures among the great musical tendencies of the postwar United States (Randel 1986, 890). In Reginald Smith Brindle's *The New Music*, Riley, closely associated with Tomás Marco, appears as an Eastern-influenced composer (1975, 136); twelve years later, he and his New York colleagues become minimalists (1987, 194–96). In both editions, however, it is still the Riley of 1964, with *In C*, that is described. Were the earlier observations on American music therefore wrong? No: this evolution owes to the fact that the substance of American music is simultaneously the origin and the end result of these controversies.

Between 1984, where we left minimalism, and 1994, where we now pick up, a vast movement in support of minimalism had taken place. Of course, some authors, such as Gilbert Chase, still balked at recognizing it. In his entry for the United States in the 1980 *New Grove* (Chase et al. 1980), he briefly mentions, with regard to the Young, Riley, Reich, and Glass, a "New Simplicity" movement that grew out of Cage's music. In his 1987 edition of *America's Music*, Chase discusses the work of Reich and Glass without ever connecting them to minimalist theory (Chase 1987, 609–11). Meanwhile other authors, such as Dan Warburton or Barney Childs, discuss various aspects of terminology (Warburton 1988; Childs 1988). Nonetheless, whether considered an aesthetic, a style, or a technique (Johnson 1994), minimalism was now being validated by a considerable number of authors. No doubt the most explicit illustration of this process of rallying to the concept of minimalism, and more generally to the composers' aesthetic, was offered by Robert T. Jones. Although this journalist for the *New York Times*, *Time* magazine, and the New York *Daily News* was among the early detractors of Glass in 1969, notably calling his music "trivial" (1969, 43), he joined the defenders of minimalism twelve years later, writing particularly laudatory articles (1981; 1983a; 1983b; 1985) and even editing a book dedicated exclusively to Glass (Glass 1987). What happened between 1969 and 1987? Indeed a new music was produced, but that was not all. Jones himself implies as much in the introduction to his book on Glass: during that time the composer made a great name for himself in the annals of the avant-garde (Glass 1987, viii); he is now inescapable. The aesthetic associated with him, minimalism—be it serious or popular—has become inescapable as well.

22. In Conquest of the Twenty-First Century

As we have seen, minimalism became inescapable, or nearly so, in the music literature of the mid-1990s. The concept now enjoyed a rare robustness, as the concepts of serialism, indeterminacy, and electronic music had a bit earlier in the century. Does that mean that the history of the reification of minimalism stops here? Does it make the notion of minimalism's arrival in the last third of the twentieth century an inalterable fact? To answer these questions, we follow minimalism through the first decade of the twenty-first century, surveying its status after a half century of struggle for its recognition.

MORE CONTROVERSIES

Although new controversies around minimalism continued to emerge in the second half of the 1990s as well as in the course of the 2000s, they proved less intense and less fundamental than those in the past. Few authors would now try to invalidate the concept of minimalism or reject its presumed place in the musical canon of the second half of the twentieth century. Few, too, would propose a competing conception of minimalism, which now almost exclusively encompassed the music of Young, Reich, Riley, and Glass. In 2000, when Ashley finally published the anthology of texts *Music with Roots in the Aether,* it was probably too late to contest Nyman's views, as he had initially intended to do (see chapter 11). The book's release in no way undermined minimalism; *Music with Roots in the Aether* did not designate an American style as the composer's opera for television did in 1976. Minimalism had quite simply become too solid, or too imposing, to be refuted or ignored anymore. Thus, the last controversies we can observe related instead to certain of its intrinsic characteristics. Developing the concept inherited from Nyman, some postulated that minimalism was not so much serious, modern, or popular as it was postmodern. Others asserted that the genre died out in the early 1970s but generated a much richer style: postminimalism.

A Postmodern Minimalism, at Last?

In the course of the 1980s, Western culture, according to some authors, underwent a fundamental change. Up to that time many had believed it to be modern, but in reality, and for some decades already, it was postmodern. We discovered as much in the writings of Lyotard ([1979] 1984) and Jameson (1991), as well as Linda Hutcheon (1988), David Harvey (1989), and Hans Bertens (1995), among many others. In spite of their differing observations and approaches, all seem to agree on one fact: modernity had broken down in the years following the Second World War. And its failure—or at least the idea that it had failed—is primarily what defines postmodernism. Beyond this consensus, points of agreement among theorists of postmodernism are rare. The term, as well as what it refers to, was the subject of controversies no less fierce than those that accompanied the emergence of minimalism. *Postmodernism* sometimes denotes culture, sometimes the way it is viewed; a historical period, a style, or an artistic position. It refers to the break with modernity or even to its continuation; it attests to the end of the grand narratives—those of modernity—for which in some ways it seems to substitute its own.

However difficult it may be to define postmodernism, postmodernity, and related expressions, music seems, in the course of the 1990s, to have definitively taken part in the movement, thus joining philosophy, architecture, and literature.[1] "Music has become postmodern as we, its early-21st-century listeners, have become postmodern," Jonathan D. Kramer wrote in 1999 (11). This declaration is far from the only one of this nature from the Columbia University professor and composer.[2] Nor was Kramer the only scholar to defend the concept of postmodernism in music, although he would best attempt to synthesize it. In 1988, in a book titled *The Time of Music*, and much more explicitly in a series of articles that he published in the mid- to late 1990s (1995; 1996; 1999), Kramer campaigned for the recognition of a new state of music. For the author, postmodernism

1. is not simply a repudiation of modernism or its continuation, but has aspects of both a break and an extension;
2. is, on some level and in some way, ironic;
3. does not respect boundaries between sonorities and procedures of the past and of the present;
4. challenges barriers between "high" and "low" styles;
5. shows disdain for the often unquestioned value of structural unity;
6. questions the mutual exclusivity of elitist and populist values;
7. avoids totalizing forms (e.g., does not want entire pieces to be tonal or serial or cast in a prescribed formal mold);
8. considers music not as autonomous but as relevant to cultural, social, and political context;
9. includes quotations of or references to music of many traditions and cultures;
10. considers technology not only as a way to preserve and transmit music but also as deeply implicated in the production and essence of music;
11. embraces contradictions;
12. distrusts binary oppositions;
13. includes fragmentations and discontinuities;
14. encompasses pluralism and eclecticism;
15. presents multiple meanings and multiple temporalities; and
16. locates meaning and even structure in listeners, more than in scores, performances, or composers.

(Kramer 1999, 10–11)

In Kramer's works, minimal music is an integral part of postmodern music. Minimal music was thought to be modern; it was thought to be serious, unitary, sometimes elitist, and predetermined in its form. Now it seems completely the opposite, or almost so, because for Kramer, at least, the postmodern is as much a continuation of the modern as a break from it. However dramatic it might be, the transfiguration of culture, music, minimalism, and, in the process, modernism itself was neither the result of the discovery of what was already there nor a pure invention by certain researchers over the last two decades of the twentieth century. The history of the connections between minimalism and postmodernity is one of translations of shared interests, as well as a chain of subtle modifications of concepts.

Postmodernism had not always been musical or minimalist, nor had it always been well regarded. To cite but one example, Lyotard's *The Postmodern Condition* ([1979] 1984), which became an indispensable resource on postmodernity in the decades that followed its publication, was above all, as its subtitle indicates, "a report on knowledge," the postulate of an incredulity toward the metanarratives of modernity: "There are several grand narratives co-existing in western thought. The postmodern condition is the result of these grand narratives ceasing to be credible. They are no longer able to legitimate, in the name of progress, the benefits and detriments that the West has bestowed upon itself and the world throughout the centuries" (Lyotard [1996] 2012, 203). For Lyotard, music only occasionally participated in the construction of the postmodern. Only his late essay "Music and Postmodernity" ([1996] 2012) contributes directly to a deeper integration of music into the movement. There, following Adorno, he postulates that "the history of western music may be thought of globally as the grand narrative of the *emancipation of sound*" (205). Under the sway of new technologies, this emancipation led to the destruction of the old rules of composition. In the absence of these foundations, a form of postmodern cynicism can appear in certain contemporary practices, according to the author, as the rules of commerce take advantage of the lack of artistic rules (Bennett 2011). This musical postmodernity is thus not explicitly minimalist, nor is it the locus of eclecticism or of the collapse of cultural hierarchies.[3] At most it brings an additional element to the landscape of a world brutalized by capitalism that the philosopher seeks to describe.

Jameson, too, briefly presented the idea of music's subordination to the laws of the market (1991). This subject would subsequently enjoy wide popularity, but it in turn would be somewhat transformed. Whereas the postmodern held a negative connotation in Lyotard or Jameson, some of their successors saw it differently. *The Postmodern Moment,* edited by Stanley Trachtenberg (1985), testifies not only to the gradual reification of postmodernity—whether the style or the period, that which existed or exists (xii–xiii)—but also to the value it has acquired. This postmodernism is not so much the result of social ruin as a potential "guerilla action, dismantling the logic of a repressive state and the political structures and social institutions that sustain it." It "renews our perception of [the art object] in the material world and so renews our perception of that object and of ourselves" (xii). In this book the postmodern is also musical: postmodern music, with its simplicity and its popular perspective on the world around it, offers a solution to the dying complexity of modern music, which has lost the capacity for communication.

Thus minimalism, with its gradual triumph, progressively came to be allied with postmodernism. The opposite was equally true: the transfigured postmodern enriched minimalism with an additional, positive meaning. Hutcheon (1988) has a much more constructive approach to postmodern art: "Even the most self-conscious and parodic of contemporary works do not try to escape, but indeed foreground, the historical, social, ideological contexts in which they have existed and continue to exist. This is as true of music as of painting; it is as valid for literature as it is for architecture" (25). In music, communication with audiences through repetitive harmonies and the crossover between genres took on a positive connotation. This outlook paved the way for Kramer's musical theories.

[Post]minimalism

The second controversy that emerged over the second half of the 1990s essentially concerned the stylistic evolution and the heritage of minimalism. Some asserted that minimalism had given rise to a variety of music genres, in particular postminimalist music. For these authors, the lifespan of minimalism was therefore shorter than it seemed.

The idea of postminimalism, however, was not entirely new. Although some authors, such as Bernard (1993) and Strickland (1993), indicated the existence of minimalism alone, others, such as Reich himself and La Barbara (1974; 1980), long postulated the existence of a minimalism "after minimalism," or at least a change in aesthetic sensibilities.[4] Indeed, since the early 1970s several authors saw the minimalists' music becoming richer, more complex, and tonal. Among the first defenders of this conception was K. Robert Schwarz, a prolific journalist for the *New York Times* and *Musical America*, among other periodicals. In the early 1980s, in a two-part article on Reich's music in *Perspectives of New Music* (1980–81 and 1981–82), the author points to the progressive enrichment of the composer's style. He furthers this idea in articles with such eloquent titles as "Maximising Minimalism" (1985), taking interest in the supposed successors of Young, Riley, Reich, and Glass, such as John Adams, to whom he devoted numerous articles (see especially Schwarz 1990). In 1996, he published a book with Phaidon that developed his postminimalist postulate: Reich and Glass were both active as minimalists before entering a "maximalist" period in the early 1970s (1996, 77–106 and 129–169), which led to the postminimalism of Adams and Meredith Monk in the second half of the decade (169–93).

Schwarz's book *Minimalists* thus incites (as much as it embodies) a new controversy on the existence of a turning point in the history of the movement, a period during which no one knows exactly whether the music was fundamentally minimal or maximal, markedly stripped down or immensely rich. It is the last great paradox to appear over the course of the decade, and not the least, because the expansiveness of postminimalism is in some ways antithetical to minimalism. Beyond this polemic, however, Schwarz's *Minimalists* indirectly reinforces the existence and arrival of minimalism. The genre should even become "a respectable field of academic pursuit," he writes (6). By superposing on minimalism a new major movement, Schwarz substantiates the early style of Young, Riley, Reich, and Glass; if postminimalism exists, then minimalism has to have existed as well. That is no doubt the main consequence of the work of Schwarz and authors such as Kyle Gann, who, over the course of the 1980s and 1990s, even alluded to the existence of a "totalist" movement in a series of articles in the *Village Voice* or in *American Music in the Twentieth Century* (1997, 355–56).[5] The concepts of ambient music and holy minimalism would have the same result. The first, under the impetus of Brian

Eno, designated a genre of static music that emphasized timbre or atmosphere to the detriment of structure, rhythm, or melody.[6] The second referred to minimalist music marked by religious themes or mysticism, such as that of Arvo Pärt, John Tavener, or Henryk Górecki.[7] Both rested on the foundations of minimalism and helped solidify them.

NEW TERRITORIES

Minimal from beginning to end or postminimal from the mid-1970s: the question would remain open throughout the 2000s. Finally, in 2014, *The Ashgate Research Companion to Minimalist and Postminimalist Music*, edited by Keith Potter, Kyle Gann, and Pwyll ap Siôn, ostensibly decided it. By contrast, the issue of the modernity or postmodernity of the genre remains, as of this writing, subject to debate. The insertion of minimalism among modern and postmodern music—two of the greatest, if not the main, late-twentieth-century movements of the musicologists' landscape—ultimately attests above all to its status as a central current of contemporaneity. Indeed, minimalism seems to have ceaselessly spread its tentacles over the musical terrain of the twentieth and even the twenty-first centuries. In 2005, Robert Fink would publish *Repeating Ourselves*, a book that connects repetitive music to the postwar evolution of an American mass consumer society. Here, as the subtitle indicates, "American minimal music" would become nothing less than "a cultural practice." Two years later, a landmark event would take place: the First International Conference on Music and Minimalism at Bangor University in Wales, in 2007, signaled the beginning of the institutionalization of a field of research dedicated to the current. In the years leading up to Fink's book and the conference, many authors and their books moved in step with minimalism's march to triumph.

Achieving Consensus

At the turn of the millennium, although reference works such as *The Harvard Concise Dictionary of Music and Musicians* (Randel 1999) and the *Nouveau Dictionnaire de la musique* (Candé 2000) had hardly any entries on minimalism, those books were now the exception. In fact, for some years already, minimalism seemed to reign supreme in twentieth-century American music, to the point that most of the country's major composers were either experimentalists or minimalists, according to Geoff Smith and Nicola Walker Smith (1994, vii). Entries devoted to minimalism thus appeared in most of the other music dictionaries: *The Harper Collins Dictionary of Music* (Ammer 1995, 249–50), the *Enciclopedia della musica Garzanti* (1996, 542–43), *The Penguin Dictionary of Music* (Jacobs 1996, 282), and *Die Musik in Geschichte und Gegenwart* (Grünzweig 1997, 294–302), among many others, not to mention the large histories of music produced by world-renowned universities, such as *The Cambridge History of American Music* (Nicholls 1998). These books most often defined minimalism as a major American repetitive style dating from the 1960s, represented by Young, Riley, Reich, and Glass. As with the *Enciclopedia della musica Garzanti* in 1996,[8] all those who during the 1980s had remained unconvinced by minimalism's arrival successively joined the ranks over the 1990s to lift the movement to the height of contemporaneity—in spite of the fact that it had not only existed but also triumphed in the 1960s and 1970s. Although still in some ways preferring the term *modular music,* even Kostelanetz, the champion of the Theatre of Mixed Means, ended up rallying to minimalism in 2000 in his *Dictionary of the Avant-Gardes* (Kostelanetz 2000, 413 and 416). The Oxford dictionaries, which ignored minimalism in 1970 (Scholes 1970), 1980 (Kennedy 1980), and 1984 (Arnold 1984), finally incorporated it twenty-five years after the now-official birth of the movement: minimalism made its entrance into the *Oxford Companion to Music* in 2002 (Davies 2002).

In 2001, minimalism also found a place in the second edition of the *New Grove* thanks to Keith Potter (Potter 2001a), the author of *Four Musical Minimalists,* published by Oxford University Press (2000). His book, like his entry on minimalism, augments and especially synthesizes what could now be read everywhere about the music of the Young, Riley, Reich, and Glass. In Potter's writings the shared composition style of the four Americans is clear, even if a few incongruities or unknowns remain, particularly on the question of popular and serious categories.

In the course of the 2000s, the movement to establish minimalism did not flag. In 2002, Reich republished his writings on music. Whereas a half century earlier the same texts had been issued by the small press of the Nova Scotia College of Art and Design, now they were published, together with later texts, by Oxford University Press and edited by the conductor Paul Hillier.[9] In his introduction, Hillier was not mistaken when he wrote of minimalism: "Much has already been written about the genesis of this style, and the question of influences and chronologies has been well documented" (Reich 2002, 14). Reich, who twenty-five years earlier had proclaimed his profound individuality, was here associated with Young, Riley, and Glass (13–16). In 2003, Jonathan Bernard viewed the label *minimalist*, as well as the movement's heritage, with a critical eye in his article "Minimalism, Postminimalism, and the Resurgence of Tonality in Recent American Music," in *American Music*. Once again, however, the result was a recognition of its force: "Minimalism strictly construed—whether as an aesthetic orientation or as a closely related group of styles—has vanished, yet its effects on present-day music are widespread and undeniable" (130). In 2005, in the introduction to his Africanist critique of Reich's "It's Gonna Rain" (1965), Martin Scherzinger was no less ignorant of the arrival of minimalism: "Defenders of the new style emphasize the cultural triumph of minimalism. For Susan McClary, minimalism is 'perhaps the single most viable extant strand of the Western art-music tradition'; for K. Robert Schwarz, a specialist in this style, minimalism is 'a potent force . . . its influence is pervasive and enduring'; and for the composer John Adams, minimalism is 'the only really interesting, important stylistic development in the past 30 years'" (Scherzinger 2005, 207; see also McClary 2004, 289; Schwarz 1997, 1; and Adams quoted in Schwarz 1996, 177).

The year before, Philip Sherburne linked minimalism to the house and techno styles. "Electronic dance music particularly foregrounds the strategies pioneered in the work of so-called minimalist composers like Steve Reich and Philip Glass," the author writes (Sherburne 2004, 319). In 2007 and 2008, monographs on composers of static or repetitive music continued to color the minimalist cast that the history of twentieth-century music had taken on. The first, by Pwyll ap Siôn (2007), was on Nyman; the second, by Branden Joseph (2008), on Tony Conrad, a notable associate of Young's. In 2009 Robert Carl published a monograph devoted entirely to Riley's *In C*, and in 2011 Jeremy Grimshaw published a work on Young, both from Oxford University Press.

Repeating Ourselves

It is impossible to consider the history of the arrival of minimalism at the beginning of the millennium without discussing *Repeating Ourselves* by Robert Fink (2005). The book crystallized a new alliance, that of minimalism and cultural studies. It thus fits within the new musicology, whose approaches the establishment was beginning to recognize and even celebrate. This new association of the rising forces of contemporary musical thought would pay off: Fink's work revitalized the study of repetitive and static music. It would enjoy acclaim and inspire many other works over the following years.

Robert Fink and the New Musicology

Arising over the course of the 1980s, the New Musicology trend challenged the research methods of traditional musicology by moving away from the positivism that permeated it. The approach borrowed from other disciplines, in particular the humanities and social sciences, to interrogate established musical knowledge. The "new musicologists"—Carolyn Abbate, Lawrence Kramer, Susan McClary, Rose Rosengard Subotnick, and Gary Tomlinson, among the best known—sought to confront music criticism and analysis with cultural studies. They gave more weight to the sociology of musicians and institutions, as well as to noncanonical genres such as jazz and popular music. In 1998, Fink barely hid his enthusiasm for this school of thought when he published "Elvis Everywhere: Musicology and Popular Music Studies at the Twilight of the Canon," calling for an alliance between new musicology and the approaches developed in popular music studies. "All too often, the positions of musicologists and popular music scholars vis-à-vis 'formalism' or 'structural analysis' harden into a pat dialectical opposition that serves neither repertory well" (Fink 1998, 151). He proposed instead "to meld precise phenomenological description of musical effects with cultural interpretation" (168). Although in this essay Fink did not deeply consider the problematic of minimal repetitive music, he would do so six years later. In 2004, his article "(Post-)minimalisms 1970–2000: The Search for a New Mainstream" appeared in *The Cambridge History of Twentieth-Century Music*, edited by Nicholas Cook and Anthony Pople.

Here Fink's approach to minimalism and postminimalism, seeking in particular to uncover their popular connections and political impact, figures in a book that appraises "the development of music in the twentieth century from the vantage-point of the twenty-first" and also aims "to set musical developments in the context of social, ideological, and technological change, and to understand reception and consumption as integral to the history of music" (Cook and Pople 2004). Also in 2004, McClary, one of the notable founders of the approaches grouped under the label *new musicology*, examined the prevalence of repetition in twentieth-century music. Her essay proposes a "genealogy of musical minimalisms that situates them in relationship to the cultural crises of the 20th century" (2004, 289).

American Minimal Music as Cultural Practice

In 2005, the approaches inherited from cultural studies, new musicology, and the research that developed around minimalism came together in Fink's *Repeating Ourselves: American Minimal Music as Cultural Practice*. An in-depth survey of the cultural contexts of the music of American repetitive composers, it "situates American (and some European) minimal music in a number of concurrent cultural activities." Over the course of his book, Fink explores the "multivalent and erotically charged teleology of minimalism and disco"; relates "the culture of repetitive advertising in the 1960s" to the music of Reich and Glass; considers the "mood-regulating therapy" of albums of baroque music played on automatic record changers; and, finally, looks at interactions between minimalism and the Suzuki method of teaching music in the United States (Haskins 2006, 147–48). The author observes that these repetitive musical and social activities paved the way for the minimal processes of the 1960s. Minimalist music thus reflects a historical transformation of consumer society: "the self-conscious postwar transfer of the repetitive structures of mass production from the material realm of the object into the symbolic realm of discourse" (Fink 2005, 81–82).

Situated at a disciplinary and epistemological turning point, Fink's book soon became a milestone. It was a "major work of . . . cultural criticism," wrote Rob Haskins in *Current Musicology* (2006, 147), that ideally should stimulate "further work that addresses other audiences for and experiences of minimal music, as well as scholarship that considers other twentieth-century concert music with respect to its wider socio-cultural aspects" (153). No doubt the story of the book's legacy continues to be written, but the years that followed its publication appear to have proven Haskins right. *Repeating Ourselves* is seen as the authoritative text not only among works that confront musical study with cultural studies or tackle the question of musical repetition (see in particular Margulis 2014), but also within the minimalist "establishment" itself. In 2013, *The Ashgate Research Companion to Minimalist and Postminimalist Music* would include a chapter by Fink titled "Going with the Flow: Minimalism as a Cultural Practice in the USA since 1945," which presented once again the thesis developed in *Repeating Ourselves*.

A First Conference on Music and Minimalism

"The last decade or so has witnessed a dramatic increase in scholarship on musical minimalism," Sumanth Gopinath wrote in 2004 (134). Indeed, this increase would lead Pwyll ap Siôn and Tristian Evans, three years later, to organize the First International Conference on Music and Minimalism at Bangor University in Wales. "This subject is sustaining more interest than ever within the wider academic community," the two organizers asserted. Their goal was clear: "[to] give rise to important future publications in this area" (ap Siôn and Evans 2007, 1). This enterprise encompassed various fields and areas of research, "aesthetic, theoretic, and analytic." In the process, the Society for Minimalist Music was founded. Subsequent conferences were organized at the University of Missouri–Kansas City, in 2009; the Katholieke Universiteit Leuven, Belgium, in 2011; California State University, Long Beach, in 2013; the University of Turku and the Sibelius Academy, Helsinki, Finland, in 2015; the University of Tennessee at Knoxville, in 2017; and Cardiff University, in 2019. The effort to institutionalize the field is evident in the publication of *The Ashgate Research Companion to Minimalist and Postminimalist Music* (Potter, Gann, and ap Siôn 2013), as well as the more recent edited volumes *Rethinking Reich* (Gopinath and ap Siôn 2019) and *Einstein on the Beach: Opera beyond Drama* (Novak and Richardson 2019), two books that gather contributions by numerous members of the Society for Minimalist Music.

Epilogue

From the start of the 1960s to the dawn of the new century, everything changed. Today the names of the great postwar composers one used to read about in the 1960s and 1970s (see chapter 1) have, for many, been erased to make room for Young, Riley, Reich, and Glass. Minimalism now commands a major place in contemporary American culture. To read some of the latest musicological publications, one would think that the second part of the twentieth century had always been minimalist. Not only do books by Potter, Fink, and other specialists on the question assert as much—along with the renowned encyclopedias and the dozens of references stacked beneath entries devoted to the movement—but so too do concert programs of orchestras and ensembles, CD booklets, and newspaper sidebars. As I write these lines, I find that the orchestra of the small city of Liège, where I live in Belgium, is presenting a concert of works by Reich and Glass. These are touted as indispensable works of minimalism, between: "the seminal movement" of twentieth-century American music. Nothing in this assertion would lead one to suspect the total ignorance or disinterest of such institutions for the movement in its prime. Indeed, behind all these affirmations, no trace of bygone struggles remains. The authors making such pronouncements are no longer "defenders" or "partisans" of the movement; they are merely spokespersons of a state of culture that they simply describe. Their words reflect nothing but the "music itself," independent of any value judgment, past or present.

Through a collective effort, in the course of various adoptions, transformations, and rejections of the theories around the music of Young, Riley, Reich, and Glass, an established fact formed. Its formation first entailed constructing a style, and the theory around it, based on other, already known, styles and theories (whether Cageian indeterminacy, serialism, or the writings of music critics). It then involved associating with this style allies of all kinds (researchers, institutions) and other musical currents, at the risk of seeing them merge (thus Tom Johnson's New York Hypnotic School faded into Michael Nyman's minimalism). Next it required fighting against competing concepts and sometimes aiding in their demise (who talks about the Theatre of Mixed Means today?). And finally, it entailed translating the interests of others so that they might latch onto and promote these ideas, which themselves had been forged by drawing on other ideas. In the end the concept first preached by Nyman won out, to become, in the course of confirmations of its truth, a proven fact—an object that we can only contemplate. Today we merely witness this reification, based on a series of other reifications and soon, potentially, the basis for further ones. Layer upon layer, ideas have solidified into things. They have become *real*—at least as long as no one is there to contest them. The teaching of Latour's *Science in Action*, mentioned in the introduction to this book, thus seems equally valid in the context of music study. Now, if musical facts are made, then it is possible to escape the circular logic of "objectively demonstrated" and "socially constructed," whereby all is determined either by objects or subjects. The facts are no less solid. Indeed they are more solid, but it is up to us to decide their fate.

To decide the fate of facts: beyond the documentary or historiographic interest of a project that aims to illuminate what lies hidden behind a fact of music history, an epistemological reform looms on the horizon of music's confrontation with actor-network theory. In this study we have sought to demonstrate the "socially constructed" nature of minimalism: minimalism as commonly accepted in the literature results from a victory won by the defenders of the concept. But even more (and this, ultimately, is what vastly differentiates the Latourian approach from the purest social constructivism), this study has aimed to shed light on the numerous mechanisms, strategies, and processes that lead to the objectification of an intellectual construct. Of course, asserting today that minimalism and its triumph are a mere invention, or even a sham, hardly has the same repercussions as contesting the theory of evolution, that of continental drift, or the effectiveness of child vaccination. Nonetheless, it runs up against the wall formed by scientific truth.

Specifically, however, if we accept that, as found in this study, the musical fact is socially constructed (essentially by a community of experts) but nonetheless objectifiable and objectified, and if we further recognize the need for a "universal" science, or at least a democratic and transparent science, then we should acknowledge that those under the sway of science, its truths and effects, should have the opportunity to participate in constructing its results.

In other words, if we acknowledge the political nature of facts and admit that they are infused with values, then the politics or values that pervade them should at least be subject to a dialogue. According to this approach, as music scholarship and knowledge become politicized, scholars, composers, and journalists no longer have sole authority over what should or should not constitute the world, and culture in particular. Far from the relativism of Paul Feyerabend, which construes science as a myth or a religion (1975), actor-network theory ultimately leads to a theory of engagement, effectively drawing those on the receiving end of science into its making (see also Hennion 2013). This new development was already envisioned in *Politics of Nature* by Bruno Latour (2004) and in *Acting in an Uncertain World* by Michel Callon, Pierre Lascoumes, and Yannick Barthe (2011). Here we merely sketch the outlines of this new development: if science (that is, music scholarship) is to "reconnect with society," the answer is perhaps not to keep popularizing or disseminating it but rather to finally acknowledge the social imprint on the construction of facts. Thus, at a time when the mistrust of science and scientists remains alive and well,[1] what actor-network theory proposes is a nonauthoritarian, democratic, and participatory science—a science whose results can be debated in meetings or forums that bring together specialists and nonspecialists. Declaring minimalism's victory in the twentieth-century musical panorama was not just a technical process but also an eminently political one. The future of minimalism therefore remains to be written—collectively, this time.

This collective history will no doubt be able to integrate numerous actors who are lamentably absent from the great minimalist narrative—not only or necessarily those left by the wayside in pursuing the advance of minimalism in this book, but many others as well. Indeed, as readers will not have failed to notice, the minimalism in triumph by the turn of the twenty-first century is one that presents all the traits of the stereotypical dominance of white Western men over forty. This minimalism pays scant attention to women composers (there is still little written on Meredith Monk or Barbara Benary) or African American musicians (what about Julius Eastman?) and merely glances over the contributions of continental Europe. The latter, up to this point, has never managed to make itself properly heard within the minimalist canon, be it the work of veterans Eliane Radigue (France), Henning Christiansen (Denmark), and Louis Andriessen (Netherlands) or that of new generations, particularly in northern Europe, with Nils Frahm, Max Richter, and Sascha Ring in Germany; Christian Fennesz in Austria; and Ólafur Arnalds, Jóhann Jóhannsson, and Valgeir Sigurðsson in Iceland. Moreover, this canonical minimalism remains impervious to the realms of popular music and has little contact with minimal techno, synthpop, doom metal, or post-rock, genres that have met with unparalleled success in recent years. I will not presume to speak of the interest of researchers—who, as we have seen, are generally quite close in terms of their social and ethnic backgrounds with the actors they observe (myself being no exception)—for an Asian, African, or South American minimal music in the twentieth century. But, on closing this work, I am heartened to see a woman scholar publish a book on a Brazilian composer whom she links to this style: *Repensando a terceira fase composicional de Gilberto Mendes: O Pós-Minimalismo nos Mares do Sul* (Santos 2019). In it the author, Rita de Cássia Domingues dos Santos, presents Gilberto Mendes as a key figure in the development of musical minimalism while also, quite fittingly, criticizing the notion of minimalism, in particular for its lack of inclusiveness. We can hope, then, that this minimalism, having become a collective object, will embark on the same path.

Notes

CHAPTER 1

1. Howard's collaborator James Lyons was the main author of this new chapter.

2. Ewen himself had published *Men of Popular Music* in 1944, and Sigmund Spaeth *A History of Popular Music in America* four years later, in 1948.

3. For a historiography of American music that contextualizes the impact of the writings of Howard, Chase, and Hugh Wiley Hitchcock on the thinking of the US musical establishment, see Crawford (1993, i–xv; 2001, 3–40).

4. For a history of the British popular music press, see Jones (2002). See also Gendron (2002) for a study of the role played by critics in defining the status of twentieth-century popular music genres.

CHAPTER 2

1. Cardew's book accompanied the score of *Treatise*, a work he composed during the years 1963–67.

2. See Stanley Sadie's editorial that looks back on 125 years of the *Musical Times* in its anniversary issue of June 1969. For a history of music journals and their respective missions, see Fellinger et al. (2001).

3. The shifting, controversial notions of the music establishment that frequently figure in this book fully deserve to be analyzed based on the same methods employed in this study. That analysis, however, far exceeds the scope of this work. Thus, *establishment* is used here in the conventional sense, to mean the officially sanctioned institutions, practices, and rules for music in a given time and place.

4. See Nicholls (2002) and Pritchett et al. (2012) on the reception of the Cage-ian aesthetic in the postwar musical landscape.

5. The work "consists of any number of performers performing any continuing activities for random but decided lengths of time within a total random but decided time" (Cardew 1962, 75).

6. The playing of "the same cluster [on a piano] six thousand one hundred and ninety-eight times" (Cardew 1962, 75).

7. See *Musical Times* 104, no. 1445 (July 1963): 528; and 104, no. 1450 (December 1963): 918.

8. "Originally, the piece was scored for 'tables, chairs, benches and other simi-lar sound sources' (these objects were pushed or pulled across the floor according to determinations effected by the same method as in *Vision*)" (Cardew 1966, 959).

9. Smalley's own work, "technically complex" and "intellectual" but not lack-ing in "sensibility," was largely permeated by the serialism of his teachers, from whom he had recently departed to draw on medieval and Renaissance music (Walsh 1968, 133).

10. In the late 1960s and early '70s, AMM for the most part did not capture the attention of the institutional music press. G. W. Hopkins evoked only the documentary interest of the group's 1967 recording (*AMM Music*, Elektra, EUK 256), even though indeed the document was "valuable and important" (Hopkins 1967, 718). The institutional press, even when lavishing praise (see Phillips 1968b), tended to ignore the group's ties to popular music, whereas jazz and rock critics focused on them (see especially the bibliography of Adams 2001).

11. See *Musical Times* 109, no. 1503 (May 1968): 430.

12. The Scratch Orchestra also played Riley's music the following year, along with works by Michael Parsons, Gustav Mahler, and Pyotr Ilyich Tchaikovsky (*Musical Times* 111, no. 1532 [October 1970]: 1070).

13. John Tilbury and John White had also joined Cardew and AMM some months earlier (see the concert announcement in the *Musical Times* 108, no. 1490 [April 1967]: 340). Thereafter, Christopher Hobbs joined as well.

14. For a history of the British experimental music groups in 1965–75, see Nyman (1976); ap Siôn (2007, 33–38); Harris (2013); and Piekut (2014).

15. For a biography of Cardew, see especially Harris (2013) and Tilbury (2008).

16. For this chapter of Cardew's history, see especially Harris (2013).

17. Indeed, Cardew himself did not reply to Smalley's criticism. In a brief note titled "62 for Henry Flynt," Skempton retorted to Smalley that it would perhaps be fitting to say of Young's work what Colin Mason had said of Stockhausen's

Momente II in 1965: "If much of [*Momente II*] cannot be called music, so much the worse for music" (Skempton 1967, 237).

18. Although history would credit Nyman as the inventor of the term *minimalist* with his October 1968 article in the *Spectator*, Phillips's use of it here, in July 1968, was the first association of Americans with the label in music literature.

19. Riley's instructions left several liberties, particularly with regard to the number of repetitions of the cells and the overall duration of the piece.

20. Parsons associated the piece not only with Cage's chance operations but also with Feldman's long silences between notes and Young's sustained sounds.

21. After Parsons's laudatory article, little would be written about Riley in the *Musical Times*. In December 1971 Paul Griffiths, who would become "one of the most influential critics of his generation" (Williamson 2001), reproached Luciano Berio for having borrowed from Riley. In Berio's *Agnus*, according to Griffiths, the composer chose to write "slow movements towards and away from a common pitch." "I hope this is just a single experiment with a current fashion," the critic asserted (Griffiths 1971, 1190). Over the following years, Griffiths's hopes would be fulfilled. Riley may have been only a fashionable composer whom the British music establishment forgot without ever really knowing him; indeed, we read in *Tempo* in 1972 that his name was unfortunately omitted in a work on notation in new music (Gilbert 1972, 47).

22. Cardew had made reference to the Third Programme broadcasts in his 1966 article on Young (Cardew 1966, 959).

23. Intermodulation notably performed these composers' works at the BBC Proms in August 1970 (see Nyman 1970). Smalley would recount years later that Intermodulation had been formed out of admiration for Cardew, Riley, and Stockhausen as much as for Cream and The Who (Mark 2012, 99).

24. In this essay Cardew used his own piece *Volo Solo* (1965) and *X for Henry Flynt* (1960) to explain how certain notations and instructions should be read or understood (Cardew 1971, xiv). He maintained that Young's piece called for uniformity but that "what is *desired* is variation," a variation that resulted from "the human (not superhuman) attempt at uniformity" (xv).

25. Thus, when authors such as Souster (1968–69) or Alan Beckett (1969) compared Young or Riley's music with popular music (in particular the Velvet Underground), they did so essentially to recall the latter's debt to the former rather than to evoke potential interconnections between hierarchically unequal worlds.

CHAPTER 3

1. Cage had by then publicly affirmed his interest in Young's work. See Cage's interview with Roger Reynolds in Dunn (1962), reprinted in Schwartz and Childs (1967, 335–48).

2. Young himself had asserted that the harmonics of these intervals could be heard after "a period of a few hours" (Hitchcock 1965, 539).

3. In the end, the first two terms would fade into the shadows of history. For a history of the construction of minimal art and the concepts developed around it over the course of the 1960s, see especially Strickland (1993) and Wagner (1995).

4. See Johnston's biography at www.jilljohnston.com/?q=node/2.

5. The two critics had moved in the same circles since at least the early 1970s, as Rose herself attests (1971, 54).

6. See especially Rose's (1967) critical history of American art, in which she gives a prominent place to Stella.

7. The following year Perreault himself noted that many critics had recently been influenced by Johnston's writing (1969, 14).

8. Bertram Jessup (1970) returned to Perreault's comments on Young, using the terms *minimal art* and *reductive art* (8), as did the critic Clement Greenberg (see Strickland 1993, 17).

9. Although Perreault had been writing on minimal art in the *Village Voice* since 1967, he does not formulate an explicit link between that art and Young.

CHAPTER 4

1. At that time, Mellers had written for *Tempo, Music & Letters,* and the *Musical Times;* he had been the music editor for the journal *Scrutiny,* and his works were widely discussed in scholarly literature. On Mellers and his central position in British academic and intellectual life, see especially East and Rumson (2008).

2. The critic John Rublowsky, in his book *Music in America* (1967), amalgamates serious and popular genres, jazz and avant-garde, following the model developed by Mellers.

3. Thompson died in 1945. Robert Sabin, who succeeded him as editor, included entries for composers such as Babbitt, Luciano Berio, Cage, and Stockhausen.

4. See, for example, reviews in *Music Educators Journal* (51, no. 3 [January 1965]: 99) and *Notes* (Millen 1965, 735). At the time of this writing, *Grove Music Online* characterizes *The International Cyclopedia of Music and Musicians* as the best general English-language music dictionary (Matthews 2001).

5. Howard would go down in history as having given the "first comprehensive account of American music, for it included . . . a discussion of folk music" (Matthews 2001).

6. Norton was widely recognized by the music establishment at that time, having published the works of Gustave Reese, Paul Henry Lang, and Alfred Einstein, among others.

7. A half century later, we read in *Grove Music Online* that "his scholarship produced a valuable body of factual material for the student of 20th-century music" (Morgan 2001a).

8. Mellers would reaffirm his thoughts on music in *Twentieth Century Music*, edited by the critic Rollo H. Myers in 1968.

9. Young is also absent in *Twentieth-Century Music* by the German musicologist and critic Hans Heinz Stuckenschmidt (1969); Stuckenschmidt's book ends the century with Stockhausen, Hans Werner Henze, and Jean Barraqué.

10. Chase's book was translated into five languages; Hitchcock calls it "the first historical study of music in the USA to treat folk and popular music as seriously as art and religious music" (Hitchcock 2001).

CHAPTER 5

1. See in particular Theodore Hoffman's (1965) description of plans for a new theater program at New York University.

2. The Performance Group was an experimental theater group. See especially Vanden Heuvel (2006).

3. On the word pieces, which consisted of a series of instructions given to the performer, see especially pp. 76, 79, and 82–83 of the lecture (Young 1965). The lecture also gave Young the opportunity to present his own views on the aesthetics of sound. Indeed, sound appears to be at the heart of his concerns (80–82). He asserts that "the trouble with most of the music of the past is that man has tried to make the sounds do what he wants them to do," whereas "we should allow the sounds to be sounds" (80). He contends that "we can learn nothing or little from [enslaved sounds] because they will simply reflect our own ideas." Instead, he likes "to get inside of a sound," which he says is easier to do "when the sounds are very long." Finally, by "giving ourselves up to them . . . we can experience another world," particularly on the level of the senses (81, 83).

4. Kirby would subsequently develop the concept of *environmental theatre* (notably in Kirby 1969, 133–52), which he defined as the way in which the spatial characteristics of the stage, as linked to the spectator, can become an aesthetic element of a particular presentation (133–34).

5. Sontag had already mentioned Young in 1966, in her collection of essays *Against Interpretation*. At that time her intent was to overthrow hermeneutics in favor of a more sensible approach to art objects. She also tried to promote a new artistic sensibility, that of Young and his "happenings" in particular (264).

6. Apart from another allusion to his work with Ann Halprin in 1972 (Sommer 1972, 136), Young would not appear in the journal again until the late 1980s. Kirby, for his part, did not mention Young in his 1965 book *Happenings*, which

presented the works of Allan Kaprow, Red Grooms, Robert Whitman, Jim Dine, and Claes Oldenburg. Four years later, when he published a collection of his essays in *The Art of Time*, Kirby included his 1965 article "The New Theatre" (1969, 75–102) but did not delve any further into his work on Young.

7. Salzman devised the term *cisum*, an anagram of *music*.

8. "Young's earliest work as a serious composer was in the Schoenberg twelve-tone tradition," writes Kostelanetz (1968, 184).

9. The second part of the chapter dedicated to Young—its main part—is an interview that Kostelanetz conducted with Young (1968, 185–218).

10. Kostelanetz's work was reviewed in the *Educational Theatre Journal* (Hobgood 1968) and the journal *New Society* (Hunt 1971). The former alleged that "his contention that these venturesome artists are creating a unique medium remains in doubt" (608). In the latter, Kostelanetz's concept is renamed the "Theatre of Boredom."

11. Among the writings in this book are "Lecture 1960" (Young 1965) and Kostelanetz's interview with Young in 1968.

12. Young thus contradicts Hitchcock's finding of European harmony in some of his works (see chapter 4).

CHAPTER 6

1. The members of Intermodulation and Gentle Fire would jointly perform works by Stockhausen for the BBC Proms of 1969. See www.bbc.co.uk/proms /archive/search/1960s/1969/august-21/8067.

2. The inventory was no longer limited to the "most prominent electronic music studios in existence in 1961" (Davies 1968b, iii).

3. The "advisory council" of the *Electronic Music Review* included not only Davies but also Lowell Cross, author of the bibliography of electronic music (1968). Other members were Larry Austin, the editor of a California journal on avant-garde music, *Source: Music of the Avant Garde* (see Austin and Kahn [2001]), as well as Oliveros, a former classmate of Young's and Riley's, then on the faculty of the music department at University of California, San Diego. Finally, Young himself belonged to the council (see *Electronic Music Review* 4 [October 1967]: 2–4).

4. Strange had already mentioned Reich in *Music Educators Journal* (1969), where he associated him with Young. This comparison, however was fortuitous: Strange was not so much seeking to link them as to defend their place (as well as that of Brant) within the music establishment. The composers' lack of interest in melodic relations should not, he argued, exclude their works from "tradition"; these composers had, after all, been schooled in well-established musical concepts. Each had continued to work within the tradition by developing these ancient

concepts (1969, 39). The following generation, he added, might in turn be educated via established musical concepts, including those of Young, Brant, and Reich.

5. His colleague Barney Childs also composed with audience participation in mind (Schwartz 1973, 165).

CHAPTER 7

1. Although he arrived on the contemporary music scene later than his two colleagues, Reich had nonetheless been active since at least 1963, the year he composed a series of soundtracks for the filmmaker Robert Nelson.

2. Although Riley was primarily active in New York from 1965 to 1969, Johnson, like many other critics, grouped him with New York rather than California composers.

3. The piece was performed at the Museum of Modern Art on December 3, 1971.

4. See especially the articles titled "Terry Riley Returns to Tonality," "Philip Glass in Twelve Parts," and "A La Monte Young Diary: April 1974" (repr. in Johnson 1991, 45, 79, 82).

5. Riley was an exception, in some respects bridging hypnotic music and jazz. Tom Johnson, "Terry Riley Returns to Tonality," *Village Voice*, September 12, 1973 (repr. in Johnson 1991, 45).

6. See *New York Times*, March 21, 1971, 9.

CHAPTER 8

1. In his "Notes on Music and Dance" from 1973, Reich again objected to Cage, this time for not focusing enough on "the basic desire for regular rhythmic movement," to which he himself was advocating a return (in Reich 1974, 43).

2. Reich again expressed his negative views on improvisation in two program notes, from 1969 and 1974 (see Reich 1974, 46, 52).

3. Also in 1973, Reich argued in his "Notes on Music and Dance" that rock gave only a superficial response to "the human desire for regular rhythmic movement" (in Reich 1974, 41).

4. See Reich's "Notes on Compositions 1965-1973" (in Reich 1974, 49-71).

5. It was also for economic reasons, says Reich, that he decided to play his own music himself (1974, 56).

6. His essay "Music as a Gradual Process," for example, was included in an exhibition catalogue for the Whitney Museum of American Arts in 1969 (Tucker and Monte 1969), translated in the French journal *VH-101* in 1970 (Reich 1970–71b), and reprinted in *Source: Music of the Avant-Garde* in 1971 (Reich [1971]

2011). "Some Optimistic Predictions about the Future of Music" was published in Elliott Schwartz's *Electronic Music* (1973, 249–50). "Postscript to a Brief Study of Balinese and African Music" in the *New York Times* (Reich 1973), "Notes on the Ensemble," and "Notes on Composition 1965–1973" were partly drawn from interviews with Nyman in the *Musical Times* (Nyman 1971b) and with Emily Wasserman in *Artforum* (Wasserman 1972).

7. See Austin (1975), Griffiths (1975), and Dickinson (1976) for enthusiastic reviews of Reich's book.

CHAPTER 9

1. The description of Nyman's background is from Pwyll ap Siôn's introduction to the *Collected Writings* (Nyman 2013, 1–23; see 1–2). On Nyman's progressive disenchantment with Stockhausen's music and his placing it in opposition to Cage's, see especially 7–11.

2. See also Nyman (2013, 13–19).

3. The journal, published by Boosey & Hawkes, would soon be edited by David Drew, who had recommended Nyman to the *Spectator* in 1968 and would obtain the commission for *Experimental Music*, which Nyman began to prepare in the early 1970s (see Nyman's foreword to Nyman 2013, xi–xii). At the time, the ties that bound Nyman, Cardew, and his fellow students together strengthened. Nyman, who collaborated on the music columns of the *Listener* with Tim Souster and Michael Parsons, took classes from Cardew at Morley College. He joined Cardew's Scratch Orchestra and then Bryars's Portsmouth Sinfonia; Brian Eno was a notable colleague in the latter.

4. Nyman, like Souster (1968–69) and Alan Beckett (1969), attempts to set the record straight. Some may indeed have been misled, the author admits, by the concert publicity, hoping to see bridges built between the two worlds, particularly with Riley and his alternative culture. But such was not the case, beyond hearing the composer's influence in Souster's *Triple Music* or in Soft Machine's new style inspired by Riley's *A Rainbow in a Curved Air* (1970, 203).

5. Riley and Young are "well known to English audiences," affirms Nyman, aware of the promotional work undertaken by his predecessors (1971, 85).

6. See the enthusiastic review of the concert by Brian Dennis (1972).

7. For the emergence of the idea of experimental music as well as the meaning of that term for composers and critics over the course of the twentieth century, see Mauceri (1997) and Beal (2006). On the construction of the experimental music canon, see also Piekut (2011).

8. This process contrasts with the approach "prescribing a defined time-object whose materials, structuring and relationships are calculated and arranged in advance" (Nyman 1974, 23).

9. When discussing Young's Fluxus period, Nyman emphasizes the pieces that rely essentially on the use of "sustained sounds" and "extended durations" (Nyman 1974, 140).

10. *Pendulum Music* is an installation for microphones that swing in a pendulum motion above speakers, creating feedback.

11. Along the same lines, Nyman argued that the "psycho-acoustic by-products" resulting from the composer's music were "not directly controlled or even foreseen by Reich" (1974, 155).

CHAPTER 10

1. Hitchcock also wrote of the composer's harmonic work, however, as in his 1965 article.

2. At this time Hitchcock was no longer writing about Young's music in terms of the Eastern harmonic developments he recounted in the *Musical Quarterly* (1965, 538–39); he now focused on Young's "static" work, *Composition 1960 #7* (1969, 248).

3. Among the book's fans was Gilbert Chase, who had sought to highlight the value of American popular music genres in his own work the year before. In Chase's prediction, "No one with a serious interest in contemporary music and aesthetics will remain indifferent to this remarkable achievement" (1968, 227).

4. On Thomson's "patriotic" work, see Tommasini (2001).

5. To elaborate his concept of minimal art, Cope drew partly on the essay "Boredom and Danger" by Dick Higgins, which had been published in the journal *Source* (Higgins 1969). Higgins, however, associated Eric Andersen rather than Young with this minimalism. Moreover, his essay deals less with a minimal aesthetic than with an aesthetic of "boredom," rooted in Satie and essentially coming to fruition in the Fluxus movement, with artists such as Brecht, Mac Low, Young, and Higgins himself. Cope's book thus reshaped Higgins's concept to associate it with Young and Cage. He included the never-ending chord repetitions of Harold Budd (*Lovely Thing*, 1969); the exact quotation of a work from the past or its verbatim reprise, as in George Rochberg and Paul Ignace; and finally the "modal" panorama of Riley's *In C* (114–15). Higgins's essay did not mark the first appearance of Young in *Source*. Over its five years of existence, from 1967 to 1972, the journal published by Larry Austin—a California composer and founder of the free improvisation group New Music Ensemble—regularly mentioned as well as published works by Young, Riley, and Reich, helping to spread their names. On Larry Austin and *Source*, see Austin and Kahn (2011, ix–xiii).

6. *In C* is nonetheless mentioned among the last works of a movement that Cope describes as "Antimusic and Return" (1971, 115).

7. Chase presents Salzman as a major representative of the new music theater in his entry on the United States in Vinton's dictionary (Chase 1974, 787). Also in this entry, Chase says nothing of the music of Young, Reich, and Glass and only briefly mentions Riley.

8. This music is distinctive in that it allows the listener, now "active," to define his own rhythm, asserts Rzewski (1974), who associates his own music in the group Musica Elettronica Viva with the work of Young, Riley, Reich, and Glass (624).

9. With the inclusion of minimalism, four movements now close Salzman's survey of twentieth-century developments. The other three are the new pop culture (Salzman 1974, 189-91), sound as image (192-93), and multimedia and music theater (194ff). Salzman would gradually come to be known as a major representative of the last.

10. Young's name appears in almost all the issues of *Source*. He is a descendant of the "Cage Group" with the Theatre of Eternal Music, according to Gordon Mumma in the third issue, from January 1968 (Austin and Kahn 2011, 95); he is associated with Fluxus for Higgins in the fifth issue, January 1969 (179); he represents the "illusion of continuity and eternity," again according to Higgins, in the seventh issue, January 1970 (239); and members of the group Fylkingen list his name in the context of mixed-media works in the eighth issue, July 1970 (264). For his part, Riley is mentioned in an editorial by Austin in July 1969 as a representative, along with Young and Jon Hassel, of a change to the "concert ritual" in which the audience applauds, approves, and appreciates, while the performer gives himself over to his feelings and his concentration (289).

11. Bertram Turetzky, following Robert Erickson, applies the term *solo ensemble* to pieces "which use a combination of live and pre-recorded music," such as Reich's *Violin Phase* (Turetzky 1970, 66-67).

12. Ewen's *The World of Twentieth-Century Music*, published in 1968 by Prentice-Hall, makes no mention of Young, Riley, Reich, and Glass.

13. John Cale, a former member of the Theatre of Eternal Music, had joined the Velvet Underground some years before.

14. For a detailed history of the discourses constructed around connections between the Velvet Underground and Young, see Levaux (2014).

15. "Loop" consists of a bass riff played in a loop and sporadically interrupted by feedback noises; it was published in the third issue of *Aspen* magazine (1966).

16. Peter Yates, who gave a history of the violin in *Twentieth Century Music* (1967, 325)—without according any place to jazz—was one such critic, Pleasants writes (1969, 229).

17. Schaeffer himself claimed the label *experimental* several times in the 1950s. See especially Schaeffer (1957). See Kahn (1999, 123-39) on the institutional support that Schaeffer received in postwar France.

18. The magazine contains a letter from Glass (Glass 1970-71); a series of notes on the *Dream House* installations (Young and Zazeela 1970-71a) taken from

Young's *Selected Writings* (Young and Zazeela 1969); an article by Young translated from the *Village Voice* and dedicated to Pandit Pran Nath (Young and Zazeela 1970–71b); as well as Reich's notes for *Pendulum Music* and a translation of his "Music as a Gradual Process" (Reich 1970–71a; 1970–71b), which had appeared in various collections and were subsequently republished in Reich (1974).

CHAPTER 11

1. At the time Reich, in particular, had on various occasions renounced electronics (see chapter 8).

2. Ashley, Behrman, Lucier, and Mumma had themselves confirmed their group identity as part of the Sonic Arts Union.

3. In 1978 the *Painted Bride Quarterly* announced the book's publication by Schirmer (Gordon 1977). It would not, however, be published until 2000. See Ashley (2000, 6–24), on the history of the publication of *Music with Roots in the Aether*.

4. See especially Childs's 1979–80 article in *Perspectives of New Music*, a journal for which he subsequently became associate editor.

5. The expression *live electronics* had been used in *The Composer*, to which Childs had contributed some years before, and was taken up by David Cope (1971) to characterize Riley's music.

CHAPTER 12

1. In the *Musical Times* of November 1971, some six months after celebrating his former teacher and current colleague White, whose music he lauded as prophetic (Dennis 1971a), Dennis called Cardew's *The Great Learning* "one of the finest and most significant works of recent times" (1971b, 1068).

2. This aspect also, "paradoxically," links systemic composition to the music of great "horizontal and vertical complexity" by Messiaen, White's mentor (Dennis 1974, 1036).

3. The difference of medium, Parsons concedes, nonetheless precludes an exact equivalence between these two modes of expression on a material and perceptual level (Parsons 1976, 816).

CHAPTER 13

1. The division that Nyman should have made, writes Smalley, is not one between postserialists and experimentalists but rather one between those who

think "*in* music" and those who think "*about* music." On that basis, the difference between Cage and, for example, Babbitt, would be smaller than it seems at first (Smalley 1975a, 25).

2. In the present chapter some of the subjects raised in chapters 11 and 12 are considered in closer connection with Nyman's work.

3. Indeed, *Composition #10* is precisely an instruction requiring the performer to "draw a straight line and follow it." Dennis, in particular, suggests the parallel with "hard-edged geometric art" (1974, 1036).

4. In this article Nyman again excluded Alvin Lucier from the musical panorama that he had constructed in *Experimental Music,* this time by presenting his work "as an alternative to repetitive, systems music" (Nyman 2013, 294).

CHAPTER 14

1. A forum on the subject had taken place on October 28, 1976, in Paris, with presentations by Caux as well as the poet and essayist Marcelin Pleynet and the musicologist Ivanka Stoïanova (see *Musique en jeu* 26 [1977]: 62–63).

2. Griffiths was referring to Berberian's *Morsicat(h)y* (1969), a piano piece for right hand only that was based on Morse code.

3. At that time Ligeti was the composer who was taking the leap from serialism to melody (Griffiths 1981, 283); certain of his works have a "proximity" to those of Reich and Riley.

4. Griffiths makes no reference to *Come Out* in his chapter on music and politics, where he mentions Rzewski's work (Griffiths 1981, 185).

CHAPTER 15

1. Indeed, Reich had recently announced that he had abandoned the medium. See chapter 8.

2. The translation is titled *American Minimal Music: La Monte Young, Terry Riley, Steve Reich, Philip Glass* (Mertens 1983). Throughout this chapter, references to Mertens's 1980 book cite the 1983 English translation.

3. In 1971, Caux was aware of the connections between Reich and the New York art world; indeed, some of Caux's writings on Reich drew on the catalogue for the exhibition *Anti-Illusion* at the Whitney Museum, in which Reich had participated (Tucker and Monte 1969).

4. See especially a review of the English edition: Kroeger (1988, 241).

5. In his preface to Mertens's book, Nyman again asserts that the group he described in 1974 is only "loosely connected" (Mertens 1983, 7).

6. For other authors Webern represented the height of complexity. Just as he did with Webern's music, Mertens would also reconfigure another supposed influence of Young's: the electronic music of Richard Maxfield, which for Mertens also contained static elements (Mertens 1983, 22).

7. Indeed, it was "after he had finished this training," Mertens reports, that Young "began to write music" (Mertens 1983, 19).

8. The extent of Young's so-called repetitive phase is theoretical, because Mertens gives no information about the way that Young used repetition during that period. From *The Tortoise, His Dreams and Journeys* to *The Well-Tuned Piano* or *Drift Studies*, the focus is on Young's work with drones or harmonics, while the subject of repetition mysteriously disappears.

9. Young even tended to dissociate himself from Cage, according to Mertens, in that he focused on a single musical event while Cage dealt with different events simultaneously in a specific period of time (Mertens 1983, 25).

10. Here Mertens draws on Young's *Lecture 1960* (Young 1965).

11. Even though he has just stated that Young's third and longest stylistic period was "repetitive," Mertens subsequently asserts, relying almost word-for-word on Nyman (Nyman 1974, 18), that this repetition was marginal in the composer's work. He later concludes, based on Young's own comment in an interview with Kostelanetz (referring to Indian music or that of Coltrane rather than Young's own work [Kostelanetz 1968, 187]), that repetition serves as a controlling mechanism for Young (Mertens 1983, 36).

12. Mertens thereby distances Young from Cage's indeterminate aesthetic. In the same way, Riley's *In C*, owing to its attention to form, is said to be a work that limits "improvisational freedom [of] the performers" (1983, 42).

13. Unlike in the Webern–Young linkage, Mertens does not explain what unites Stockhausen and Riley and offers no hypothesis as to the former's influence in terms of repetition in the latter's work.

14. Mertens does not consider the role of popular music in compositions ranging from *Five-Legged Stool* (1961) to *Persian Surgery Dervishes* (1970–71), which he places after the development of Riley's language and not before (36).

15. On Adorno's writings and commentary on his work, see especially the bibliography in Paddison 2001.

16. Stoïanova (1977) placed emphasis on repetition in American minimalism as well, in her case to help elaborate a Freudian connection.

17. This antidialectical movement culminated with Cage, Mertens writes, but Cage's orientation is completely absent from repetitive music (Mertens 1983, 87).

18. See Schnebel's 1972 article on Young (translated into French the following year in *Musique en jeu* [Schnebel 1973]).

19. The title translates as "From serialism to minimalism: the development of a mannerism. The case of Goeyvaerts, 'minimalist avant la lettre.'"

20. Sabbe himself was initially a specialist in serialism. See his thesis, *Het muzikale serialisme als techniek en als denkmethode* (Sabbe 1977).

21. The concept of minimal music, we read in Fahres's introduction to the collection, was formulated by Nyman (Fahres 1982b).

22. Boulez emphasized the irreversible nature of serialism (Sabbe 1982b, 1).

23. The gist of Sabbe's argument linking serial music with minimalism is on pages 1 and 2 of his article, where he writes that Webern emphasized repetition and sound "as a quality in itself," as well as on pages 5 and 6, where we read that Schoenberg's *Klangfarbenmelodie*, Goeyvaerts's *Nr. 3* and *Nr. 4*, Feldman's isolated treatment of sounds, and Young's *Composition 1960 #7* all reflected "the notion that the whole is contained in the singular: a series, a chord, a sound."

24. The approach aimed at integrating Cage into the history of the genre is doubtless "complementary," Sabbe affirms (1982b, 4), but minimal music "has nothing to do with the composer's 'aleatoric music'" (10).

25. The bibliography to Fahres's compilation includes numerous references to the works of Lyotard, who had synthesized part of his thought in his 1979 book *The Postmodern Condition* (Lyotard [1979] 1984).

CHAPTER 16

1. See especially Jameson's lecture at the Whitney Museum in autumn 1982 (Jameson 1982).

2. Adorno did not directly discuss repetition per se, as Middleton notes (1983, 241), but rather a "standardization [in popular songs] that extends from the most general features to the most specific ones. Best known is the rule that the chorus consists of thirty-two bars and that the range is limited to one octave and one note" (Adorno [1941] 2000, para. 3).

3. See, among many other writings in musicology, Beard and Gloag (2005, 141), which views Lyotard as the founder of the concept of postmodernism.

4. On *Musique en jeu* and its place within French avant-garde intellectual and art circles in the 1970s, see Donin (2010).

5. "It is not novelty that gives rise to *jouissance*, but a subtle balance between old or known elements that are constantly repeated and new elements that create an event," writes Avron (1972, 106), following Lyotard ([1971] 2012).

6. Stoïanova is alluding to Gadamer (2013, 151).

CHAPTER 17

1. See the manifesto on the back cover of the first volume of *Popular Music* in 1981.

2. The use of repetition in certain "'minimalist' groups" or its practice "for 'aesthetic' reasons" is beyond the scope of the article, Middleton writes (1983, 253n).

3. In his article Middleton does not emphasize the difference that Barthes makes between the *jouissance* repetition of traditional musics and the "humiliated repetition" of mass culture, where "the superficial forms are varied" (Barthes 1975, 42).

4. Young was interviewed in the context of this article.

5. Jones, a member of the Rolling Stones, had released *Brian Jones Presents the Pipes of Pan at Joujouka* in 1968 on the group's label.

6. Palmer returned to Jajouka in 1973 accompanied by the saxophonist Ornette Coleman. There they recorded a series of tracks, including "Midnight Sunrise," which would appear on Ornette Coleman's 1977 album *Dancing in Your Head* (Horizon, SP-722). In 1988 Palmer published "Into the Mystic" in *Rolling Stone*, in which he related his trance experiences in the Moroccan mountains (2009, 350–61).

7. In *Deep Blues* (Palmer 1982), one of his "most important books" (Rockwell 2002), Palmer presents the blues through connections extending from Africa to the Mississippi Delta to Chicago. For a biography of Palmer, see Rockwell (2002). On the East-West connection and the effort to transcend cultural hierarchies in his writings, see Anthony DeCurtis's introduction to Palmer (2009, xiv–xv), as well as Palmer's "What Is American Music?" (1975, reprinted in Palmer 2009, 1–12).

8. Palmer was also one of the few authors to bring out Young's connections to jazz in his youth and to present the Theatre of Eternal Music as a group in which he improvised on solo saxophone (1975; Palmer 2009, 395).

9. In 1983, in the *New York Times*, Young even became a "pioneering minimalist composer" (Palmer 1983, 17).

10. *Come Out* (1966) is based on the repetition of a phrase uttered by Daniel Hamm, a young African American beaten by the police during the Harlem riots in 1964.

11. The following year he called Reich's music "minimal" (Henahan 1970).

12. Rockwell mentions in particular "minimal, pop, op, concept, kinetic and process painting and sculpture" (1970c); see also Rockwell (1970b) on the analogy with the visual arts.

13. For Rockwell, however, the music of Riley and Young was stylistically dissimilar to that of Reich and Glass (Rockwell 1973c; 1974b). The first two focused on Indian music and the teachings of their "guru" Pandit Prân Nath (Rockwell 1974b). The latter two, in particular Glass, even tended to abandon the austere minimal aesthetic that had characterized their earlier pieces (Rockwell 1974d, 21).

14. "As opposed to avant-garde jazz or 'serious' music," Rockwell wrote in 1977, "rock offers clean-cut, exactly focused formal clarity" (Rockwell 1977a, 11).

15. The content of minimal music is largely the same over the dozen years of Rockwell's reviews: even though at the end of the 1970s, we read, Reich and Glass

did enrich their vocabulary in terms of texture, harmony, and melody (see Rockwell 1977b; 1982; 1983a), and even though "post-minimalism" now seems to prevail (Rockwell 1983b), the art of the New York composers is that of repetition and simplicity.

CHAPTER 18

1. See Cage's interview in Reynolds (1979, 576-77).
2. See Young's interview in Reinhard (1982-83).

CHAPTER 19

1. On formalism, see especially Fink (1998, 161).
2. The sole exception was a two-part article by K. Robert Schwarz on the music of Reich (Schwarz 1980-81 and 1981-82).
3. Pulse is understood here as the exact opposite of pause.
4. On the history of *Perspectives of New Music,* see Berger, Boritz, and Tichenor (1987); Berry (2006); and Boretz (2012).
5. The authors announced this intention in their opening to the first issue (Berger and Boretz 1962, 4).
6. Among the many studies discussing new musicology or postmodern musicology, see Beard and Gloag (2005, 92-93), for a brief introduction, or J. D. Kramer (1995); Fink (1998); and Cook and Everist (1999) for more substantial works.
7. See especially Boulez's declarations in Reich (1987); Fink (2005), 19; and Gann (2010).
8. Boulez's comments are from a translation of an interview he had given two years earlier in the journal *Le Débat* (see Boulez, Menger, and Bernard 1990, 6).
9. The first minimalist forum, in *Perspectives of New Music* 30, no. 2 (summer 1992), consists of "Transpositional Combination of Beat-Class Sets in Steve Reich's Phase-Shifting Music," by Richard Cohn, and "Generating Modal Sequences (A Remote Approach to Minimal Music)," by Anatol Vieru. The latter deals not with the music of the New York composers but rather with "the usage of the 'sieve of Eratosthenes' (an ancient algorithm for finding prime numbers) in music," which, according to the author, approaches the use of loops (178-79). The second minimalist forum, in *Perspectives of New Music* 31, no. 1 (winter 1993), contains "The Minimalist Aesthetic in the Plastic Arts and in Music," by Jonathan W. Bernard, and "La Monte Young's *The Well-Tuned Piano,*" by Kyle Gann.
10. See chapter 8 of the present volume and "Music as a Gradual Process" (Reich 1974, 9-11).

11. For an introduction to musical set theory, see Andreatta and Schaub (2003).

12. The lecture would finally be published in the collection *Classic Essays on Twentieth-Century Music,* ed. Richard Kostelanetz (Hitchcock 1996).

CHAPTER 20

1. "He cannot be incognizant of the potency of his judgments, opinions," writes Barkin (1983–84, 536).

2. Rockwell's book would garner further accolades both within the academic establishment (for example, a review by the American music scholar Peter Dickinson (1986) and beyond. The *New York Times,* his employer, included it in its list of "notable books of the year" (December 4, 1983, 38) and sanctioned Rockwell's "report" on the collapse of musical hierarchies.

3. Bergman founded the Planet Rock series for Quill, the publisher of *Recombinant Do Re Mi.* Horn notably wrote a piece of "audio-musical theater" in collaboration with Phil Kline, the singer and guitarist of the no-wave group the Del-Byzanteens (which included Jim Jarmusch and occasionally John Lurie).

4. See especially Strickland (1987) and the introduction to Strickland (1991) for his views on jazz.

5. In particular, see Strickland's insistent return to the question on 114–15.

6. See Strickland (1993, 17–118 and 257–80) on painting and in particular sculpture.

CHAPTER 21

1. Paul Griffiths refers the reader to the entry for "System" instead (see the end of chapter 12, this volume). Five years later, however, in an article in the *Musical Times,* Griffiths too used the term *minimal* for the American composers' music (Griffiths 1985).

CHAPTER 22

1. On the definition of postmodernism, see especially Bertens (1995, 3). On the first associations between minimalism and postmodernity, see chapter 16. For a brief introduction to postmodernism in music, see Gloag (2012).

2. Kramer was to become known precisely for a style with resolutely "postmodern" traits (see Chute 2001).

3. When Lyotard mentions minimalism in "The Inaudible: Music and Post-modernity," he refers to the aleatoric procedure of Cage (Lyotard [1996] 2012, 211).

4. See also Stoïanova (1977) and Mertens (1980), as well as Rockwell's articles in the *New York Times* from the late 1970s.

5. See Fink (2004) for a critical reflection on the concept of postminimalism.

6. On ambient music, see especially Gagne (1990) and Toop (1995).

7. See Karnes (2017, 9–13), on the use of the label *holy minimalism*.

8. Minimalism was absent from the 1983 edition.

9. The 2002 edition was essentially augmented with writings by Reich on his individual works and interviews with the composer. These texts are presented in chronological order for the period 1965–2000.

EPILOGUE

1. As a recent Ipsos study surveying fourteen countries showed, a great many people still mistrust science. See *3M State of Science Index*, www.3m.com/3M /en_US/state-of-science-index-survey/.

References

Articles from *Grove Music Online* (www.oxfordmusiconline.com/grovemusic) are cited with the years 2001, 2002, or 2004 (the respective publication dates of the most recent editions of *New Grove Dictionary of Music and Musicians, New Grove Dictionary of Jazz,* and *New Grove Dictionary of Opera*), unless the website specifies a different publication date. These articles, as well as all the other online sources listed below, were last consulted on November 1, 2019.

Adams, Simon. 2001. "AMM." *Grove Music Online* in Oxford Music Online, Oxford University Press.

Adorno, Theodor W. (1941) 2000. "On Popular Music." *Soundscapes.info: Journal on Media Culture* 2 (January), www.icce.rug.nl/~soundscapes /DATABASES/SWA/On_popular_music_1.shtml.

———. (1949) 2005. *Philosophy of New Music.* Translated by Robert Hullot-Kentor. Minneapolis: University of Minnesota Press.

Akrich, Madeleine, Michel Callon, and Bruno Latour, eds. 2006. *Sociologie de la traduction: Textes fondateurs.* Paris: Presses de l'Ecole des Mines.

Ammer, Christine. 1995. *The HarperCollins Dictionary of Music.* New York: HarperPerennial.

Andreatta, Moreno, and Stéphan Schaub. 2003. "Une introduction à la Set Theory: Les concepts à la base des théories d'Allen Forte et de David Lewin." *Musurgia* 10, no. 1: 73–92.

Apel, Willi. 1969. *Harvard Dictionary of Music.* Cambridge, MA: Belknap Press of Harvard University Press.

Appleton, Jon H. 1979. "Commentary I: Electronic Music: Questions of Style and Compositional Technique." *Musical Quarterly* 65, no. 1 (January): 103–10.

ap Siôn, Pwyll. 2007. *The Music of Michael Nyman: Texts, Contexts and Intertexts.* Aldershot, England: Ashgate.

ap Siôn, Pwyll, and Tristian Evans. 2007. Introduction to *Programme of Events,* First International Conference on Music and Minimalism, Bangor University Wales, August 31–September 2. http://minimalismsociety.org/wp-content/uploads/2016/01/Conference-booklet.pdf.

ap Siôn, Pwyll, Keith Potter, and Kyle Gann, eds. 2013. *The Ashgate Research Companion to Minimalist and Postminimalist Music.* Aldershot: Ashgate.

Arnold, Denis, ed. 1984. *The New Oxford Companion to Music.* Oxford: Oxford University Press.

Aronowitz, Stanley, John Brenkman, and Fredric Jameson. 1979. "Prospectus." *Social Text,* no. 1 (Winter): 3–6.

Ashley, Robert, ed. 2000. *Music with Roots in the Aether.* Cologne: MusikTexte.

Attinello, Paul. 2001. "Schnebel, Dieter (Wolfgang)." *Grove Music Online* in Oxford Music Online, Oxford University Press.

Austin, Larry, and Douglas Kahn, eds. 2011. *Source: Music of the Avant-Garde, 1966–1973.* Berkeley: University of California Press.

Austin, William W. 1966. *Music in the Twentieth Century: From Debussy through Stravinsky.* New York: W. W. Norton.

———. 1975. Review of *Writings about Music,* by Steve Reich. *Notes: The Quarterly Journal of the Music Library Association* 31, no. 4 (June): 780.

Avron, Dominique. 1972. "Notes pour introduire une métapsychologie de la musique." *Musique en jeu,* no. 9 (November): 102–10.

Babbitt, Milton. 1955. "Some Aspects of Twelve-Tone Composition." *Score,* no. 12 (June): 53–61.

Baker, Kenneth. 1988. *Minimalism: Art of Circumstance.* New York: Abbeville Press.

Ballantine, Christopher. 1977. "Towards an Aesthetic of Experimental Music." *Musical Quarterly* 63, no. 2 (April): 224–46.

Barkin, Helen. 1983–84. Review of *All American Music: Composition in the Late Twentieth Century,* by John Rockwell. *Perspectives of New Music* 22, no. 1/2 (Autumn–Summer): 533–44.

Barnes, Barry. 1974. *Scientific Knowledge and Sociological Theory.* London: Routledge K. Paul.

Barthes, Roland. 1975. *The Pleasure of the Text.* New York: Hill and Wang.

Basso, Alberto. 1984. *Dizionario Enciclopedico Universale della Musica e dei Musicisti.* Turin: Unione Tipografico-Editrice Torinese.

Battcock, Gregory. 1968. *Minimal Art: A Critical Anthology.* New York: E. P. Dutton.

Béar, Liza, and Willoughby Sharp. 1972. "Phil Glass: An Interview in Two Parts." *Avalanche*, no. 5 (Summer): 26–35.

Beal, Amy C. 2006. *New Music, New Allies: American Experimental Music in West Germany from the Zero Hour to Reunification*. Berkeley: University of California Press.

Beard, David, and Kenneth Gloag. 2005. "Postmodernism." In *Musicology: The Key Concepts*, 106–9. Oxon: Routledge.

Beckett, Alan. 1969. "Mapping Pop." *New Left Review* 1, no. 54 (March–April): 82–84.

Bellows, George Kent. 1957. "John Tasker Howard." *Notes: The Quarterly Journal of the Music Library Association* 14, no. 4 (September): 501–6.

Bennett, David. 2011. "Music." In *The Lyotard Dictionary*, edited by Stuart Sim, 147–49. Edinburgh: Edinburgh University Press.

Berger, Arthur, and Benjamin Boretz. 1962. "Editorial Note." *Perspectives of New Music* 1, no. 1 (Autumn): 4–5.

Berger, Arthur, Benjamin Boretz, and Marjorie Tichenor. 1987. "A Conversation about *Perspectives*." *Perspectives of New Music* 25, no. 1/2 (Summer): 592–607.

Bergman, Billy, and Richard Horn. 1985. *Recombinant Do Re Mi: Frontiers of the Rock Era*. New York: Quill.

Bernard, Jonathan W. 1993. "The Minimalist Aesthetic in the Plastic Arts and in Music." *Perspectives of New Music* 31, no. 1 (Winter): 86–132.

———. 2003. "Minimalism, Postminimalism, and the Resurgence of Tonality in Recent American Music." *American Music* 21, no. 1 (Spring): 112–33.

Berry, David Carson. 2006. "*Journal of Music Theory* under Allen Forte's Editorship." *Journal of Music Theory* 50, no. 1 (Spring): 7–23.

Bertens, Hans. 1995. *The Idea of the Postmodern: A History*. London: Routledge.

Blaikley, D. J., William C. Smith, and Peter Ward Jones. 2001. "Boosey & Hawkes." *Grove Music Online* in Oxford Music Online, Oxford University Press.

Blanks, Fred R. 1970. "Reports: Australia." *Musical Times* 111, no. 1531 (September): 917–18.

Bloor, David. 1976. *Knowledge and Social Imagery*. London: Routledge.

Boretz, Benjamin. 2012. "The Zeitgeist of *Perspectives*, ab origine." *Perspectives of New Music* 50, no. 1–2 (Winter–Summer): 9–17.

Boretz, Benjamin, and Edward T. Cone, eds. 1971. *Perspectives on American Composers*. New York: W. W. Norton.

Born, Georgina. 1995. *Rationalizing Culture: IRCAM, Boulez, and the Institutionalization of the Musical Avant-Garde*. Berkeley: University of California Press.

Borroff, Edith. 1971. *Music in Europe and the United States: A History*. Englewood Cliffs, NJ: Prentice-Hall.

Boulez, Pierre, Pierre-Michel Menger, and Jonathan W. Bernard. 1990. "From the Domaine Musical to IRCAM." *Perspectives of New Music* 28, no. 1 (Winter): 6–19.

Bracefield, Hilary. 1988. "Editorial." *Contact,* no. 33 (Autumn): 4–5.

Brindle, Reginald Smith. 1975. *The New Music: The Avant-Garde since 1945.* New York: Oxford University Press.

———. 1987. *The New Music: The Avant-Garde since 1945.* 2nd ed. New York: Oxford University Press.

Broder, Nathan. 1966. "Vereinigte Staaten: C. Nach 1920." In *Die Musik in Geschichte und Gegenwart: Allgemeine Enzyklopädie der Musik* 13: 1475–79. Kassel: Bärenreiter.

Burge, David. 1976. Review of *Spaces,* by Tom Johnson. *Notes: The Quarterly Journal of the Music Library Association* 32, no. 4: 879.

Cage, John. 1955. "Experimental Music." *Score,* no. 12 (June): 65–68.

———. 1960. "Winter Music." *New Departures,* no. 2/3: 57–77.

———. 1961. *Silence: Lectures and Writings.* Middletown, CT: Wesleyan University Press.

———. 1968. *A Year from Monday.* Middletown, CT: Wesleyan University Press.

Callerdo, Francesco, and Charles Girard. 2011. "La neutralité." In *Philosophie des sciences humaines: Concepts et problèmes,* edited by Florence Hulak and Charles Girard, 243–72. Paris: Vrin.

Callon, Michel, Pierre Lascoumes, and Yannick Barthe. 2011. *Acting in an Uncertain World: An Essay on Technical Democracy.* Translated by Graham Burchell. Cambridge, MA: MIT Press.

Candé, Roland de. 2000. *Nouveau dictionnaire de la musique.* Rev. ed. Paris: Seuil.

Cardew, Cornelius. 1959a. "Piano Piece." *New Departures,* no. 1 (Summer): 49–52.

———. 1959b. "Musical Space." *New Departures,* no. 1 (Summer): 53–56.

———. 1961a. "Notation: Interpretation, etc." *Tempo,* no. 58 (Summer): 21–33.

———. 1961b. "Report on Stockhausen's 'Carré.'" *Musical Times* 102, no. 1424 (October): 619–22.

———. 1962. "In re La Monte Young." *New Departures,* no. 4: 75–77.

———. 1964. "Cage and Cunningham." *Musical Times* 105, no. 1459 (September): 659–60.

———. 1966. "One Sound: La Monte Young." *Musical Times* 107, no. 1485 (November): 959–60.

———. 1967a. "The Sounds of La Monte Young." *London Magazine* 7, no. 1 (April): 88–90.

———. 1967b. "Sextet. The Tiger's Mind." *Musical Times* 108, no. 1492 (June): 527–30.

———. 1968. "Sitting in the Dark." *Musical Times* 109, no. 1501 (March): 233–34.

———. 1969. "A Scratch Orchestra: Draft Constitution." *Musical Times* 110, no. 1516 (June): 617–19.

———. 1971. *Treatise Handbook*. London: Peters.

———. 1974. *Stockhausen Serves Imperialism*. London: Latimer New Dimensions Limited.

Carl, Robert. 2009. *Terry Riley's "In C."* New York: Oxford University Press.

Cassaro, James P. 2001. "Salzman, Eric." *Grove Music Online* in Oxford Music Online, Oxford University Press.

Caux, Daniel. 1969. "La nouvelle musique américaine contemporaine." *Chroniques de l'art vivant*, no. 5 (November): 28–29.

———. 1970. "Terry Riley." *Chroniques de l'art vivant*, no. 13 (August–September): 27.

———. 1971a. "Live/Electric Music: Steve Reich." *Chroniques de l'art vivant*, no. 18 (March): 25.

———. 1971b. "The Mood of Terry Riley." *Chroniques de l'art vivant*, no. 25 (November): 26–27.

———. 1972. "La Monte Young." *Chroniques de l'art vivant*, no. 30: 24–32.

———. 1973. "Phil Glass." *Chroniques de l'art vivant*, no. 39 (May): 24–27.

Chase, Gilbert. 1955. *America's Music: From the Pilgrims to the Present*. New York: McGraw-Hill.

———. 1968. Review of *Music, the Arts, and Ideas: Patterns and Predictions in Twentieth-Century Culture*, by Leonard B. Meyer. *Notes: The Quarterly Journal of the Music Library Association* 25, no. 2 (December): 225–27.

———. 1974. "United States." In *Dictionary of Contemporary Music*, edited by John Vinton, 781–88. New York: E. P. Dutton.

———. 1987. *America's Music: From the Pilgrims to the Present*. 3rd ed. Urbana: University of Illinois Press.

Chase, Gilbert, Charles Seeger, Alan Jabbour, and Eileen Southern. 1980. "United States of America." In *The New Grove Dictionary of Music and Musicians*, edited by Stanley Sadie, 20:424–52. London: Macmillan.

Childs, Barney. 1966. "Articulation in Sound Structures: Some Notes toward an Analytic." *Texas Studies in Literature and Language* 8, no. 3 (Autumn): 423–45.

———. 1969. "Indeterminacy and Theory: Some Notes." *Composer* 1, no. 1: 15–34.

———. 1974. "Indeterminacy." In *Dictionary of Contemporary Music*, edited by John Vinton, 336–39. New York: E. P. Dutton.

———. 1975a. "Directions in American Composition since the Second World War." *Music Educators Journal* 61, no. 7 (March): 34–35.

———. 1975b. Review of *Experimental Music*, by Michael Nyman. *Music Educators Journal* 61, no. 9 (May): 79–80, 82.

——. 1977. "To the Editor." *Notes: The Quarterly Journal of the Music Library Association* 33, no. 3 (March): 723.

——. 1979–1980. "The University of Redlands New Music Ensemble." *Perspectives of New Music* 18, no. 1/2 (Autumn–Summer): 517–19.

——. 1989. "Aporia as Parataxis or 'I Had One of Them Once, but the Wheels Came Off.'" Paper delivered at the Society of Composers Twenty-third Annual Conference, University of Kansas, April 27–May 1, 1988. *Ex tempore* 5, no. 1 (Spring–Summer), n.p. www.ex-tempore.org/CHILDS.htm.

Chute, James. 2001. "Kramer, Jonathan D." *Grove Music Online* in Oxford Music Online, Oxford University Press.

Clark, Thomas. 2001. "Austin, Larry (Don)." *Grove Music Online* in Oxford Music Online, Oxford University Press.

Clarke, Henry Leland. 1965. "Current Chronicle." *Musical Quarterly* 51, no. 3 (July): 530–60.

Coe, Robert. 1981. "Philip Glass Breaks Through." *New York Times*, October 25, 1981 117.

Cohn, Richard. 1992. "Transpositional Combination of Beat-Class Sets in Steve Reich's Phase-Shifting Music." *Perspectives of New Music* 30, no. 2 (Summer): 146–77.

Collaer, Paul. 1955. *La musique moderne.* Brussels: Elsevier.

——. 1961. *A History of Modern Music.* New York: Grosset & Dunlap.

Collaer, Paul, and Albert Vander Linden. 1960. *Atlas historique de la musique.* Paris: Elsevier.

Collins, Randall. 1998. *The Sociology of Philosophies: A Global Theory of Intellectual Change.* Cambridge, MA: Harvard University Press.

Collins, Harry, and Trevor Pinch. 1993. *The Golem: What You Should Know about Science.* Cambridge: Cambridge University Press.

Cook, Nicholas. 1999. "Analysing Performance and Performing Analysis." In *Rethinking Music,* edited by Nicholas Cook and Mark Everist, 239–61. Oxford: Oxford University Press.

Cook, Nicholas, and Mark Everist, eds. 1999. *Rethinking Music.* Oxford: Oxford University Press.

Cook, Nicholas, and Anthony Pople, eds. 2004. *The Cambridge History of Twentieth-Century Music.* Cambridge: Cambridge University Press.

Cope, David. 1969. "Soundhouse." *Composer* 1, no. 1: 48–49.

——. 1971. *New Directions in Music.* Dubuque, IA: Wm. C. Brown.

Covach, John. 1999. "Popular Music, Unpopular Musicology." In *Rethinking Music,* edited by Nicholas Cook and Mark Everist, 452–70. Oxford: Oxford University Press.

Crawford, Richard. 1984. "United States of America." In *The New Oxford Companion to Music,* edited by Denis Arnold, 1878–92. Oxford: Oxford University Press.

———. 1993. *The American Musical Landscape*. Berkeley: University of California Press.

———. 2001. *America's Musical Life: A History*. New York: W. W. Norton.

Cross, Lowell M. 1968. *A Bibliography of Electronic Music*. Toronto: University of Toronto Press.

Cummings, Conrad, and David Hicks. 1980–81. "Computer Music Conference in New York, 1980." *Perspectives of New Music* 19, no. 1/2 (Autumn–Summer): 442–48.

Dahlhaus, Carl. [1977] 1983. *Foundations of Music History*. Translated by J. Bradford Robinson. Cambridge: Cambridge University Press.

Davies, Hugh. 1964. "A Discography of Electronic Music and Musique Concrète." *Recorded Sound*, no. 14, 205–24.

———. 1966. "Aleatory Procedures." *Musical Times* 107, no. 1480 (June): 503–4.

———. 1968a. "Electronic Workshop." *Musical Times* 109, no. 1501 (March): 235.

———. 1968b. *Répertoire international des musiques* électroacoustiques. Cambridge, MA: MIT Press.

———. 2001. "Gentle Fire: An Early Approach to Live Electronic Music." *Leonardo Music Journal* 11: 53–60.

Davies, Lucy. 2002. "Minimalism." In *The Oxford Companion to Music*, edited by Alison Latham, 781–82. Oxford: Oxford University Press.

Davis, Peter G. 1970. "3 Pieces by Glass Probe the Sonic Possibilities." *New York Times*, January 17, 22.

Davis, Ronald L. 1981. *A History of Music in American Life*. Vol. 3, *The Modern Era, 1920–Present*. Malabar, FL: R. E. Krieger.

Delaere, Mark. 2004. "Goeyvaerts, Karel (August)." *Grove Music Online* in Oxford Music Online, Oxford University Press.

De La Motte-Haber, Helga. 1969. "Internationale Seminare für Neue Musik in Smolenice." *Die Musikforschung* 22, no. 2 (April–June): 215–16.

de la Vega, Aurelio. 1965. "Electronic Music: Tool of Creativity." *Music Journal* 23, no. 6 (September): 52–53.

Demuth, Norman. 1952. *Musical Trends in the Twentieth Century*. London: Rockliff.

Dennis, Brian. 1969. "Roger Smalley's Pulses for 5 × 4 Players and Transformation I for Piano." *Tempo*, no. 90 (Autumn): 28–30.

———. 1970. *Experimental Music in Schools: Towards a New World of Sound*. London, Oxford University Press.

———. 1971a. "The Music of John White." *Musical Times* 112, no. 1539 (May): 435–37.

———. 1971b. "Cardew's 'The Great Learning.'" *Musical Times* 112, no. 1545 (November): 1066–68.

———. 1972. "Drumming, cpe." *Musical Times* 113, no. 1550 (April): 374–85.

———. 1974. "Repetitive and Systemic Music." *Musical Times* 115, no. 1582 (December): 1036–38.

DeNora, Tia. 2000. *Music in Everyday Life*. Cambridge: Cambridge University Press.

de Vries, Gerard. 2016. *Bruno Latour: Une introduction*. Paris: La Découverte.

Dickinson, Peter. 1960. "The Avant-Garde in New York: Spring 1960." *Musical Times* 101, no. 1408 (June): 377–78.

———. 1964. Review of *Music in a New Found Land: Themes and Developments in the History of American Music*, by Wilfrid Mellers. *Musical Times* 105, no. 1459 (September): 660–61.

———. 1968. "Noise and Silence." *Musical Times* 109, no. 1509 (November): 1026–27.

———. 1971. "Manifesto." *Contact*, no. 1 (Spring): 15.

———. 1975. *First American Music Conference. Keele University, England. Friday, April 18–21, 1975*. Keele: University of Keele.

———. 1976. Review of *Genesis of a Music: An Account of a Creative Work, Its Roots and Its Fulfilments*, by Harry Partch, and *Writings about Music*, by Steve Reich. *Tempo*, no. 119, (December): 41–43.

———. 1986. Review of *The Life and Music of George Antheil, 1900–1959*, by Linda Whitesitt, and *All American Music: Composition in the Late Twentieth Century*, by John Rockwell. *Tempo*, no. 158 (September): 59–61.

Dockstader, Tod. 1968. "New Sounds in Electronic Music." *Electronic Music Review*, no. 7 (July): 33–34.

Dolan, Robert Emmett. 1967. *Music in Modern Media: Techniques in Tape, Disc, Film Recording, Motion Picture and Television Scoring and Electronic Music*. New York: G. Schirmer.

Donin, Nicolas. 2010. "Le moment *Musique en jeu*." *Circuit: Musiques Contemporaines* 20, no. 1/2: 25–31.

Dreier, Ruth. 1986. "Minimalism." In *The New Grove Dictionary of American Music*, edited by Stanley Sadie, 3:240–42. London: Macmillan.

Drott, Eric. 2006. "Class, Ideology, and *il caso Scelsi*." *Musical Quarterly* 89, no. 1: 80–120.

———. 2013. "The End(s) of Genre." *Journal of Music Theory* 57, no. 1 (Spring): 1–45.

East, Leslie, and Gordon Rumson. 2008. "Mellers, Wilfrid (Howard)." *Grove Music Online* in Oxford Music Online, Oxford University Press.

Eisen, Jonathan, ed. 1969. *The Age of Rock: Sounds of the American Cultural Revolution*. New York: Vintage.

Emmerson, Simon, and Denis Smalley. 2001. "Electro-Acoustic Music." *Grove Music Online* in Oxford Music Online, Oxford University Press.

Emons, Hans. 1982. "Minimalism: A World Vision's World Versions." In *Das Europäische Minimal-Musik-Projekt*, edited by Michael Fahres, 1–23. Munich: Goethe Institut.

Enciclopedia della musica Garzanti. 1996. 9th ed., revised and augmented. [Milan]: Redazioni Garzanti.

Engel, Gerhard. 1990. *Zur Logik der Musiksoziologie: Ein Beitrag zur Philosophie der Musikwissenschaft.* Tübingen: Mohr Siebeck Verlag.

Epstein, Paul. 1986. "Pattern Structure and Process in Steve Reich's Piano Phase." *Musical Quarterly,* no. 72: 494–502.

Erickson, Robert. 1975. *Sound Structure in Music.* Berkeley: University of California Press.

Ericson, Raymond. 1972. "'Four Note Opera' Clever and Funny." *New York Times,* May 13, 1972, 17.

Ewen, David. 1944. *Men of Popular Music.* Chicago, New York: Ziff-Davis.

———. 1952. *The Complete Book of 20th Century Music.* New York: Prentice-Hall.

———. 1957. *Panorama of American Popular Music.* Englewood Cliffs, NJ: Prentice-Hall.

———. 1962. *David Ewen Introduces Modern Music.* Philadelphia: Chilton.

———. 1968. *The World of Twentieth-Century Music.* Englewood Cliffs, NJ: Prentice-Hall.

———. 1971. *Composers of Tomorrow's Music: A Non-Technical Introduction to the Musical Avant-Garde Movement.* New York: Dodd, Mead.

Fabbri, Paolo, and Bruno Latour. 1977. "La rhétorique de la science: Pouvoir et devoir dans un article de science exacte." *Actes de la recherche en sciences sociales* 13 (February, "L'économie des biens symboliques"): 81–95.

Fahres, Michael, ed. 1982a. *Das Europäische Minimal-Musik-Projekt = European Minimal Music Project.* Munich: Goethe Institut.

———. 1982b. "Vorwort." In *Das Europäische Minimal-Musik-Projekt,* edited by Michael Fahres. Munich: Goethe Institut.

———. 1982c. "Interview mit La Monte Young." In *Das Europäische Minimal-Musik-Projekt,* edited by Michael Fahres, 1–8. Munich: Goethe Institut.

Fellinger, Imogen, et al. 2001. "Periodicals." *Grove Music Online* in Oxford Music Online, Oxford University Press.

Feyerabend, Paul. 1975. *Against Method: Outline of an Anarchistic Theory of Knowledge.* London: NLB; Atlantic Highlands, NJ: Humanities Press.

Fink, Robert. 1998. "Elvis Everywhere: Musicology and Popular Music Studies at the Twilight of the Canon." *American Music* 16, no. 2 (Summer): 135–79.

———. 2004. "(Post-)minimalisms 1970–2000: The Search for a New Mainstream." In *The Cambridge History of Twentieth-Century Music,* edited by Nicholas Cook and Anthony Pople, 539–56. Cambridge: Cambridge University Press.

———. 2005. *Repeating Ourselves: American Minimal Music as a Cultural Practice.* Berkeley: University of California Press.

———. 2013. "Going with the Flow: Minimalism as a Cultural Pratice in the USA since 1945." In *The Ashgate Research Companion to Minimalist and*

Postminimalist Music, edited by Keith Potter, Kyle Gann, and Pwyll ap Siôn, 201–18. Farnham, England: Ashgate.

Flynt, Henry. 1996. "La Monte Young in New York, 1960–62." In *Sound and Light: La Monte Young, Marian Zazeela,* edited by William Duckworth and Richard Fleming, 44–97. Lewisburg, PA: Bucknell University Press.

Forte, Allen. 1959. "Schenker's Conception of Musical Structure." *Journal of Music Theory* 3, no. 1: 1–30.

Fox, Charles. 1962. "New Departures in Jazz." *New Departures,* no. 4: 66–74.

Frank, Peter. 1970. "Discography of Electronic Music on Recordings." *BMI: The Many Worlds of Music* (Summer): 14–22.

———. 1979. "Fluxus Music." *Southern California Art Magazine,* no. 22. http:// ricochet.cc/FLUXUS/fluxus_txt.html.

Friend, Howard C. 1971. "11th November: St. Francis Hall, Birmingham University." *Contact,* no. 3 (Autumn): 38–39.

Gadamer, Hans-Georg. 2013. *Truth and Method.* London: Bloomsbury, 2013.

Gagne, Cole. 1990. *Sonic Transports: New Frontiers in Our Music.* New York: De Falco.

Gann, Kyle. 1993. "La Monte Young's *The Well-Tuned Piano.*" *Perspectives of New Music* 31, no. 1 (Winter): 134–62.

———. 1997. *American Music in the Twentieth Century.* New York: Schirmer.

———. 2010. "Boulez on Music 22 Years Ago." www.artsjournal.com/postclassic /2010/02/boulez_on_music_22_years_ago.html.

Garland, David. 1983. "Philip Glass. Theater of Glass." *Downbeat* 50, no. 11 (December): 16–18.

Gendron, Bernard. 2002. *Between Montmartre and the Mudd Club: Popular Music and the Avant-Garde.* Chicago: University of Chicago Press.

Geysen, Frans. 1974. "Eigen Kompositorische Bevindingen in Vergelijking met het Werk van de Jonge Amerikaanse School." *Adem: Driemaandelijks tijdschrift voor musikalischen Volkskunde,* no. 10 (January–February): 24–30.

Gieseler, Walter. 1975. *Komposition im 20. Jahrhundert.* Celle, Germany: Moek Verlag.

Gilbert, Anthony. 1972. Review of *Notation in New Music,* by Erhard Karkoschka and Ruth Koenig. *Tempo,* no. 103: 46–48.

Gill, Dominic. 1973. "Music in London." *Musical Times* 114, no. 1559 (January): 56–57.

Gingras, Yves, ed. 2014. *Controverses: Accords et désaccords en sciences humaines et sociales.* Paris: CNRS.

Glass, Philip. 1970–71. "Une lettre de Philip Glass." *VH 101,* no. 4 (Winter): 46–48.

———. 1987. *Music by Philip Glass.* Edited by Robert T. Jones. New York: Harper & Row.

Gloag, Kenneth. 2012. *Postmodernism in Music.* Cambridge: Cambridge University Press.

Glock, William. 1955. "Comment." *Score,* no. 12 (June): 4.

Glueck, Grace. 1967. "The Park Place Puts on a Stoner." *New York Times,* March 11, 1967, 25.

———. 1971. "No More Ta-Rum, Ta-Rum." *New York Times,* October 24, 1971, 20.

Godfrey, Daniel S. 2002. "Schwartz, Elliott (Shelling)." *Grove Music Online* in Oxford Music Online, Oxford University Press.

Goodwin, Andrew. 1991. "Popular Music and Postmodern Theory." *Cultural Studies* 5, no. 2:174–90.

Gopinath, Sumanth S. 2004. "'A Composer Looks East': Steve Reich and Discourse on Non-Western Music." *Glendora Review* 3, no. 3/4: 134–45.

Gopinath, Sumanth S., and Pwyll ap Siôn, eds. 2019. *Rethinking Reich.* Oxford: Oxford University Press.

Gordon, Peter. 1977. "Landscape with Philip Glass." *Painted Bride Quarterly* 4, no. 2 (Summer): 57–62.

Griffiths, Paul. 1971. "Recitals: The Matrix." *Musical Times* 112, no. 1546 (December): 1190.

———. 1972. "Ballista." *Musical Times* 113, no. 1548 (February): 168–69.

———. 1975. Review of *Writings about Music,* by Steve Reich. *Musical Times* 116, no. 1589 (July): 627.

———. 1978. *A Concise History of Modern Music: From Debussy to Boulez.* London: Thames and Hudson.

———. 1980. "System." In *The New Grove Dictionary of Music and Musicians,* edited by Stanley Sadie, 18:481. London: Macmillan.

———. 1981. *Modern Music: The Avant Garde since 1945.* London: J. M. Dent & Sons.

———. 1984a. "Reich, Steve." In *The New Oxford Companion to Music,* edited by Denis Arnold, 1553. Oxford: Oxford University Press.

———. 1984b. "Riley, Terry." In *The New Oxford Companion to Music,* edited by Denis Arnold, 1569. Oxford: Oxford University Press.

———. 1984c. "Young, La Monte." In *The New Oxford Companion to Music,* edited by Denis Arnold, 2002. Oxford: Oxford University Press.

———. 1985. "Opera Glass." *Musical Times* 126, no. 1708 (June): 337–39.

Grimshaw, Jeremy Neal. 2011. *Draw a Straight Line and Follow It: The Music and Mysticism of La Monte Young.* New York: Oxford University Press.

Grünzweig, Werner. 1997. "Minimal Music." In *Die Musik in Geschichte und Gegenwart: Allgemeine Enzyklopädie der Musik,* edited by Friedrich Blume, 16:294–301. Kassel: Bärenreiter.

Hamm, Charles. 1971. "Music and Higher Education in the 1970's: A Needed Change in Attitude." *College Music Symposium* 11 (Autumn): 94–95.

———. 1983. *Music in the New World.* New York: W. W. Norton.

Hansen, Peter S. 1961. *An Introduction to Twentieth Century Music.* Boston: Allyn and Bacon.

———. 1967. *An Introduction to Twentieth Century Music.* 2nd ed. Boston: Allyn and Bacon.

Harkins, Paul. 2019. *Digital Sampling: The Design and Use of Music Technologies.* London: Routledge.

Harris, Tony. 2007. *The Legacy of Cornelius Cardew.* Aldershot, England: Ashgate.

Hartog, Howard. 1957. *European Music in the Twentieth Century.* London: Routledge & Kegan Paul.

Harvey, David. 1989. *The Condition of Postmodernity: An Enquiry into the Origins of Cultural Change.* Oxford: Blackwell.

Haskell, Barbara. 1984. *Blam! The Explosion of Pop, Minimalism, and Performance, 1958–1964.* New York: Whitney Museum of American Art and W. W. Norton.

Haskins, Rob. 2006. Review of *Repeating Ourselves: American Minimal Music as Cultural Practice,* by Robert Fink. *Current Musicology* 81 (Spring): 147–54.

Hayes, Malcolm. 1982. Review of *Modern Music: The Avant Garde since 1945,* by Paul Griffiths. *Tempo,* no. 140 (March): 35–36.

Henahan, Donal. 1969a. "Multimedia's Mother of Them All." *New York Times,* April 13, 1969, 17.

———. 1969b. "Repetition, Electronically Aided, Dominates Music of Steve Reich." *New York Times,* May 28, 1969, 37.

———. 1969c. "Who Dreams of Being a Beethoven." *New York Times,* June 29, 1969, 17.

———. 1970. "Steve Reich Presents a Program of Pulse Music at Guggenheim." *New York Times,* May 9, 1970, 15.

———. 1971. "Reich? Philharmonic? Paradiddling?" *New York Times,* October 24, 1971, 13.

———. 1981. "The Going-Nowhere Music and Where It Came From." *New York Times,* December 6, 1981, 1.

Hennion, Antoine. 1997. "Baroque and Rock: Music, Mediators and Musical Taste." *Poetics* 24, no. 6: 415–35.

———. 2013. "Enquêter sur nos attachements: Comment hériter de William James?" *SociologieS,* http://journals.openedition.org/sociologies/4953.

Martin, Jim. 1969. "Interview with Lou Reed." *Open City,* no 78. Reprinted in Clinton Heylin, *All Yesterdays' Parties: The Velvet Underground in Print, 1966–1971,* 109–17. Cambridge: Da Capo, 2005.

Higgins, Dick. 1969. "Boredom and Danger." In *Source: Music of the Avant-Garde, 1966–1973,* edited by Larry Austin and Douglas Kahn, 178–80. Berkeley: University of California Press, 2011.

Higgins, Hannah. 2002. *Fluxus Experience.* Berkeley: University of California Press.

Hiller, Lejaren A. Jr., and Leonard M. Isaacson. 1959. *Experimental Music: Composition with a Computer.* New York: McGraw-Hill.

Hitchcock, H. Wiley. 1962. "Current Chronicle." *Musical Quarterly* 48, no. 2 (April): 244–48.

———. 1965. "Current Chronicle." *Musical Quarterly* 51, no. 3 (July): 530–40.

———. 1966. Review of *Music in the 20th Century from Debussy through Stravinsky,* by William W. Austin. *Notes: The Quarterly Journal of the Music Library Association* 23, no. 2 (December): 254–57.

———. 1969. *Music in the United States: A Historical Introduction.* Englewood Cliffs, NJ: Prentice-Hall.

———. 1974. *Music in the United States: A Historical Introduction.* 2nd ed. Englewood Cliffs, NJ: Prentice-Hall.

———. 1983. Review of *All American Music: Composition in the Late Twentieth Century,* by John Rockwell, and *Music in the New World,* by Charles Hamm. *Journal of Musicology* 2, no. 3 (Summer): 334–39.

———. 1988. *Music in the United States: A Historical Introduction.* 3rd ed. Englewood Cliffs, NJ: Prentice-Hall.

———. 1996. "Minimalism in Art and Music: Origins and Aesthetic." In *Classic Essays on Twentieth-Century Music,* edited by Richard Kostelanetz and Joseph Darby, 308–19. New York: Schirmer.

———. 2000. *Music in the United States: A Historical Introduction.* 4th ed. Englewood Cliffs, NJ: Prentice-Hall.

———. 2001. "Chase, Gilbert." *Grove Music Online* in Oxford Music Online, Oxford University Press.

Hobgood, Burnet M. 1968. Review of *The Theatre of Mixed Means* by Richard Kostelanetz. *Educational Theatre Journal* 20, no. 4 (December): 608.

Hodeir, André. 1961. *Since Debussy: A View of Contemporary Music.* Translated by Noel Burch. New York: Grove Press.

Hoffman, Alan. 1982. Review of *Modern Music: The Avant Garde since 1945,* by Paul Griffiths; *Cage,* by Paul Griffiths; and *Experimental Music: Cage and Beyond,* by Michael Nyman. *Notes: The Quarterly Journal of the Music Library Association* 39, no. 1: 97–98.

Hoffman, Theodore. 1965. "Corrigan's Analogy or What We Will Do at NYU." *Tulane Drama Review* 10, no. 2 (Winter): 15–22.

Hopkins, Bill. 1975. Review of *Experimental Music: Cage and Beyond,* by Michael Nyman. *Tempo,* no. 112 (March 1975): 39–40.

Hopkins, G. W. 1967a. Review of *Amm Music,* by Cornelius Cardew, Lou Gare, Eddie Prévost, Keith Rowe, and Lawrence Sheaff. *Musical Times* 108, no. 1494 (August): 718.

———. 1967b. "Potatoes." *Musical Times* 108, no. 1494 (August): 739.

Horovitz, Michael. 1962. "Live New Departures." *New Departures,* no. 4: 25–34.

Howard, John Tasker. 1939. *Our American Music: Three Hundred Years of It.* 2nd ed. New York: Thomas Y. Crowell.

———. 1954. *Our American Music: Three Hundred Years of It.* 3rd ed. New York: Thomas Y. Crowell.

———. 1957. *Modern Music: A Popular Guide to Greater Musical Enjoyment.* New York: Crowell.

———. 1965. *Our American Music: Three Hundred Years of It.* 4th ed. New York: Thomas Y. Crowell.

Howard, John Tasker, and George Kent Bellows. 1957. *A Short History of Music in America.* New York: Thomas Y. Crowell.

Hughes, Langston. 1962. "Jazz Is a Heartbeat." *New Departures,* no. 4: 14–21.

Hunt, Albert. 1971. "The Theatre of Boredom." *New Society,* no. 11 (March): 405–6.

Hutcheon, Linda. 1988. *A Poetics of Postmodernism: History, Theory, Fiction.* New York: Routledge.

Isaacs, Alan, and Elizabeth Martin, ed. 1983. *Dictionary of Music.* New York: Facts on File.

Jacobs, Arthur. 1958. *A New Dictionary of Music.* New York: Penguin.

———. 1996. *The Penguin Dictionary of Music.* 6th ed. New York: Penguin.

Jameson, Fredric. 1979. "Reification and Utopia in Mass Culture." *Social Text,* no. 1 (Winter, 1979): 130–48.

———. 1982. "Postmodernism and Consumer Society." http://art.ucsc.edu/sites /default/files/Jameson_Postmodernism_and_Consumer_Society.pdf.

———. 1984. "Postmodernism, or the Cultural Logic of Late Capitalism." *New Left Review* 146 (July–August): 53–92.

———. 1991. *Postmodernism or the Cultural Logic of Late Capitalism.* Durham, NC: Duke University Press.

Jessup, Bertram. 1970. "Crisis in the Fine Arts Today." *Journal of Aesthetics and Art Criticism* 29, no. 1 (Autumn): 3–10.

Johnson, Timothy A. 1994. "Minimalism: Aesthetic, Style, or Technique?" *Musical Quarterly* 78, no. 4 (Winter): 742–73.

Johnson, Tom. 1972. "Teachers, Step Up to the Avant-Garde!" *Music Educators Journal* 58, no. 9 (May): 30–32.

———. 1982. "The Original Minimalists." *Village Voice,* July 27, 1982, 68–69.

———. 1991. *The Voice of New Music: New York City, 1972-1982: A Collection of Articles Originally Published in the "Village Voice."* Eindhoven, Netherlands: Apollohuis.

Johnston, Ben. 1974. "Microtones." In *Dictionary of Contemporary Music,* edited by John Vinton, 483–84. New York: E. P. Dutton.

Johnston, Jill. 1963. "Walter De Maria." *Art News* (February): 19.

———. 1964. "La Monte Young." *Village Voice,* November 19, 1964, 14 and 20.

Jones, Robert T. 1969. "3 Films by Serra and Glass's Music Offered at Whitney." *New York Times,* May 21, 1969, 43.

———. 1981. "The Sound of Glass." *Opera News*, no. 46 (July): 17–18.

———. 1983a. "An Outburst of Minimalism." *High Fidelity/Musical America* 33, no. 2 (February): 26.

———. 1983b. "Minimalist Philip Glass' Insistent Beat Is Luring a Wide Range of Choreographers." *Ballet News* 5, no. 4 (October): 23–24, 42.

———. 1985. "Philip Glass: Musician of the Year." *High Fidelity/Musical America* 35, no. 1 (January): 9.

Jones, Steve, ed. 2002. *Pop Music and the Press*. Philadelphia: Temple University Press.

Joseph, Branden W. 2008. *Beyond the Dream Syndicate: Tony Conrad and the Arts after Cage*. New York: Zone Books.

Karkoschka, Erhard. 1972. *Notation in New Music: A Critical Guide to Interpretation and Realisation*. New York: Praeger.

Karnes, Kevin. 2017. *Arvo Pärt's "Tabula Rasa."* New York: Oxford University Press.

Kaye, Lenny. 1970. "The Velvet Underground." *New Times*, April 20. Reprinted in Clinton Heylin, *All Yesterdays' Parties: The Velvet Underground in Print, 1966–1971*, 155–65. Cambridge: Da Capo, 2005.

Kennedy, Michael, ed. 1980. *The Concise Oxford Dictionary of Music: Based on the Original Publication by Percy Scholes*. 3rd ed. London: Oxford University Press.

Kerman, Joseph. 1958. "American Music: The Columbia Series." *Hudson Review* 11, no. 3 (Autumn): 420–30.

———. 1961. "American Music: The Columbia Series (II)." *Hudson Review* 14, no. 3 (Autumn): 408–18.

———. 1963. "'The Proper Study of Music': A Reply." *Perspectives of New Music* 2, no. 1 (Autumn–Winter): 151–59.

———. 1985. *Contemplating Music: Challenges to Musicology*. Cambridge, MA: Harvard University Press.

Kirby, Michael. 1965a. "The New Theatre." *Tulane Drama Review* 10, no. 2 (Winter): 23–43.

———, ed. 1965b. *Happenings*. New York: Dutton.

———. 1969. *The Art of Time: Essays on the Avant-Garde*. New York: Dutton.

Kirkeby, Marc. 1982. "Philip Glass Alters the Shape of Classical Music." *Rolling Stone*, January 21, 1982, 40.

Knockaert, Yves. 2013. "Geysen, Frans." *Grove Music Online* in Oxford Music Online, Oxford University Press.

Knox, Kenneth. 1967. "The Parametric Music of Terry Riley." *Jazz Monthly* 13, no. 5: 9–12.

Knox, Kenneth, and Rita Knox. 1970. "Relax and Fully Concentrate: The Time of Terry Riley." *Friends*, no. 3 (February 20).

Kostelanetz, Richard. 1966. "'La Monte Young's *The Tortoise: The Dream and Journeys*." *Art Voices* 5, no. 4 (Autumn): 23–24.

———. 1967. "Modern Music and the Literate Layman." *Perspectives of New Music* 6, no. 1 (Autumn–Winter): 119–33.

———. 1968. *The Theatre of Mixed Means*. New York: Dial Press.

———. 1969. *Master Minds: Portraits of Contemporary American Artists and Intellectuals*. Toronto: Macmillan.

———. 1970. *John Cage*. New York: Praeger.

———. 2000. *A Dictionary of the Avant-Gardes*. New York: Schirmer.

Kostelanetz, Richard, ed. 1965. *The New American Arts*. New York: Horizon Press.

Kozinn, Allan. 1992. "John Cage, 79, a Minimalist Enchanted with Sound, Dies." *New York Times*, August 13, 1992.

Kramer, Jonathan D. 1988. *The Time of Music: New Meanings, New Temporalities, New Listening Strategies*. New York: Schirmer.

———. 1995. "Beyond Unity: Toward an Understanding of Postmodernism in Music and Music Theory." In *Concert Music, Rock, and Jazz since 1945*, edited by Elizabeth West Marvin and Richard Hermann, 11–33. Rochester, NY: Rochester University Press.

———. 1996. "Postmodern Concepts of Musical Time." *Indiana Theory Review* 17, no. 2 (Autumn): 21–61.

———. 1999. "The Nature and Origins of Musical Postmodernism." *Current Musicology* no. 66 (Spring): 7–20.

Kramer, Lawrence. 1995. *Classical Music and Postmodern Knowledge*. Berkeley: University of California Press.

Krauss, Rosalind. 1977. *Passages in Modern Sculpture*. New York: Viking Press.

Kroeger, Karl. 1988. Review of *American Minimal Music: La Monte Young, Terry Riley, Steve Reich, Philip Glass*, by Wim Mertens. *American Music* 6, no. 2 (Summer): 241–43.

Kuhn, Thomas S. 1962. *The Structure of Scientific Revolutions*. Chicago: University of Chicago Press.

Kunst, Jos. 1988. *Filosofie van de muziekwetenschap*. Leiden: Nijhoff.

La Barbara, Joan. 1974. "Philip Glass and Steve Reich: Two from the Steady State School." *Data: Pratica e teoria delle arti*, no. 13 (Winter): 36–39.

———. 1980. "Three by Reich." *High Fidelity/Musical America* 29, no. 6: 12.

Larner, Gerald, and David C. F. Wright. 2013. "Smith Brindle, Reginald." *Grove Music Online* in Oxford Music Online, Oxford University Press.

Latour, Bruno. 1987. *Science in Action: How to Follow Scientists and Engineers through Society*. Cambridge, MA: Harvard University Press.

———. 1993. *We Have Never Been Modern*. Translated by Catherine Porter. Cambridge, MA: Harvard University Press.

———. 2004. *Politics of Nature: How to Bring the Sciences into Democracy*. Translated by Catherine Porter. Cambridge, MA: Harvard University Press.

———. 2005. *Reassembling the Social: An Introduction to Actor-Network-Theory*. Oxford: Oxford University Press.

——. 2010. *Cogitamus: Six lettres sur les humanités scientifiques*. Paris: La Découverte.

Leech-Wilkinson, Daniel. 2002. *The Modern Invention of Medieval Music: Scholarship, Ideology, Performance*. Cambridge: Cambridge University Press.

Levaux, Christophe. 2015. "La Monte Young vs The Velvet, Minimalisme vs Punk, savant vs populaire: Constructions et déconstructions postmodernes." *Volume! La revue des musiques populaires* 11, no. 2: 101–21.

——. 2016. "Loop." *Rock Music Studies* 3, no. 2: 167–79.

——. 2017. "The Forgotten History of Repetitive Audio Technologies." *Organised Sound* 22, no. 2: 187–94.

Lippard, Lucy R. 1968. "Constellation by Harsh Daylight: The Whitney Annual." *Hudson Review* 21, no. 1 (Spring): 174–82.

Lockwood, Larry. 1975. Review of *Experimental Music: Cage and Beyond*, by Michael Nyman. *Notes: The Quarterly Journal of the Music Library Association* 32, no. 1 (September): 57–58.

Lovisa, Fabian R. 1996. *Minimal-music: Entwicklung, Komponisten, Werke*. Darmstadt: Wissenschaftliche Buchgesellschaft.

Lyotard, Jean-François. [1971] 2011. *Discourse, Figure*. Translated by Antony Hudek and Mary Lydon. Minneapolis: University of Minnesota Press.

——. [1971] 2012. "'A Few Words to Sing': *Sequenza III*." In Jean-François Lyotard, *Miscellaneous Texts II: Contemporary Artists*, edited by Herman Parret, 56–93. Louvain: Leuven University Press, 2012.

——. 1972. "Plusieurs silences." *Musique en jeu*, no. 9 (November): 65–77.

——. (1979) 1984. *The Postmodern Condition: A Report on Knowledge*. Translated by Geoff Bennington and Brian Massumi. Manchester: Manchester University Press.

——. (1996) 2012. "The Inaudible: Music and Postmodernity." In *Miscellaneous Texts I: Aesthetics and Theory of Art*, edited by Herman Parret, translated by Vlad Ionescu, Erica Harris, and Peter W. Milne, 201–23. Louvain: Leuven University Press.

Machlis, Joseph. 1961. *Introduction to Contemporary Music*. New York: W. W. Norton.

Magaudda, Paolo. 2019. "Infrastructures de la musique numérisée: Les promesses de la 'révolution' de la *blockchain*." *Revue d'anthropologie des connaissances* 13, no. 3: 849–69.

Marengo, Silvio Riolfo, ed. 1983. *La nuova enciclopedia della musica Garzanti*. Milan: Garzanti.

Margulis, Elizabeth Hellmuth. 2014. *On Repeat: How Music Plays the Mind*. New York: Oxford University Press.

Mark, Christopher. 2012. *Roger Smalley: A Case Study of Late Twentieth-Century Composition*. Farnham, England: Ashgate.

Mason, Colin. 1968–69. Introduction. *Tempo*, no. 87 (Winter): 1.

Mauceri, Frank X. 1997. "From Experimental Music to Musical Experiment." *Perspectives of New Music* 35, no. 1 (Winter 1997): 187–204.

Matthews, Ramona H. 2001. "Thompson, Oscar." *Grove Music Online* in Oxford Music Online, Oxford University Press.

McClary, Susan. 1989. "Terminal Prestige: The Case of Avant-Garde Music Composition." *Cultural Critique*, no. 12 (Spring): 57–81.

———. 2004. "Rap, Minimalism, and Structures of Time in Late Twentieth-Century Culture." In *Audio Culture: Readings in Modern Music,* edited by Christoph Cox and Daniel Warner, 289–98. New York: Continuum.

McGuire, Wayne. 1968. "The Boston Sound." *Crawdaddy,* no. 17 (August): 43–47.

McKenna, Kristine. 1979. "Philip Glass: The Future Is Now." *Rolling Stone,* March 8, 1979, 19–20.

Mellers, Wilfrid. 1955. "Music, Theatre and Commerce." *Score,* no. 12 (June): 69–76.

———. 1957. *Romanticism and the 20th Century, from 1800.* London: Rockliff, 1957.

———. 1964. *Music in a New Found Land: Themes and Developments in the History of American Music.* London: Barrie & Rockliff.

———. 1965. *Music in a New Found Land: Themes and Developments in the History of American Music.* First American edition. New York: Alfred A. Knopf.

———. 1967. *Caliban Reborn: Renewal in Twentieth-Century Music.* New York: Harper & Row.

———. 1968. "The New Music in a New World." In *Twentieth Century Music,* edited by Rollo H. Myers, 241–52. New York: Orion Press.

———. 1973. *Twilight of the Gods: The Beatles in Retrospect.* London: Faber & Faber.

———. 1975. *Music in a New Found Land: Themes and Developments in the History of American Music.* 2nd ed. New York: Hillstone-Stonehill.

———. 1984a. "Modern Music—Seen from America." *Musical Times* 125, no. 1694 (April): 206–7.

———. 1984b. "A Minimalist Definition." *Musical Times* 125, no. 1696 (June): 328.

———. 1987. *Music in a New Found Land: Themes and Developments in the History of American Music.* Rev. ed. Oxford: Oxford University Press.

Mertens, Wim. 1979. *Non-narratieve en a-teleologische aspekten in de muziek van de Amerikaanse repetitieven.* Diss. lic. kunstgeschiedenis en oudheid-kunde: musicologie, Universiteit Gent, Ghent.

———. 1980. *Amerikaanse repetitieve muziek: in het perspectief van de Westeu-ropese muziekrevolutie.* Bierbeek, Belgium: Vergaelen. (Translated as Mertens 1983.)

———. 1983. *American Minimal Music: La Monte Young, Terry Riley, Steve Reich, Philip Glass.* Translated by J. Hautekiet. London: Kahn & Averill.

Meyer, Leonard B. 1956. *Emotion and Meaning in Music*. Chicago: University of Chicago Press.

———. 1963. "The End of Renaissance?" *Hudson Review* 16, no. 2 (Summer): 169–86.

———. 1967. *Music, the Arts, and Ideas*. Chicago: University of Chicago Press.

Michel, François, ed. 1958–61. *Encyclopédie de la musique*. Paris: Fasquelle.

Middleton, Richard. 1971. "The Musical Significance of Pop." *Contact*, no. 1 (Spring):10–13.

———. 1972. *Pop Music and the Blues: A Study of the Relationship and Its Significance*. London: Gollancz.

———. 1974. Review of *Philosophy of Modern Music*, by Theodor W. Adorno, Anne G. Mitchell, Wesley W. Bloomster; and *Faust as Musician: A Study of Thomas Mann's Novel "Doctor Faustus,"* by Patrick Carnegy. *Music & Letters* 55, no. 2 (April): 219–24.

———. 1975. Review of *Experimental Music: Cage and Beyond*, by Michael Nyman. *Music & Letters* 56, no. 1 (January): 85–86.

———. 1983. "'Play It Again Sam': Some Notes on the Productivity of Repetition in Popular Music." *Popular Music* 3: 235–70.

Millen, Irene. 1965. Review of *The International Cyclopedia of Music and Musicians* by Oscar Thompson and Robert Sabin. *Notes: The Quarterly Journal of the Music Library Association* 22, no. 19 (Autumn): 733–35.

Milner, Anthony. 1957. "English Contemporary Music." In *European Music in the Twentieth Century*, edited by Howard Hartog, 132–51. London: Routledge & Kegan Paul.

Moore, Carman. 1966. "Park Place Electronics." *Village Voice*, June 9, 1966, 17.

———. 1967. "Park Place Pianos." *Village Voice*, March 23, 1967, 15.

———. 1968. "Zukofsky." *Village Voice*, January 18, 1968, 25 and 28.

———. 1969. "Zukofsky." *Village Voice*, May 1, 1969, 28.

Moore, Allan F. 2001. "Categorical Conventions in Music Discourse: Style and Genre." *Music & Letters* 82, no. 3: 432–42.

Morgan, Paula. 2001a. "Austin, William W(eaver)." *Grove Music Online* in Oxford Music Online, Oxford University Press.

———. 2001b. "Hitchcock, H. Wiley." *Grove Music Online* in Oxford Music Online, Oxford University Press.

———. 2001c. "Stein, Leonard." *Grove Music Online* in Oxford Music Online, Oxford University Press.

Morris, Robert. 1988. "Generalizing Rotational Arrays." *Journal of Music Theory*, no. 32: 91–93.

Nadeau, Roland. 1981. Review of *Modern Music: The Avant Garde since 1945*, by Paul Griffiths. *Music Educators Journal* 68, no. 4 (December 1981): 63–64.

Nettl, Bruno. 1991. "The Dual Nature of Ethnomusicology in North America: The Contributions of Charles Seeger and George Herzog." In *Comparative*

Musicology and Anthropology of Music, edited by Bruno Nettl and Philip V. Bohlman, 266–74. Chicago: University of Chicago Press.

———. 1999. "The Institutionalization of Musicology: Perspectives of a North American Ethnomusicologist." In *Rethinking Music*, edited by Nicholas Cook and Mark Everist, 287–310. Oxford: Oxford University Press.

Nettl, Bruno, and Philip V. Bohlman, eds. 1991. *Comparative Musicology and Anthropology of Music: Essays on the History of Ethnomusicology.* Chicago: University of Chicago Press.

Neumann, Frederick. 1991. "The Vibrato Controversy." *Performance Practice Review* 4, no. 1: 14–27.

Nicholls, David, ed. 1998. *The Cambridge History of American Music.* Cambridge: Cambridge University Press.

———. 2002. *The Cambridge Companion to John Cage.* Cambridge: Cambridge University Press.

Nice, James. 2006. "From Brussels with Love." Les Disques du Crépuscule. http://lesdisquesducrepuscule.com/from_brussels_with_love_ltmcd2479.html.

Niebur, Louis. 2018. "'There Is Music in It, but It Is Not Music: A Reception History of Musique Concrète in Britain." *Twentieth-Century Music* 15, no. 2: 211–30.

Norrington, Roger. 1965. "Peter Dickinson." *Musical Times* 106, no. 1464 (February): 109–10.

"Notes: Tempo and the New Music." 1961. *Tempo*, no. 58 (Summer): 1.

Novak, Jelena, and John Richardson, eds. 2019. *Einstein on the Beach: Opera beyond Drama.* London: Routledge.

Nyman, Michael. 1970. "Tim Souster's Night Out at the Proms." *Tempo*, no. 94 (Autumn): 20–24.

———. 1971a. "The Music of Steve Reich." *Time Out*, February 21–March 7, 1971, 85.

———. 1971b. "Steve Reich." *Musical Times* 112, no. 1537 (March): 229–31.

———. 1974. *Experimental Music: Cage and Beyond.* New York: Cambridge University Press.

———. 2013. *Michael Nyman: Collected Writings.* Edited by Pwyll ap Siôn. Farnham, England: Ashgate.

Oehlman, Werner. 1961. *Die Musik des 20. Jahrhunderts.* Berlin: Walter De Gruyter.

Offenstadt, Nicolas. 2011. *L'historiographie.* Paris: Presses Universitaires de France.

Oliveros, Pauline. 1969. "Tape Delay Techniques for Electronic Music Composition." *Composer* 1, no. 3 (1969): 135–43.

Osterreich, Norbert. 1977. "Music with Roots in the Aether." *Perspectives of New Music* 16, no. 1 (Autumn–Winter): 214–28.

Paddison, M. 2001. "Adorno, Theodor (Ludwig) W(iesengrund)." *Grove Music Online* in Oxford Music Online, Oxford University Press.

Page, Tim. 1981. "Framing the River: A Minimalist Primer." *High Fidelity/ Musical America* 31, no. 11 (November): 64–68.

Palmer, Robert. 1975a. "Trance Music: A Trend of the 1970's." *New York Times,* January 12, 1975, 1, 17.

———. 1975b. "Non-Electric Jazz Is a Gas." *New York Times,* March 9, 1975, 24, 29.

———. 1978. "Philip Glass Comes to Carnegie Hall—At Last." *New York Times,* May 28, 1978, 13, 15.

———. 1981. "A Father Figure for the Avant-Garde." *Atlantic Monthly* 247, no. 5 (May): 48–56.

———. 1982. *Deep Blues: A Musical and Cultural History of the Mississippi Delta.* New York: Penguin.

———. 1983. "Get Ready for the Music of Harmonics." *New York Times,* July 17, 1983, 17 and 30.

———. 2009. *Blues and Chaos: The Music Writing of Robert Palmer.* Edited by Anthony DeCurtis. New York: Scribner.

Palmer, Tony. 1970. "Hard Rock in the Albert Hall: Two Views of the First-Ever Pop Prom, Which Took Place Last Week. Relying on Chance." *Observer,* August 16, 19.

Parsons, Michael. 1968. "Sounds of Discovery." *Musical Times* 109, no. 1503 (May): 429–30.

———. 1976. "Systems in Art and Music." *Musical Times* 117, no. 1604 (October): 815–18.

Pegg, Carole, Helen Myers, Philip V. Bohlman, and Martin Stokes. 2001. "Ethnomusicology." *Grove Music Online* in Oxford Music Online, Oxford University Press.

Perkins, John Mac Ivor. 1966. "Arthur Berger: The Composer as Mannerist." *Perspectives of New Music* 5, no. 1 (Autumn–Winter): 75–92.

Perreault, John. 1967. "Minimal Art: Clearing the Air." *Village Voice,* January 12, 1967, 11.

———. 1968. "La Monte Young's Tracery: The Voice of the Tortoise." *Village Voice,* February 22, 1968, 27 and 29.

———. 1969. "A Sort of Sacrifice." *Village Voice,* May 29, 1969, 14–16.

Phillips, Jill. 1968a. "Sounds of Discovery." *Musical Times* 109, no. 1505 (July): 644–45.

———. 1968b. "Music in London." *Musical Times* 109, no. 1506 (August): 741.

———. 1969a. "New Music." *Musical Times* 110, no. 1513 (March): 288–89.

———. 1969b. "Music Now." *Musical Times* 110, no. 1517 (July): 756.

Piekut, Benjamin. 2011. *Experimentalism Otherwise: The New York Avant-Garde and Its Limits.* Berkeley: University of California Press.

———. 2014a. "Actor-Networks in Music History: Clarifications and Critiques." *Twentieth-Century Music* 11, no. 2 (September): 1–25.

———. 2014b. "Indeterminacy, Free Improvisation, and the Mixed Avant-Garde: Experimental Music in London, 1965–1975." *Journal of the American Musicological Society* 67, no. 3 (Autumn): 769–824.

Pinch, Trevor. 2015. "Moments in the Valuation of Sound: The Early History of Synthesizers." In *Moments of Valuation: Exploring Sites of Dissonance*, edited by Ariane Berthoin Antal, Michael Hutter, and David Stark, 15–36. Oxford: Oxford University Press.

Pinch, Trevor, and Wiebe Bijker. 1984. "The Social Construction of Facts and Artefacts; or How the Sociology of Science and the Sociology of Technology Might Benefit Each Other." *Social Studies of Science*, no. 14: 388–441.

Pinch, Trevor, and Frank Trocco. 2004. *Analog Days: The Invention and Impact of the Moog Synthesizer*. Cambridge, MA: Harvard University Press.

Pincus-Witten, Robert. 1977. *Postminimalism*. New York: Out of London Press.

Pleasants, Henry. 1955. *The Agony of Modern Music*. New York: Simon & Schuster.

———. 1969. *Serious Music and All that Jazz!* New York: Simon & Schuster.

Poirier, Richard. 1967. "Learning from the Beatles." *Partisan Review* (Autumn): 526–46.

Potter, Keith. 1974. "Schoenberg Today." *Contact*, no. 9 (Autumn): 3–5.

———. 2000. *Four Musical Minimalists: La Monte Young, Terry Riley, Steve Reich, Philip Glass*. Cambridge: Cambridge University Press.

———. 2001a. "Minimalism." *Grove Music Online* in Oxford Music Online, Oxford University Press.

———. 2001b. "Skempton, Howard." *Grove Music Online* in Oxford Music Online, Oxford University Press.

Potter, Keith, Kyle Gann, and Pwyll ap Siôn, eds. 2013. *The Ashgate Research Companion to Minimalist and Postminimalist Music*. Farnham, England: Ashgate.

Potter, Keith, and Chris Villars. 1971. "Editorial." *Contact*, no. 1 (Spring): 1.

Prior, Nick. 2008. "Putting a Glitch in the Field: Bourdieu, Actor Network Theory and Contemporary Music." *Cultural Sociology* 2, no. 3: 301–19.

Pritchett, James, Laura Kuhn, and Charles Hiroshi Garrett. 2012. "Cage, John." *Grove Music Online* in Oxford Music Online, Oxford University Press.

Radano, Ronald M. 1984. Review of *All American Music: Composition in the Late Twentieth Century*, by John Rockwell. *Ethnomusicology* 28, no. 1 (January): 148–49.

Randel, Don Michael, ed. 1978. *Harvard Concise Dictionary of Music*. Cambridge, MA: Belknap Press of Harvard University Press.

———. 1986, ed. *Harvard Concise Dictionary of Music*. Cambridge, MA: Belknap Press of Harvard University Press.

———, ed. 1999. *The Harvard Concise Dictionary of Music and Musicians.* Cambridge, MA: Belknap Press of Harvard University Press.

Rehding, Alexander. 2009. *Music and Monumentality: Commemoration and Wonderment in Nineteenth-Century Germany.* New York: Oxford University Press.

Reich, Howard. 1987. "Composer/Conductor Boulez Stays on the Cutting Edge." *Chicago Tribune*, November 8, 1987, 20.

Reich, Steve. 1970–71a. "*Pendulum Music.*" *VH 101*, no. 4 (Winter): 94–95.

———. 1970–71b. "La musique comme processus graduel." *VH 101*, no. 4 (Winter): 96–97.

———. (1971) 2011. "Music as a Gradual Process." In *Source: Music of the Avant-Garde, 1966–1973*, edited by Larry Austin and Douglas Kahn, 317–18. Berkeley: University of California Press.

———. 1973. "A Composer Looks East." *New York Times*, September 2, 1973, 95.

———. 1974. *Writings about Music.* Halifax: The Press of the Nova Scotia College of Art and Design.

———. 2002. *Writings on Music, 1965–2000.* Edited by Paul Hillier. New York: Oxford University Press.

Reinhard, Johnny. 1982–83. "A Conversation with La Monte Young and Marian Zazeela." *Ear* 7, no. 5: 4–6.

Reynolds, Roger. 1962. "Interview with John Cage." In *John Cage*, edited by Robert Dunn, 45–52. New York: Henmar Press.

———. 1968. "It(')s Time." *Electronic Music Review*, no. 7 (July): 12–17.

———. 1975. *Mind Models: New Forms of Musical Experience.* New York: Praeger.

———. 1979. "John Cage and Roger Reynolds: A Conversation." *Musical Quarterly* 65, no. 4 (October): 573–94.

Rich, Alan. 1969. "Music to Stay Home With." *New York Magazine*, March 10, 1969, 50.

———. 1970. "Over and Over and Over and..." *New York Magazine*, May 25, 1970, 54.

———. 1972a. "The Only Thing We Have to Fear." *New York Magazine*, March 6, 1972, 66–67.

———. 1972b. "Is There a Tweedle in Your Future?" *New York Magazine*, June 12, 1972, 59–60.

Rinck, Fanny. 2010. "L'analyse linguistique des enjeux de connaissance dans le discours scientifique: Un état des lieux." *Revue d'anthropologie des connaissances* 4, no. 3: 427–50.

Roberts, David. 2005. "Davies, Hugh." *Grove Music Online* in Oxford Music Online, Oxford University Press.

Rosenbaum, Ron. 1970. "Eternal Music in a Dreamhouse Barn." *Village Voice*, February 12, 1970, 5–6.

Robijns, J., and Miep Zijlstra. 1983. *Algemene Muziek Encyclopedie*. Haarlem: De Haan.

Rockwell, John. 1970a. "Leedy, Dissident Composer, Wars with Custom." *Los Angeles Times*, March 27, 1970, 1, 8.

———. 1970b. "Terry Riley's 'In C' Offered at Festival." *Los Angeles Times*, July 28, 1970, 10.

———. 1970c. "Reich and Riley: Violent Reactions to Simple Works." *Los Angeles Times*, September 6, 1970, 37.

———. 1971a. "Terry Riley at Beckman." *Los Angeles Times*, April 20, 1971, 13.

———. 1972a. "Boulez and Young: Enormous Gulf or Unwitting Allies." *Los Angeles Times*, February 13, 1972, 38, 41.

———. 1972b. "Alla Breve." *Los Angeles Times*, September 24, 1972, 48–49.

———. 1973a. "Sound of New Music Is Likened to Art." *New York Times*, January 3, 1973, 48.

———. 1973b. "Synthesized Music by Behrman Offers Beguiling Sounds." *New York Times*, January 24, 1973, 33.

———. 1973c. "11 Players Perform Terry Riley's 'In C.'" *New York Times*, April 27, 1973, 28.

———. 1973d. "Music: Reich Meditations." *New York Times*, May 19, 1973, 28.

———. 1973e. "Sonic Arts Union Playing 72 Hours of the New Music." *New York Times*, May 27, 1973, 37.

———. 1973f. "Philip Glass Works to Broaden Scope beyond 'In' Crowd." *New York Times*, June 28, 1973, 58.

———. 1973g. "David Behrman's Synthesizer, Modified, Makes Soho Music." *New York Times*, December 19, 1973, 60.

———. 1974a. "Rzewski, Pianist, Plays New Music by Tom Johnson." *New York Times*, January 21, 1974, 36.

———. 1974b. "Guru Brings Composers New Voice." *New York Times*, March 27, 1974, 32.

———. 1974c. "La Monte Young Plays at Kitchen." *New York Times*, May 2, 1974, 67.

———. 1974d. "There's Nothing Like the Sound of Glass." *New York Times*, May 26, 1974, 11, 21.

———. 1974e. "Face of Jazz Is Changing Visibly." *New York Times*, June 4, 1974, 33.

———. 1975a. "Music: 'In Twelve Parts.'" *New York Times*, February 17, 1975, 29.

———. 1975b. "The Pop Life: In Progressive Rock, the Classical Touch." *New York Times*, May 9, 1975, 23.

———. 1976. "*Crawdaddy* Party Mirrors Magazine." *New York Times*, June 9, 1976, 31.

———. 1977a. "Report from New York's Rock 'Underground.'" *New York Times*, February 20, 1977, 11 and 20.

———. 1977b. "Concert: Philip Glass Ensemble." *New York Times*, May 2, 1977, 41.

———. 1977c. "Pop: Reich in Review." *New York Times*, May 18, 1977, 70.

———. 1977d. "Video Portraits of Avant-Garde Composers." *New York Times*, May 29, 1977, 13, 30.

———. 1977e. "Today's Blank Art Explores the Space behind the Obvious." *New York Times*, July 17, 1977, 1, 14.

———. 1977f. "The Pop Life." *New York Times*, December 9, 1977, 13.

———. 1977g. "The Pop Life." *New York Times*, December 23, 1977, 67.

———. 1978a. "The Pop Life." *New York Times*, November 17, 1978, 12.

———. 1978b. "The Pop Life: One Critic's Top 10 for 1978." *New York Times*, December 22, 1978, 21.

———. 1978c. "Disco, Progressive Rock and Comebacks Were '78 High Notes." *New York Times*, December 31, 1978, 10, 16.

———. 1979a. "The Pop Life: Journey to the Outer Edges of Rock." *New York Times*, January 12, 1979, 20.

———. 1979b. "Reich without Reich." *New York Times*, January 18, 1979, 12.

———. 1979c. "Glass's 'Einstein' Is Aural Magic." *New York Times*, March 11, 1979, 23.

———. 1979d. "Rock: Steve Reich." *New York Times*, March 20, 1979, C-6.

———. 1979e. "The Pop Life: Robert Fripp Makes Personal Statement." *New York Times*, April 27, 1979, 17.

———. 1979f. "Avant-Garde: 2 New-Music Concerts." *New York Times*, November 5, 1979, 17.

———. 1980a. "The Rich Diversity of New American Music." *New York Times*, April 27, 1980, 21 and 27.

———. 1980b. "Which Works of the 70's Were Significant?" *New York Times*, July 27, 1980, 19.

———. 1981a. "Critics' Choices." *New York Times*, February 22, 1981, 3.

———. 1981b. "Rhys Chatham: Classical Road to Rock." *New York Times*, April 17, 1981, 15.

———. 1982. "The Evolution of Steve Reich." *New York Times*, March 14, 1982, 23.

———. 1983a. "Music: Glass's Ensemble Performs 2 New Works." *New York Times*, May 11, 1983, 16.

———. 1983b. "Concert: New Music of California." *New York Times*, June 6, 1983, 13.

———. 1983c. *All American Music: Composition in the Late Twentieth Century.* New York: Alfred A. Knopf.

———. 1984. "An Evening of Minimalism at Tanglewood." *New York Times*, July 31, 1984, 13.

———. 1985a. "Expanding on Minimalist Music." *New York Times*, February 10, 1985, 96.

———. 1985b. "Fresh Light on Minimalism's Founding Trio." *New York Times,* September 29, 1985, 25.

———. 1986. "The Death and Life of Minimalism." *New York Times,* December 21, 1986, 1.

———. 1992. "Feldman's Minimalism in Maximal Doses." *New York Times,* January 12, 1992, 28.

———. 1993. "In East Europe, Minimalism Meets Mysticism." *New York Times,* July 4, 1993, 24.

———. 2002. "Palmer, Robert." *Grove Music Online* in Oxford Music Online, Oxford University Press.

Rose, Barbara. 1965. "A B C Art." *Art in America,* no. 53: 56–69.

———. 1967. *American Art since 1900: A Critical History.* New York: Praeger.

———. 1969. "Television as Art, 'Inevitable.'" *Vogue,* August 15, 1969, 36.

———. 1971. "In Andy Warhol's Aluminum Foil, We All Have Been Reflected." *New York Magazine,* May 31, 1971, 54–56.

Rosen, Charles. 1962. "The Proper Study of Music." *Perspectives of New Music* 1, no. 1 (Autumn): 80–88.

Rosolato, Guy. 1972. "Répétitions." *Musique en jeu,* no. 9 (November): 33–44.

Rostand, Claude. 1970. *Dictionnaire de la musique contemporaine.* Paris: Librairie Larousse.

Rothstein, Joel. 1981. "Terry Riley." *Down Beat* 48, no. 5 (May): 26–28, 63.

Rublowsky, John. 1967. *Music in America: From the Psalms and Ballads of Colonial Days to the Jazz, Folk-Rock and Electronic Sounds of Today.* New York: Crowell-Collier.

Ruppenthal, Stephen, and David Patterson. 2001. "Strange, (John) Allen." *Grove Music Online* in Oxford Music Online, Oxford University Press.

Russcol, Herbert. 1972. *The Liberation of Sound: An Introduction to Electronic Music.* Englewood Cliffs, NJ: Prentice-Hall International.

Rzewski, Fredric. 1974. "Prose Music." In *Dictionary of Contemporary Music,* edited by John Vinton, 593–95. New York: E. P. Dutton.

Sabbe, Herman. 1972a. "Ac' Art." *Kunst- en Cultuuragenda* 4, no. 5 (February 17): 20–21.

———. 1972b. "Philosophie der neuesten Musik: Ein Versuch zur Extrapolation von Adornos 'Philosophie der neuen Musik.'" *Philosophica Gandensia,* no. 9: 90–111.

———. 1977. *Het muzikale serialisme als techniek en als denkmethode: Een onderzoek naar de logische en historische samenhang van de onderscheiden toepassingen van het seriërend beginsel in de muziek van de periode 1950–1975.* Ghent: Rijksuniversiteit te Gent.

———. 1979. "Stroop uit de Kosmos." *Kunst- en Cultuuragenda* 12, no. 1 (January 1): 20–23.

————. 1982a. "Vom Serialismus zum Minimalismus: der Werdegang eines Manierismus. Der Fall Goeyvaerts, 'Minimalist avant la lettre.'" *Neuland: Ansätze zur Musik der Gegenwart*, no. 323: 203–8.

————. 1982b. "Minimalism: A World Vision's World Versions." In *Das Europäische Minimal-Musik-Projekt*, edited by Michael Fahres, 1–17. Munich: Goethe Institut.

Sadie, Stanley. 1969. "Editorial." *Musical Times* 110, no. 1516 (June): 581.

————. 1988. *The Grove Concise Dictionary of Music*. London: Macmillan, 1988.

————. 2001a. "Preface to the Revised Edition." In *The New Grove Dictionary of Music and Musicians*, edited by Stanley Sadie, vii–ix. London: Macmillan.

————. 2001b. "Preface to the 1980 Edition." In *The New Grove Dictionary of Music and Musicians*, edited by Stanley Sadie, xi–xiv. London: Macmillan.

Salzman, Eric. 1961. "Modern Stirrings: Works in Avant-Garde Idioms Heard on Piano Program by Toshi Ichiyanagi." *New York Times*, May 15, 1961, 34.

————. 1965. "Music." In *The New American Arts*, edited by Richard Kostelanetz, 237–64. New York: Horizon Press.

————. 1967. *Twentieth-Century Music: An Introduction*. Englewood Cliffs, NJ: Prentice-Hall.

————. 1974a. *Twentieth-Century Music: An Introduction*. 2nd ed. Englewood Cliffs, NJ: Prentice-Hall.

————. 1974b. "Mixed Media." In *Dictionary of Contemporary Music*, edited by John Vinton, 489–92. New York: E. P. Dutton.

————. 1988. *Twentieth-Century Music: An Introduction*. 3rd ed. Englewood Cliffs, NJ: Prentice-Hall.

————. 2001. *Twentieth-Century Music: An Introduction*. 4th ed. Englewood Cliffs, NJ: Prentice-Hall.

Samson, Jim. 1999. "Analysis in Context." In *Rethinking Music*, edited by Nicholas Cook and Mark Everist, 35–54. Oxford: Oxford University Press.

Sandow, Gregory. 1980. "Steve Reich: Something New." *Village Voice*, March 10, 1980, 74.

Santos, Rita de Cássia Domingues dos. 2019. *Repensando a terceira fase composicional de Gilberto Mendes: o Pós-Minimalismo nos Mares do Sul*. Curitiba, Brazil: Editora CRV.

Schaefer, John. 1987. *New Sounds: A Listener's Guide to New Music*. New York: Harper & Row.

Schaeffer, Pierre. (1952) 2012. *In Search of a Concrete Musique*. Translated by John Dack and Christine North. Berkeley: University of California Press.

————. 1957. *Vers une musique expérimentale*. Paris: Richard-Masse.

Scherzinger, Martin. 2005. "Curious Intersections, Uncommon Magic: Steve Reich's *It's Gonna Rain*." *Current Musicology*, no. 79/80 (2005): 207–44.

Schnebel, Dieter. 1972. *Denkbare Musik: Schriften 1952–1972*. Cologne: M. DuMont Schauberg.

———. 1973. "Composition 1960: La Monte Young (1971)." *Musique en jeu*, no. 11 (June): 7–16.

———. 1978. "Tendenzen in der neuen amerikanischen Musik." In *Avantgarde, Jazz, Pop: Tendenzen zwischen Tonalität und Atonalität*, edited by Reinhold Brinkmann, 9–17. Mainz: Schott.

Scholes, Percy A., ed. 1970. *The Oxford Companion to Music*. London: Oxford University Press.

Schonberg, Harold C. 1969a. "The Medium Electric, the Message Hypnotic." *New York Times*, April 15, 1969, 42.

———. 1969b. "Music: Loud Last Word." *New York Times*, May 7, 1969, 37.

———. 1969c. "One-Note Nirvanas? Music as Ritual? Phooey!" *New York Times*, July 20, 1969, 13.

———. 1973a. "Music: A Concert Fuss." *New York Times*, January 20, 1973, 36.

———. 1973b. "Carter, Cage, Reich... Speak to Me." *New York Times*, February 4, 1973, 15.

———. 1974. "Music: New Amsterdam." *New York Times*, April 4, 1974, 54.

Schwartz, Elliott. 1972. "Current Chronicle: The Netherlands." *Musical Quarterly* 58, no. 4 (October): 653–58.

———. 1973. *Electronic Music: A Listener's Guide*. New York: Praeger.

———. 1978. "Electronic Music: A Thirty-Year Retrospective." *Music Educators Journal* 64, no. 7 (March): 36–41.

———. 1989. *Electronic Music: A Listener's Guide*. Rev. ed. New York: Da Capo.

Schwartz, Elliott, and Barney Childs, eds. 1967. *Contemporary Composers on Contemporary Music*. New York: Holt, Rinehart & Winston.

Schwarz, K. Robert. 1980–81. "Steve Reich: Music as a Gradual Process, Part I." *Perspectives of New Music* 19, no. 1/2 (Autumn–Summer): 373–92.

———. 1981–82. "Steve Reich: Music as a Gradual Process, Part II." *Perspectives of New Music* 20, no. 1/2 (Autumn–Summer): 225–86.

———. 1985. "Maximising Minimalism." *Listener*, July 25, 1985, 36.

———. 1990. "Process vs. Intuition in the Recent Works of Steve Reich and John Adams." *American Music* 8, no. 3 (Autumn): 245–73.

———. 1996. *Minimalists*. London: Phaidon.

———. 1997. "Minimalism/Music." In *Perceptible Processes: Minimalism and the Baroque*, edited by Claudia Swan, 1–17. New York: Eos Music.

Searle, Humphrey. 1954. "Twelve-Tone Music." In *Grove's Dictionary of Music and Musicians*, edited by Eric Blom, 8:617–24. New York: St. Martin's Press.

———. 1961a. "Electronic Music." In *Grove's Dictionary of Music and Musicians*, edited by Eric Blom, 20:120. New York: St. Martin's Press.

———. 1961b. "Musique concrète." In *Grove's Dictionary of Music and Musicians*, edited by Eric Blom, 20:80–81. New York: St. Martin's Press.

Shepherd, John. 2013. "Sociology of Music." *Grove Music Online* in Oxford Music Online, Oxford University Press.

Sheppard, David. 2008. *The Life and Times of Brian Eno*. Chicago: Chicago Review Press.

Sherburne, Philip. 2004. "Digital Discipline: Minimalism in House and Techno." In *Audio Culture: Readings in Modern Music*, edited by Christoph Cox and Daniel Warner, 319–28. New York: Continuum.

Shirley, Wayne D. 1973. "North America." In *Music in the Modern Age*, edited by Frederick W. Sternfeld, 365–406. London: Weidenfeld & Nicholson.

Skempton, Howard. 1967. "62 for Henry Flynt." *Musical Times* 108, no. 1489 (March): 237.

Slonimsky, Nicolas. 1971. *Music since 1900*. New York: Charles Scribner's Sons.

Slowik, Edward. 2007. "The Structure of Musical Revolutions." *Philosophy Now*, no. 59: 9–11.

Smalley, Roger. 1967a. "La Monte Young." *Musical Times* 108, no. 1488 (February): 143.

———. 1967b. "Unconventional Conventions." *Musical Times* 108, no. 1497 (November): 1029–30.

———. 1968. "Royan." *Musical Times* 109, no. 1504 (June): 563.

———. 1971. "Avant Garde 3." *Musical Times* 112, no. 1540 (June): 567.

———. 1972a. "Colin Mason: A Memoir." *Tempo*, no. 100: 23–24.

———. 1972b. "Brian Dennis." *Musical Times* 113, no. 1547 (January): 30–33.

———. 1972c. "The New Music." *Musical Times* 113, no. 1552 (June): 593–95.

———. 1972d. "Avant-Garde Piano." *Musical Times* 113, no. 1558 (December): 1222.

———. 1975a. "Experimental Music." *Musical Times* 116, no. 1583 (January): 23–26.

———. 1975b. "Accord." *Musical Times* 116, no. 1594 (December): 1054–56.

Smith, Geoff, and Nicola Walker Smith. 1994. *American Originals: Interviews with 25 Contemporary Composers*. Boston: Faber and Faber.

Smith, Patrick J. 2001. "Schonberg, Harold C." *Grove Music Online* in Oxford Music Online, Oxford University Press.

Sollberger, Harvey. 2001. "Reynolds, Roger (Lee)." *Grove Music Online* in Oxford Music Online, Oxford University Press.

Sommer, Sally. 1972. "Equipment Dances: Trisha Brown." *Drama Review* 16, no. 3 (September): 135–41.

Sontag, Susan. 1966. *Against Interpretation*. New York: Farrar, Straus & Giroux.

———. 1967. "Film and Theatre." *Tulane Drama Review* 11, no. 1 (Autumn): 24–37.

Souster, Tim. 1968–69. "Notes on Pop Music." *Tempo*, no. 87 (Winter): 2–6.

Spaeth, Sigmund. 1948. *A History of Popular Music in America*. New York: Random House.

Staehelin, Martin. 1980. Review of *The Medici Codex of 1518: A Choirbook of Motets Dedicated to Lorenzo de'Medici, Duke of Urbino*, ed. Edward E. Lowinsky. *Journal of the American Musicological Society* 33, no. 3 (Autumn): 575–87.

Stella, Frank. 1986. *Working Space*. Cambridge: Harvard University Press.

Stephan, Rudolf. 1958. *Neue Musik: Versuch einer kritischen Einführung*. Göttingen: Vandenhoeck & Ruprecht.

Sterne, Jonathan. 2012. *MP3: The Meaning of a Format*. Durham, NC: Duke University Press.

Stoïanova, Ivanka. 1977. "Musique répétitive." *Musique en jeu*, no. 26 (February): 64–74.

Stoner, Thomas. 1969. "Analysis of 20th-Century Music." *Current Musicology*, no. 9: 20–21.

Strange, Allen. 1969. "Musical Tradition Is Alive and Well." *Music Educators Journal* 55, no. 9: 37–39.

———. 1970. "Tape Piece." *Composer* 2, no. 1: 12–15.

———. 1972. *Electronic Music: Systems, Techniques, and Controls*. Dubuque, Iowa: Wm. C. Brown.

Strickland, Edward. 1980. "Riley: *Shri Camel*." *Fanfare* 4, no. 1 (September–October). http://fanfarearchive.com.

———. 1984. "Glass: *Einstein on the Beach*." *Fanfare* 8, no. 2 (November–December). http://fanfarearchive.com.

———. 1985. "Riley: *Cadenza on the Night Plain and other String Quartets: Sunrise of the Planetary Dream Collector; G Song; Mythic Birds Waltz; Cadenza on the Night Plain*." *Fanfare* 9, no. 2 (November–December). http://fanfarearchive.com.

———. 1986a. "Reich: *The Desert Music*." *Fanfare* 9, no. 3 (January–February). http://fanfarearchive.com.

———. 1986b. "Glass: *Songs from Liquid Days*." *Fanfare* 10, no. 1 (September–October). http://fanfarearchive.com.

———. 1987. "Want List for Edward Strickland." *Fanfare* 11, no. 2 (November–December). http://fanfarearchive.com.

———. 1989. "Glass: *Dance 1–5*." *Fanfare* 12, no. 4 (March–April). http://fanfarearchive.com.

———. 1990. "Riley: *Salome Dances for Peace*." *Fanfare* 13, no. 4 (March–April). http://fanfarearchive.com.

———. 1991. *American Composers: Dialogues on Contemporary Music*. Bloomington: Indiana University Press.

———. 1993. *Minimalism: Origins*. Bloomington: Indiana University Press.

Strongin, Theodore. 1967. "When Teen-agers Get to College." *New York Times*, December 10, 1967, 32, and 36.

———. 1968a. "Sound-Light Show Drags Slowly On." *New York Times*, February 19, 1968, 50.

———. 1968b. "Too Loud? Too Soft? Sometimes You Can't Win." *New York Times*, November 10, 1968, 25.

———. 1969. "Is Timelessness Out of Style?" *New York Times*, December 21, 1969, 26.

Stuckenschmidt, Hans Heinz. 1958. *Schöpfer der neuen Musik: Portraits und Studien*. Frankfurt: Suhrkamp Verlag.

———. 1969. *Twentieth Century Music*. New York: McGraw-Hill.

Swift, Richard, and Paul Attinello. 2001. "Childs, Barney (Sanford)." *Grove Music Online* in Oxford Music Online, Oxford University Press.

Szendy, Peter. 2002. *Tristan Murail*. Paris: L'Harmattan.

Tack, Lieven. 1998. "Ouverture(s). L'objet musico-littéraire: pour une analyse théorique de l'interférence." *Revue belge de philologie et d'histoire* 76, no. 3: 763–91.

Taruskin, Richard. 2014. "Agents and Causes and Ends, Oh My." *Journal of Musicology* 31, no. 2: 272–93.

Tebbel, John. 1987. *Between Covers: The Rise and Transformation of Book Publishing in America*. New York: Oxford University Press.

Thomson, Virgil. 1971. *Twentieth-Century Composers: American Music since 1910*. New York: Holt, Rinehart and Winston.

Thompson, Oscar, ed. 1964. *The International Cyclopedia of Music and Musicians*. 9th ed. New York: Dodd, Mead.

———, ed. 1975. *The International Cyclopedia of Music and Musicians*. 10th ed. New York: Dodd, Mead.

———, ed. 1985. *The International Cyclopedia of Music and Musicians*. 11th ed. New York: Dodd, Mead.

Tilbury, John. 2001. "Cardew, Cornelius." *Grove Music Online* in Oxford Music Online, Oxford University Press.

———. 2008. *Cornelius Cardew (1936–1981): A Life Unfinished*. Essex: Copula.

Tommasini, Anthony. 2001. "Thomson, Virgil (Garnett)." *Grove Music Online* in Oxford Music Online, Oxford University Press.

Toop, David. 1995. *Ocean of Sound: Aether Talk, Ambient Sound and Imaginary Worlds*. London: Serpent's Tail.

Toop, Richard. 1974. "Messiaen/ Goeyvaerts, Fano/ Stockhausen, Boulez." *Perspectives of New Music* 13, no. 1 (Autumn–Winter): 141–69.

———. 2008. "Stockhausen, Karlheinz." *Grove Music Online* in Oxford Music Online, Oxford University Press.

Trachtenberg, Stanley. 1985. *The Postmodern Moment: A Handbook of Contemporary Innovation in the Arts*. Westport, CT: Greenwood Press.

Treitler, Leo. 1989. *Music and the Historical Imagination*. Cambridge, MA: Harvard University Press.

Tucker, Marcia, and James Monte. 1969. *Anti-Illusion: Procedures/Materials*. New York: Whitney Museum of American Art.

Turetzky, Bertram. 1970. "The Solo-Ensemble Piece." *Composer* 2, no. 3: 66–67.

Vanden Heuvel, Jean. 1966. "The Fantastic Sounds of La Monte Young." *Vogue* (May): 198, 206.

Vanden Heuvel, Mike. 2006. "A Different Kind of Pomo: The Performance Group and the Mixed Legacy of Authentic Performance." In *Restaging the Sixties: Radical Theaters and Their Legacies*, edited by James M. Harding and Cindy Rosenthal, 332–52. Ann Arbor: University of Michigan Press.

Van der Merwe, Peter. 1989. *Origins of Popular Style: The Antecedents of Twentieth-Century Popular Music*. Oxford: Clarendon Press.

Vieru, Anatol. 1992. "Generating Modal Sequences (A Remote Approach to Minimal Music)." *Perspectives of New Music* 30, no. 2 (Summer): 178–200.

Vinton, John, ed. 1974. *Dictionary of Contemporary Music*. New York: E. P. Dutton.

Wagner, Anne. 1995. "Reading Minimal Art." In *Minimal Art: A Critical Anthology*, edited by Gregory Battcock, 3–18. Berkeley: University of California Press.

Walsh, Stephen. 1967. Review of *Twentieth-Century Music: An Introduction*, by Eric Salzman. *Tempo*, no. 82 (Autumn): 35.

———. 1968. "Roger Smalley." *Musical Times* 109, no. 1500 (February): 131–34.

———. 1969. Review of *Twentieth-Century Music*, by H. H. Stuckenschmidt. *Tempo*, no. 90 (Autumn): 43–45.

———. 1970. "Hard Rock in the Albert Hall: Two Views of the First-Ever Pop Prom, Which Took Place Last Week. Not Worth the Fuss." *Observer*, August 16, 1970, 19.

Warburton, Dan. 1988. "A Working Terminology for Minimal Music." *Integral*, no. 2: 135–59.

Wasserman, Emily. 1972. "An Interview with Composer Steve Reich." *Artforum* 10, no. 9 (May): 44–48.

Westergaard, Peter. 1962. "Some Problems in Rhythmic Theory and Analysis." *Perspectives of New Music* 1, no. 1 (Autumn): 180–91.

Whittall, Arnold. 1977. *Music since the First World War*. London: J. M. Dent & Sons.

Wilder, Robert D. 1969. *Twentieth-Century Music*. Dubuque, IA: Wm. C. Brown.

Williamson, Rosemary. 2001. "Griffiths, Paul." *Grove Music Online* in Oxford Music Online, Oxford University Press.

Witts, Richard. 2006. *The Velvet Underground*. London: Equinox.

Wollheim, Richard. 1965. "Minimal Art." *Arts Magazine* 39, no. 4 (January): 26–32.

Wright, David. 1992. Review of *American Composers: Dialogues on Contemporary Music*, by Edward Strickland. *Musical Times* 133, no. 1795 (September): 462.

Wyatt, Lucius R. 2001. "Moore, Carman (Leroy)." *Grove Music Online* in Oxford Music Online, Oxford University Press.

Yates, Peter. 1967. *Twentieth Century Music: Its Evolution from the End of the Harmonic Era into the Present Era of Sound*. New York: Pantheon.

Young, La Monte. 1960. "Lecture 1960." *Kulchur*, no. 10 (1963): 18–21.

———. 1965. "Lecture 1960." *Tulane Drama Review* 10, no. 2 (Winter): 73–83.

———. 1970. "The Sound Is God." *Village Voice*, April 1, 1970.

Young, La Monte, and Jackson Mac Low. 1963. *An Anthology of Chance Operations*. New York.

Young, La Monte, and Marian Zazeela. 1969. *Selected Writings*. Munich: Heiner Friedrich.

———. 1970–71a. "Dream House." *VH 101*, no. 4 (Winter): 70–74.

———. 1970–71b. "Le chant de Pran Nath: Le son est Dieu." *VH 101*, no. 4 (Winter): 75–79.

Index

Founded in 1893,
UNIVERSITY OF CALIFORNIA PRESS
publishes bold, progressive books and journals
on topics in the arts, humanities, social sciences,
and natural sciences—with a focus on social
justice issues—that inspire thought and action
among readers worldwide.

The UC PRESS FOUNDATION
raises funds to uphold the press's vital role
as an independent, nonprofit publisher, and
receives philanthropic support from a wide
range of individuals and institutions—and from
committed readers like you. To learn more, visit
ucpress.edu/supportus.